IS THERE LIFE AFTER FOOTBALL?

IS THERE
LIFE AFTER
FOOTBALL?
SURVIVING THE NFL

JAMES A. HOLSTEIN, RICHARD S. JONES &
GEORGE E. KOONCE, JR.

NEW YORK UNIVERSITY PRESS
New York and London

NEW YORK UNIVERSITY PRESS
New York and London
www.nyupress.org

References to Internet websites (URLs) were accurate at the time of writing. Neither the author nor New York University Press is responsible for URLs that may have expired or changed since the manuscript was prepared.

ISBN: 978-1-4798-6286-3

For Library of Congress Cataloging-in-Publication data, please contact the Library of Congress.

New York University Press books are printed on acid-free paper, and their binding materials are chosen for strength and durability. We strive to use environmentally responsible suppliers and materials to the greatest extent possible in publishing our books.

Manufactured in the United States of America

10 9 8 7 6 5 4 3 2 1

Also available as an ebook

Dedicated to
the players of the NFL,
past and present

CONTENTS

ACKNOWLEDGMENTS

Above all, we thank the NFL players and former players who talked to us about their football lives. They are a genuinely impressive and interesting cast of characters.

The book also reflects the generous input of friends, colleagues, and students who talked football with us over the course of the project. At Marquette University our friend and chair, Roberta Coles, encouraged our efforts and, despite her Chicago roots, became a Packers fan along the way. We also thank our colleagues and students in the Department of Social and Cultural Sciences, and across the university: Jimmy Butler, Junior Cadougan, Louise Cainkar, John Cotton, Alexandra Crampton, Deb Crane, Tom Ford, Steve Franzoi, Beth Godbee, Angie Harris, Kim Salas Harris, Heather Hlavka, Ed Inderreiden, Gale Miller, Matt Mitten, Dawne Moon, Sameena Mulla, Paul Nollette, David Nowacek, Alex Peete, Jane Peterson, Adrienne Ridgeway, Ryan Seebruck, Olga Semukhina, Meghan Stroshine, John Su, Nick Szczech, Darren Wheelock, Marcia Williams, and Amelia Zurcher. Our appreciation also extends to those outside the university: Jun Ayukawa, Mitch Berbrier, Nancy Berns, Susan Chase, Jeffrey Chin, Suzy Clarkson Holstein, Chris Corey, Dana Ellingson, Bob Emerson, Kerry Ferris, Jessie Garcia, Scott Harris, Ray Hinojosa, Doni Loseke, Kathe Lowney, Linda Permaul, Nad Permaul, Jack Spencer, the Rev. Arthur Webb, Jr., Joseph E. Williams, and Pansy Yee.

Special thanks go to Joel Best, who encouraged us to venture outside the staid academic realm and masterfully showed us the way. Jim Holstein took a hiatus from his career-long collaboration with Jay Gubrium to work on this project, and thanks Jay for the space and support. His work always bears Jay's intellectual imprint.

Ilene Kalish, our editor at NYU Press, has been enthusiastic and demanding from the start. Her insight, expertise, and professionalism are evident throughout. Thanks for the superb guidance that's made the book so much better. We definitely appreciate everything the rest of the staff at NYU Press did to bring the project to fruition, especially Caelyn Cobb, Dan Geist, and Dorothea Halliday.

Finally we thank the anonymous reviewers of the manuscript for their helpful insights and suggestions.

Note to the Reader

George Koonce plays a unique role in this book: he is both an author and the subject of many sections of the text. To distinguish his subject and author voices, we have italicized all direct quotations from Koonce, as they have been elicited through interviews. Thus, his subject voice is always in italics. Many of the interviews for the book were conducted with promises of confidentiality. Pseudonyms for players and teams were used in these instances. Consequently, some of the names of players quoted in the book cannot be found in NFL records. Player interviews from public media are attributed to actual sources and the names in these are authentic.

INTRODUCTION

"IT'S ALL OVER!"

"George, don't you realize, that's it!"

She said it with love and compassion, but Tunisia, my wife, was telling me that my NFL career was over. I didn't want to hear it.

I asked her, "Why the hell would you say some shit like that?"

"George, you're done," she repeated. "It's all over!"

I didn't talk to her for a couple of weeks. That's when I started going to the beach and spending three or four days by myself. I would say, "Tunisia, I'm going to the beach on Thursday. I'll be back on Monday," and she would say, "Really? OK." And the beach was about two hours away. I was pissed off, hurt, angry, depressed. I just wanted to get out of there. I didn't really want to be around people who were asking me, "George have you talked to anybody, have any teams given you a call?" I didn't have an answer. Well, I had the answer, but I didn't want to tell people. I was basically a failure in my mind. I was totally numb. I was in a dark and lonely place. I was embarrassed to talk with friends in the league. I envied them. So I'd get in my Chevy Suburban and whatever happened that day was going to happen. I didn't really care. . . .

It was on the drive back home one day that I took a turn at 75 miles per hour just to see what would happen. I flew off the road and the truck ended upside down in a ditch. Thank God, I didn't hit anyone. But I survived. By the grace of God, I survived. Maybe, in retrospect, it was a suicide attempt. At the time I just didn't care.

But the paramedics weren't going to cart me off. No chance. The football tough guy in me refused to get into that ambulance. Tunisia drove me to the house and saved my life with words, not medicine.

1

*"George," she said, "I don't understand what you're going through, but I sym-
pathize. We cannot reinvent who you are, but we can redefine who you are."*

*After we got home, Tunisia said to me, "Well, did you accomplish what you
intended?"*

I told her, "Yeah, and that part of me is dead now and I'm ready to move on."

After nine years as a starting linebacker in the NFL, George Koonce's
football days had come to an end.[1] He was depressed. Perhaps suicidal.
Emotionally estranged from his wife. Avoiding his friends. Why had such
a rewarding career boiled down to this? Is this what retirement amounts
to for NFL players? What can they expect from life after football?

George Koonce's account of "the end" may not be typical, but it's not
unique. It expresses many common themes of how ex-NFL players get
on with their lives. Like Koonce's account, the stories are complex and
often paradoxical. NFL careers are relatively short—3.5 years according
to the National Football League Players Association (NFLPA)—yet their
impact lasts far longer.[2] Recently, the spotlight has focused on tragedies,
poignantly and publicly exemplified in the suicide of former All-Pro linebacker Junior Seau. At age 43, Seau shot himself to death in May 2012.
Seau had been out of the game for less than 18 months. He had actually
first "retired" several years earlier, in 2006. At the time, Seau referred to
the move as his "graduation" because he was simply not going to stop
working. He was moving to the next phase of his life, which lasted only
four days before he signed to play several more seasons for the New
England Patriots. Retirement on both occasions proved difficult, and
ultimately tragic. His heartbreaking story epitomizes the difficulties
confronted by many former NFL players. Seau's untimely struggles and
ultimate demise literally prompt the question: Is there life after football?

Junior Seau's death launched a firestorm of speculation and investigation into the relation between head injuries and post-career troubles for
NFL players.[3] Other incidents contributed to the headlines. Since 2011
at least seven NFL players or former players have committed suicide,
including Seau, Ray Easterling, Dave Duerson, Kurt Crain, O.J. Murdock,

Jovan Belcher, and Paul Oliver. Belcher also killed his girlfriend.[4] These painful stories might shed new light on the frequently overlooked tragedies of older ex-players like Jim Tyrer, who was involved in a 1980 murder-suicide.[5] The same might hold for the emotionally wrenching cases of dementia tormenting Super Bowl quarterback Jim McMahon and former Charger, Dolphin, and Raider Dave Kocourek.[6] Then it's just a short inferential leap to questioning the connection between playing in the NFL and the debilitating mental health problems, prescription drug addiction, and depression that plagued former players such as Mike Webster, Ray Lucas, and Lionel Aldridge.[7]

But the stories are not just about head injuries. The general physical condition of former NFL players and the aftermath of their injuries are monumental legacies of this quintessentially violent game. Most retired players are scarred by major surgery, some from dozens of trips to the operating room. Many—Hall of Fame running back Earl Campbell, for example—can barely walk. Hundreds have had joint replacement surgery. Some—quarterbacking legend John Unitas comes to mind—lost use of their hands and fingers. And a few—Kurt Marsh and Jim Otto, in particular—have lost limbs to football injuries. In response to mounting health concerns, the NFL has instituted drastic rule changes and injury treatment protocols. In addition, in September 2012, the NFL announced a $30 million grant to the National Institutes of Health to study brain injuries and other sports-related health issues, and in 2013 the league and NFLPA announced a huge financial payout to players suffering the aftermath of head injuries.[8]

If the ravages of injury aren't enough, former players by the dozen face financial disaster. Despite their lucrative contracts, ex-players are showing up flat broke shortly after retirement. Terrell Owens is nearly penniless despite earning top dollar for years. He reportedly owes the IRS $438,000 in unpaid taxes. Seven-time Pro Bowl defensive tackle—and one-time multimillionaire—Warren Sapp has filed for bankruptcy. Court documents show he owes more than $6.7 million to creditors and in unpaid child support.[9] The NFLPA says that between 1999 and 2002, at least 78 players and former players were swindled out of more than \$42 million. *Sports Illustrated* claims that over three quarters of former NFL players are in desperate financial straits within two years of retirement.[10]

Still looking for trouble? Late in 2013, Patriots tight end Aaron Hernandez was arrested and placed under investigation for double homicide. Ryan Leaf, the second player taken in the 1998 draft (after Peyton Manning) and retired since 2002, was arrested in March 2012 on burglary, theft, and drug charges. Four days later he was rearrested for similar offenses. Leaf pled guilty to burglary and drug charges and has been sentenced to five years in a Montana state prison. In late April 2012, Texas authorities issued two additional warrants for his arrest. Leaf is just one of several recent additions to the list of convicted felons among NFL alumni. Some examples:

- Billy Cannon: counterfeiting
- Thomas "Hollywood" Henderson: sexual assault
- Dave Meggett: sexual misconduct and burglary
- Eugene "Mercury" Morris and Nate Newton: drug trafficking
- Lawrence Phillips: multiple assault convictions
- Art Schlichter: forgery and over 20 gambling-related felonies
- Lawrence Taylor: tax evasion, sexual misconduct, and patronizing a prostitute

While no one can forget O.J. Simpson, his actual convictions pale in comparison to some of his fellow alums'. Former Patriot and Colt Erik Naposki was convicted of homicide and received a life sentence without parole, but the standard may have been set by Keith Wright, a defensive lineman who lurked at the fringes of the NFL from 2003 to 2006. In 2012, Wright was found guilty on 19 charges including armed robbery, burglary, kidnapping, and false imprisonment, for which he was sentenced to a combined 234 years in prison.[11]

The litany of horror stories goes on and on. But are they the entire story of life after the NFL? Are there other stories to tell, other chapters being written? Former players have coached Super Bowl winners and college national champions. NFL front offices are full of NFL vets. Fans love media personalities who graduated from the NFL: Michael Strahan, Troy Aikman, Howie Long, Terry Bradshaw, Boomer Esiason, and Herman Edwards, just to name a few. The list of NFL alums among successful local broadcasters is burgeoning as talk show radio and TV employ ex-jocks to talk sports 24/7, nonstop. While they've certainly capitalized on their football fame, there's also a long list of serious actors among NFL alums, including Jim Brown, Fred Williamson, Merlin Olsen, Carl Weathers, and, of course, O.J.

But former players succeed offstage, too. Ex-Viking Alan Page is a justice of the Minnesota Supreme Court. Jack Kemp, formerly of the Chargers and Bills, was a nine-term congressman from New York and U.S. Secretary of Housing and Urban Development. Steve Largent and Heath Schuler were elected to the U.S. House of Representatives. Duane Benson, member of the "badass" Oakland Raiders, was a Minnesota state senator. There's a catalog of other successful professionals—physicians, dentists, attorneys, and educators, among others—who've launched successful second careers after the NFL. Willie Davis, Jerry Richardson, and Eugene Profit have made millions of dollars in business and investments. Herbert Blumer, an All-Pro for the Chicago Cardinals in 1929, went on to become one of the foremost sociologists of all time.

In light of these contradictory stories, the question *"Is there life after football?"* demands a complex and nuanced answer. Perhaps several answers. The recent cascade of tales of lives gone awry has predisposed the popular media and sports journalists to emphasize the perils of both playing and retiring from football. But these hazards have been around for a long time. For decades, former NFL players have complained— sometimes bitterly—of being discarded and forsaken. They contend that *both* the league and their own union have abandoned retired players once they can't produce on the field. Many have decried the NFL's and NFLPA's indifference to the plight of old-timers, and the media have been especially eager to offer sensationalized accounts, sometimes corroborated with poignant, sympathetic personal stories. But the media tend to bury more mundane success stories in the process, leaving the public with little but visions of life after football as a cataclysmic mess. And they rarely have the patience for nuanced answers. Why do relatively young, capable men who are seemingly on top of the world so frequently fall off the cliff after retirement? Why has the lucrative financial situation of NFL players not translated into rich lives after football? What are most lives after football really like?

Is There Life after Football? offers an "insider's" look at the challenges facing NFL players when they leave the game, but it also provides an analytic distance from which to approach the many paradoxes of NFL life. The book draws upon the experience and stories of hundreds of former players as they describe their lives after their playing days are over. But it also incorporates stories about their playing careers, as well as times before entering the NFL, to provide context for understanding their current situations. The research is inspired by the NFL life and "afterlife" of former player George Koonce. Koonce initiated the project with his doctoral research on the "life course" of professional football players. This research draws upon his many years of experience in and around the NFL and its players, as well as a decade coming to grips with his own retirement. Koonce was a starting linebacker on the Green Bay Packers' Super Bowl teams of the 1990s. He also spent a year with the Seattle Seahawks at the end of his career. After continuing his education—he now has a master's degree from East Carolina University and a Ph.D. from Marquette University—he returned to Green Bay to work for the Packers in a number of off-field capacities, such as director of player development. Koonce also held positions in the athletic and advancement departments at Marquette, and served as director of athletics at the University of Wisconsin–Milwaukee. He is currently the vice president of advancement at Marian University. His involvement with retired players has deepened as a result of his research, and he is presently a member of the National Football League Player Engagement Advisory Board.

In a sense, Koonce is the consummate "participant observer"—a researcher who has been embedded in his research subject most of his life. He's an authentic insider who has seen and done it all. Koonce's observations and insights inform the analysis throughout the book. In addition, the other authors (Jim Holstein and Rick Jones, both sociologists at Marquette) spent dozens of hours interviewing Koonce, conducting in-depth life history interviews. These interview data also appear throughout the book, with Koonce's stock of experiential knowledge of football, the NFL, and retirement supplying the empirical bedrock for this study. In addition, the book draws upon dozens of formal, in-depth life history interviews as well as many more informal interviews conducted with former NFL players—players with experience on a variety of teams, from different eras, playing different positions, from diverse social, economic, and racial backgrounds, and experiencing varying degrees of success and financial reward in the NFL. Several other academic studies of NFL players, former players, and their families also provide revealing first-hand data. Finally, the book draws on narratives and interviews on retirement-related issues from a wide variety of media sources, citing hundreds of players.[12]

The sports and entertainment media provide plenty of sensationalized, sweeping generalizations and judgmental conclusions about life after football. An anecdote here and there is usually deemed sufficient to warrant the claims. But an empirically narrow, predetermined focus often distorts players' lived realities. It's likely to ignore complexity and discount the mundane. Life after football is as complex and variegated as it is in any other segment of society. It's just lived in a spotlight, or under a microscope, but there's more to discover if we recognize and honor the complexity, nuance, and paradoxes of ex-players' lives that defy easy characterization.[13]

Recently, head injuries have been the big story. Prior to that, money dominated the discussion, with reports of monumental TV deals and collective bargaining agreements juxtaposed with lurid tales of profligate spending and bankruptcy. Crime, domestic violence, social relationships, sexuality, isolation, and addiction claimed the sidebars. But none of these issues emerges in a vacuum. Nor do they develop in stereotypic lockstep with media images. Like everyone else in 21st-century America, former NFL players live at the complicated intersection of race, social class, gender, and the economy. Everyone faces the mundane challenges of getting by from day to day in a world of jobs, bills, ailments, and relationships. Life after football is no different. If the challenges are distinctive, it's due in large part to the radical social changes that players encounter when they exit the game. When NFL players leave football, they encounter a version of culture shock. They aren't just retiring from a job or a career. They're leaving a way of life, entering a world that is foreign to them. They know the language—sort of—but they speak a distinctive dialect. They've seen the sights from afar, but they're no longer tourists or disinterested onlookers. Now they live in the neighborhood. The world after football for some players is so different from what they've experienced for their entire adult lives that it leaves them disoriented.

NFL players are tough, talented, and well-compensated. Their lives revolve around competition and commitment. Violence and injury lurk around every corner. Teamwork, loyalty, and camaraderie are transcendent themes, juxtaposed with individual glory and respect. Beyond question, the NFL is a *man's* world, where masculine pride and character are constantly challenged. Even though players occupy the spotlight much of the time, they also occupy a private world, shielded, if not isolated, from the mundane world of everyday life around them. They live in a "fishbowl"—an arena where they are scrutinized, but also insulated from many of the routine demands of everyday life.

When a player leaves the league, everything changes. It's not just the money or the lifestyle. The codes and principles by which players live in the NFL bubble no longer apply. Players are no longer part of the locker room culture. Everything they're used to is up for grabs. But old ways die hard; the NFL imprint is deep. How players adapt to radical post-career changes can be excruciatingly personal, even if they might seem avoidable, trivial, or absurd to outsiders. On top of that, former players are challenged daily to work things out at the intricate nexus of celebrity and oblivion.

George Koonce's personal story provides a point of departure for examining these changes. As informative as his accounts are, however, they aren't definitive. Instead, his experience provides the narrative anchor for telling the broader range of players' stories. Koonce faced his fair share of challenges and changes. He's met with plenty of setbacks and successes. But his story isn't everyone's story. Sometimes it confirms broader patterns; sometimes it serves as instructive counterpoint.

To grasp the range of challenges, we must carefully consider what life was like while players were still *in the game*, as well as the standards to which ex-players compare their post-NFL experience. Players' lives both before the NFL and while they played serve as the backdrop for their lives after football. Understanding how players carve their niches within the NFL and embody the game's culture helps us to appreciate how they make their peace with life after football.

1

PURSUING "THE DREAM"

I had dreams of being a football player since I was a little kid. It was some-thing I wanted from as far back as I can remember, something I've been striving for from the very beginning. Sometimes it was all that mattered.[1]

NFL careers start with a childhood dream. On NFL draft day, absolutely the most frequent comment by players just drafted is, "It's a dream come true!" Of course, most American boys at one time or another dream of being football players, firefighters, or superheroes. But NFL players have devoted their lives to pursuing their dream through a combination of work, talent, and opportunity. George Koonce recalls his dream.

When I was a kid, I was going to be a football player, a basketball player, some-thing like that. When I was nine years old, but even before that, I used to play behind the houses. I would go to the high school football games with my sister. I would be up under the bleachers with a bunch of kids. I wouldn't really be watching the game. I was trying to play my own game with other kids of my own age. But I really got involved at nine years old officially, when I started playing Pop Warner. Then it was official, when I had a uniform and there were guys [referees] out there in pinstripes. About that time, I started thinking about it seriously. My mom was going to night school to become a beautician, going to cosmetology school. Like a lot of parents, she told me, "You stay out of my room when I'm not there!" Well, I went into her room, and I turned the television on and there was a Monday Night Football game on. I went and got my shoulder pads, my uniform, and put it on while I watched the game. Howard Cosell was up there talking. I think the Houston Oilers were playing. I said, "I'm gonna play on Monday night!" From that day forward, I said I am going to do everything I possibly can to make that happen. I watched the Sunday games and read the papers. I would save my money and get the Street and Smith [magazine] from the grocery store. I would ask my grandma to buy me sport magazines. I didn't know anybody personally who ever played, but I knew from watching on television that being a big-time player was special. For whatever reason, I thought I was special, and I wanted to be a part of that scene.[2]

Compared to some, Koonce started dreaming late in life. Retired quarterback Brett Favre claims he got his first football uniform—complete with helmet and shoulder pads—when he was one year old. "By the time I was in second grade," he adds, "sports were my life."[3] Journeyman running back Brandon Gold's dream was just as poignant, and perhaps more prescient:

I always knew I was going to go to the NFL as a little kid. Even from the second grade, I signed my autograph and said, "You better keep it," because I had dreamed it and thought it, and I knew I was going to the NFL. . . . I wanted to be an NFL player. That is all I wanted to be—period! So, that is when I made my goal. . . . I wanted to go to the Pro Bowl. I wanted to go to the Super Bowl.[4]

Gold accomplished everything he dreamed of, but simply wanting it isn't enough. Initially, the excitement of the fantasy propels the dream, but eventually physical talent, opportunity, encouragement, and hard work take over. Growing bigger, stronger, and faster than the other kids is usually crucial. Prospects for five-foot-three, 113-pound high schoolers are pretty dim. Of course, not all big, fast kids turn into elite athletes. They need direction, as Koonce recounts.

I really fell in love with the sport once I got involved. That was because of my mom. She thought maybe I needed something structured. Needed something that would keep me out of trouble. She knew I was aggressive growing up. She didn't want to—she actually used these words—she didn't want to lose me to the streets or to prison or anything like that. So she thought the best way to keep me busy and keep me out of trouble was to get me involved in sports. And that was genius on her part because she didn't have any models for this but she came to it on her own. She just felt like, hopefully, it's something that can keep him occupied. . . . She thought if I wasn't involved in sports she didn't know what I would get in to.[5]

Opportunity and encouragement set the table for Koonce. He grew big, strong, and fast, and with his mother's foresight and guidance, the dream took shape.

At first, I had no plan. I was just a kid. I didn't know what the steps were at nine years old, but as time went on from talking with different coaches as I went from Pop Warner to middle school, from middle school to high school, it became clear that to get the dream that I saw when I was nine years old in my mom's room, there was a process. There was a lot of work. And college had to be a part of that, to get to Monday Night Football. You had to go to college to play in the NFL.[6]

Other players didn't see real career possibilities until they had some life experience and organized sports under their belts. Former defensive back Charles Nobles, who played cornerback for several teams during his 11-year career in the 1990s and 2000s, speaks about his turning point: "It was high school for me. Coming from a poor family, you realize you only have so many different ways out of getting yourself that education. My football dream came from a high school that was a pretty much football school, and I knew that was the start of it right there."[7]

Dreaming of a *lucrative* NFL career is a relatively recent phenomenon. Members of earlier generations of NFL retirees dreamed of playing an exciting game at an elite level of competition, but big money wasn't yet part of it. Their dream was relatively innocent, highly romanticized, and almost never commercial or economic. In his autobiographical reflection on football in the 1960s and 1970s, cultural historian and former Kansas City Chief and Notre Dame grad Michael Oriard argues that football captured his boyish imagination like no other sport or game because of its "heroic" qualities.[8] From the perspective of a young boy, football was more exciting, dangerous, and intense than other sports. Players were more courageous, braver, larger-than-life heroes in outsized body armor. But Oriard never thought about the money. Others, such as Will Siegel, whose ten-year NFL career spanned the 1950s and 1960s, never gave football as a livelihood a second thought: "I really didn't think about it [playing in the NFL] until my senior year [in college]. I didn't anticipate going that far. I think we all thought about it, but never thought it would come to reality."[9] A dream was merely a dream.

Television, marketing, Pete Rozelle, and Joe Namath changed all that, as the NFL became "America's game" by the 1970s. It was *Monday Night Football*, after all, that inspired George Koonce. Oriard and Siegel grew up in the infancy of televised sports, before it was a multibillion-dollar industry. Subsequent generations came to know football as a grand spectacle with great financial allure. For Koonce, football was heroic, but it also promised a way to make a better life for himself. Like Charles Nobles, he learned that football had financial promise, that it was a way of getting an education, of improving his lot in life.

As the NFL's financial promise blossomed, the dream took on new significance in relation to the dreamer's socioeconomic status, social class, and even race. Middle-class kids' dreams of making it big in sports are often simply fantasies. For poor kids—often African Americans—the dream has more practical significance. If pursued with purpose, it has a compelling material payoff. So when poor kids dream of becoming NFL players, they may very well be plotting a practical life course that middle-class kids don't necessarily contemplate. The upshot, of course, is that boys of relatively limited means may actually invest more of themselves in the pursuit of their dreams than do middle-class kids.[10] This isn't necessarily the case for everyone. NFL players from middle-class backgrounds—Michael Oriard included—worked hard and sacrificed to bring their fantasies to life. But they probably played out those dreams alongside other dreams, if not plans, for adult success. Ultimately, these differences permeate the ways that players approach their NFL careers, and eventually, their lives after football.

The Path to the Dream

The dream doesn't come easy. Childhood play turns into practice, commitment, and conditioning. For George Koonce, this meant honing his focus and specializing his efforts. A good all-around athlete, he started out playing all sports, but by high school, his priorities changed:

After my sophomore year, I basically just quit basketball. I didn't want to play varsity. I just wanted to concentrate all of my attention on football. I was probably about 185 pounds and six foot tall, and I knew that I needed to get bigger if I wanted the chance to play at the next level in college. . . . My mom didn't like it. She asked me what was going on with me. I said that I just wanted to concentrate on football. She said, "Are you sure?" I went like, "Yeah." And she said, "OK." I said I want to join a gym, and after school I went there and worked out. . . . I thought that it would better my chances of going to college. I needed to truly concentrate on just one sport. And I focused on football all of the time.[11]

Today, such dedication is common. Boys with athletic potential know that it must be finely honed, not squandered in mere "play." Elite athletes "work" at their craft, on playgrounds, in gyms and weight rooms, and at elite sports camps, their dreams turning to goals. Work to be bigger, stronger, faster. Develop their skills, their games. Get "known" in order to improve their prospects of moving to "the next level." It may not be this way for all former NFL players, but for most of those growing up after the 1960s, football became as much a job as a game.

Sometimes the dream becomes a virtual reality itself, played out across myriad forms of communication media that originally inspired it. For example, De'Anthony Thomas, who eventually played for the University of Oregon, was a standout as a 12-year-old youth league player. Before long, hip hop superstar and entertainment mogul Snoop Dogg took a special interest in this "superstar," christening him the "Black Mamba."

By the time he was 17, Thomas was reading in *Sports Illustrated* that he was already a sports legend on his way to a spot in the NFL and an acting career after that.[12]

Thomas isn't the only "kid" in the limelight. *Friday Night Lights,* H.G. "Buzz" Bassinger's detailed chronicle of Odessa (Texas) Permian High School's 1988 football season, became a major motion picture and long-running NBC TV series.[13] The nonfiction book illuminates the degree to which local cultures elevate prep football players, highlighting their importance to the life of the community. Boys become heroes to grown men, public icons upon whom the self-esteem of the entire community depends. This is all part of the football "career" of many NFL players.

Football stardom often means more than adulation. Certainly not everyone, but plenty of teenaged stars reap tangible rewards for being special. Every high school has its mythology regarding the perks of being a star player: dating cheerleaders, lower expectations in the classroom, rules that can be bent if not ignored. Raised a notch, players get highly paid summer jobs requiring little work. Merchants offer "discounts." School officials and law enforcement officers are particularly lenient and "understanding" regarding players' childish "mishaps" or legal transgressions.[14]

George Koonce got a few perks early on, but nothing extravagant:

[I got some] attention from girls, better summer job opportunities. Help in the classroom as teachers gave me more opportunities. Most teachers and staff wanted to see a talented student-athlete graduate from high school and then go on to college. Students were willing to help with classroom assignments and offered assistance as tutors. There were even students in the class asking me if I needed help with a project, or if I wanted to be a part of the smart kids' group.[15]

Onto the "Conveyor Belt"

Most players realize that going to college is the only route to the NFL. If the odds are astronomically against making it to the NFL, the chances of earning a Division I football scholarship aren't that much better. Annually, more than one million boys play high school football, but only about 19,500 earn scholarships to Division I and II schools *combined*. There are roughly 10,000 players on scholarship at any one time at all major college football schools (the Football Bowl Subdivision—FBS) combined. Less than three out of every 1,000 high school players will get football scholarships to one of these big-time schools.[16] Undaunted, most players set out to become one of the chosen few. For many, college is simply a stepping stone to the NFL, a path that's entered earlier and earlier every year. De'Anthony Thomas may have been exceptional, but more and more he epitomizes a new rule: "Get the players with 'the program' as soon as possible."

In the summer of 2012, for example, Southeastern Conference (SEC) powerhouses Alabama and LSU began recruiting an eighth grader. LSU offered 12-year-old Dylan Moses a scholarship to play ball in Baton Rouge. Not to be outdone, Alabama matched the offer. Was this a dream come true for Moses, or had everyone lost perspective? Imagine the scenario of coaching legends Nick Saban and Les Miles—both winners of national championships—pleading with 12-year-old Moses, promising him the experience of a lifetime based on his *preteen* gridiron talents.[17]

From the very inception of college football in the 19th century, special incentives—inducements, promises, and bribes—have been the stock-in-trade of college recruiting. In recent times, "legitimate" recruiting expenses are extravagant. On one routine recruiting weekend hosted by the University of Oregon, the Ducks spent over $140,000 on 25 recruits. The entire point of the weekend, according to Coach Mike Belotti, was to make the young men "feel special." Dawn to dusk attention is mandatory. Coaches text, use Facebook, and call recruits dozens, even hundreds of times—leading to frequent "improper contact" violations of NCAA recruiting rules over the past few years.[18] In February 2013, the NCAA Board of Directors addressed this problem, opening the recruiting floodgates by removing nearly all restrictions on the type and number of contacts coaches can employ in recruiting prospective players.[19] By spring of

2013, recruits were reporting landslides of recruiting pitches. The University of Mississippi made headlines by sending at least 54 *handwritten* recruiting messages to a recruit *in one day*. All the letters conformed to NCAA guidelines.[20] Clifton Garrett, one of the top high school prospects in the country, tweeted: "#OleMiss aint playin no games!! 54 hand written letters today #RebelNation!!" Not to be outdone, Ole Miss defensive line coach Chris Kiffin, the coach responsible for recruiting Laremy Tunsil, exchanged more than 800 Facebook messages with Tunsil and more than 400 with Tunsil's *girlfriend*. Ole Miss also had 14 staff members write letters to Tunsil and other people close to him. These tactics are all within NCAA rules, and, with electronic communication restrictions relaxed, they will likely become more and more common in future recruiting classes.[21]

Not only are players on college radars from childhood, colleges and their agents often act like Santa Claus 12 months a year. Illicit payments and extravagant inducements are commonplace and well documented. High profile recruits such as Reggie Bush and Cam Newton reportedly reaped or solicited hundreds of thousands of dollars in benefits during their recruitment and college years.[22] In January 2013, Ole Miss five-star recruit Laquon Treadwell posted a series of online photos showing himself surrounded by attractive young women and holding $100 bills during his recruiting trip to the school. Whether the photos are documentary or merely suggestive, they convey the prevalent attitude among some recruiters that football talent can literally be bought and sold.[23]

Stories like these may be part mythology, but they are so commonplace that their underlying truths can't be discounted. Consider, for example, how University of Michigan quarterbacks Denard Robinson and Devin Gardner reflected on their recruiting experiences. On one visit to an SEC school, one of them arrived at his hotel room, only to discover two attractive coeds in the room, already in his bed. "It was weird, man." On another trip, one of them was given a rental car and told, "You don't have to return that." Another SEC school offered to pay for a relative's tuition. "Man, am I the only one to do it clean?" lamented

Gardner. "Michigan didn't give me anything!" he continued in mock outrage. "This place sucks."[24]

Such perks have been dangled in front of recruits for decades. Hakeem Chapman, an all-city player from the West Coast in the 1950s, tells his recruiting tale: "I was offered money, cars, women, by all the big schools. My mom asked me what everyone was promising me and I told her. She asked, 'What did [one college] say they'd give you?' I said, 'They didn't offer anything.' 'Good,' she said. 'That's where you're going.'"[25] The inducements offered "back in the day" may be small change by today's standards, but they were ubiquitous. For decades we've probably seen a mere tip of the inducement iceberg, generally when a school gets caught violating NCAA rules.[26]

Some college recruiters will say or do just about anything to entice a prospect. In addition to material inducements, college football programs are willing to "overlook" recruits' academic deficiencies in order to bring them into the program. Many players are enrolled with grades and/or test scores far below those of regularly admitted students. A 2008 study conducted by the *Atlanta Journal-Constitution* found that for a cross section of FBS schools, football players were admitted with mean (average) SAT scores that were 220 points below the mean of the full student body. The largest gap was at the University of Florida, where the average SAT score for football players was 890 (out of a possible 1600 points), compared to the university's 1236 average—a gap of 346 points.[27] Instances of individual players being enrolled without minimal academic qualifications are legendary. Dexter Manley—who went on to an 11-year NFL career (but who was also suspended for life for repeated drug use)—provides an egregious example. Manley confessed that he was functionally illiterate when he enrolled at Oklahoma State University. He had scored an 8 on the ACT (the equivalent of 400 on the SAT).[28]

Journalist William Rhoden has adopted the term "conveyor belt" to characterize how the big-time collegiate athletic/financial machine captures and co-opts young athletes. He argues that the best are funneled into college programs via the conveyor belt, which runs through a feeder system of youth leagues, camps, clubs, clinics, summer leagues, and scholastic leagues. "The Conveyor Belt transports young athletes from the innocent fun and games to clubs and specialized leagues—where they find increasingly rigorous competition and better training and coaching—and finally to colleges and pro leagues. . . . The contemporary Conveyor Belt is a streamlined mechanism for developing players and offering training and showcases where talented players display their talents for college scouts." Unfortunately, precious few of them succeed in fashioning NFL careers, notes Rhoden, and even those who make it to the pros pay a steep price in terms of personal autonomy and identity. By the time an elite player is ready for college, he may already be convinced that he is entitled to the opportunity—and a whole lot more.[29]

While Rhoden is skeptical about the conveyor belt and what it ultimately does to young athletes, there's no doubt that, in recent years, players have eagerly jumped on board. Their sense of entitlement aside, many have studiously mapped out the realization of their dreams. That route now runs through weight rooms, nutritional supplements, elite summer camps, personal trainers, and recruiting gurus and street agents.[30] For top-flight teenaged players, football is more than a dream. It's a full-fledged commitment. And by the time a player signs a college letter of intent, he's likely convinced that he's an exceptional player and a special person. He goes on national TV to announce his college choice. His self-esteem is on steroids.

The Dream Goes to College

Most elite players go to college to play ball. Were it not for football, most big-time players wouldn't have attended the universities where they enrolled. College educations and degrees are valuable perks, but they aren't the main course on players' menus. Football is *the* centerpiece of the college experience, and being a top-tier player requires nearly total investment of time, energy, and attention. George Koonce was typical.

Football was pretty much year-round. Spring training ran February through April. June and July consisted of working out, running, and conditioning. In season, we played from late August through December. . . . I would get to the stadium around 2:00 p.m. each day and leave after study hall around 9:00 p.m. . . . Somewhere, we'd fit in dinner. . . . I'd go to bed dead tired. Get up the next morning and do it again.[31]

Twenty years later, a midseason day for Michigan quarterback Denard Robinson provides a variation on the same theme. Up at 6:30 a.m. to make it to Schembechler Hall (the football facility) by seven for treatment for his swollen knee. An hour for Kenesio taping, electrical shock treatments, stretching, ultrasound treatment, and laser therapy, then into to another training room for rehabilitation exercises. After this, a trip to the cold tub to reduce pain and swelling. By 9:00 a.m., Robinson was in the swim tank. At least this was warmer. Finally, like all other players, he had his ankles taped to be ready for that afternoon's practice. From 10:00 a.m. to 2 p.m., it was classes and lunch. Then Robinson was back in the cold tub. At 2:30, he had a quarterbacks' position meeting and film study. Then practice. After practice, he headed immediately for the training room for more treatment. A quick dinner at 7:30, then back to Schembechler Hall for unsupervised film study. Robinson finally left the building at around 10:30. There he ran into autograph hounds for whom he signed photographs ostensibly for charities and children (but in all likelihood, to be sold as Michigan memorabilia, with no cut given to Robinson). He was in bed by 11. That's a 16-hour work day, 11 hours devoted to football-related activities. The next day would be different. He had to fit in "study table."[32]

In 1991, the NCAA instituted rules limiting actual practice/contact hours for varsity sports to 20 hours per week during the season. Organized off-season workouts were also severely restricted. Nevertheless, the widespread practice of "voluntary" conditioning and film sessions, plus time devoted to physical therapy and rehabilitation, mock the 20-hour rule. Denard Robinson's 11-hour football days were all legitimately within guidelines.[33] A few years back, an NCAA survey of football players at FBS programs reported that players devoted an average of 44.8 hours per week to football. Moreover, during the past two decades, the college schedule has been extended from ten games to 12 (or even 13 in special circumstances) plus approximately 35 postseason bowl games for the top 70 teams.[34] The college football season itself extends for nearly six months for some players—and this doesn't count spring and fall practices. Even summers are far from "free," with individual voluntary workouts paired with organized activities to make football a full-time, year-round enterprise.

So it goes in pursuit of the dream. Of course, there are compelling reasons to forge on. An athletic scholarship and a college education are themselves integral parts of the playing package—a valuable inducement, opportunity, and reward in its own right. Even though it's not the *ultimate* dream for many players—after all, the NFL is still the Holy Grail—it's a precious commodity, worth tens of thousands of dollars over the course of a college career. But as we discuss the value of athletic scholarships— and how they are used and misused—let's be crystal clear on one point. College football players put an extraordinary amount of time, energy, and sacrifice into their sport. They literally lay their bodies and futures on the line. The sport is typically both an emotional cornerstone for the college and the source of immense revenue for athletic departments. But even though they often put in 40-plus-hour work weeks on top of being full-time students, football players aren't directly paid a penny for their labor. They get free tuition and comfortable living arrangements, but colleges don't come close to covering all reasonable living expenses or compensating players for their contributions to the financial enterprise. College football is big business, and players are cheap labor.[35]

The basic reward for playing college football is an athletic scholarship—a grant-in-aid. The *2012–13 NCAA Division I Manual* specifies that a full grant-in-aid, more commonly known as the "full ride"—cannot exceed the typical "cost of attendance" for a particular institution. This is the amount calculated by an institution's financial aid office, using federal guidelines, that includes the total cost of tuition and fees, room and board, books and supplies, transportation, and other expenses typically considered in the cost of attending a college.[36] Tuition, room, and board are the "big ticket" items, but there are a variety of other minor benefits to which student-athletes are entitled, including medical insurance, a small number of complimentary tickets provided by the university, institutional awards (and gifts) given to all team members, and summer school and preseason training expenses, among other things. All grants-in-aid are awarded on a one-year basis, so no player is actually guaranteed a four-year college education. If a player is a bust on the field, his scholarship can be terminated.[37]

The standard grant-in-aid at an FBS school is worth about $50,000 annually, give or take a few thousand dollars. Near the top of the heap, for example, a full scholarship at the University of Southern California (USC)—a private institution and perennial football powerhouse—might cost more than $62,000: $45,602 for tuition, $13,000 for room and board, $1,500 for books ands supplies, plus other sundry expenses. Among private schools, Stanford, Miami, and Duke are a little less expensive. At top public institutions such as the University of Texas, out-of-state tuition is only $34,000, helping to keep costs down, while Alabama weighs in with an economical tuition rate of $23,000 a year.[38] Nevertheless, full-ride scholarships fail to cover many typical college expenses and don't provide players with funds for minimal discretionary spending.

School Days

> Why should we have to go to class if we came here to play FOOTBALL, we ain't come to play SCHOOL classes are POINTLESS

Third-string Ohio State quarterback Cardale Jones's 2012 tweet caused a social media buzz when it openly proclaimed sentiments many have long suspected regarding how big-time college athletes approach their educational opportunities.[39] Public perception—right or wrong—holds that college football players are single-minded, "dumb jocks" for whom education is more of a nuisance than reward or opportunity. While Cardale Jones does nothing to dispel this belief, let's not single him out for castigation. As legendary Alabama coach Bear Bryant once put it, "At the level we play, the boy is an athlete first and a student second."[40]

"Student" Athletes?

The student-athlete situation is even more complex than these comments suggest. In general, Division I football players enter college less qualified and less prepared than their non-athlete counterparts.[41] Nevertheless, Division I players graduate from college at rates only slightly lower than comparable college students in general—about 59 percent compared to 63 percent. Black college players graduate at substantially higher rates than their black student counterparts. At the same time, however, many elite football programs have substantially lower graduation rates.[42] "Dumb jock" image aside, college players are relatively successful students, not all that different from members of their age cohorts. Martin Willis, who played 16 years in the NFL, sounds just like the computer geek next door as he recounts his college experience: "I majored in computer science. I always loved math, and I got involved in a couple of computer classes back in high school. When I got to college, I already knew what I wanted to do. I wanted to be a software analyst . . . so I immediately pursued computer science, and that's what I graduated with my degree in."[43] Stories like this—of direction, purpose, and success—aren't uncommon among former NFL players.

Still, they aren't as common as tales of indifference, lack of preparation, and neglected opportunities. In many respects, George Koonce's college experience was typical. He dutifully attended classes, followed a recommended course of studies, maintained his eligibility, and set school aside after his eligibility ran out. The dream took precedence over school: "*After my last season, I signed up for classes my spring semester, but I didn't go to class. I was enrolled in four courses and got four incompletes. I needed to be enrolled so I could have access to the dorm and the meal plan while*

I worked out trying to get ready for the draft."[44] Koonce, however, did eventually earn bachelor's and master's degrees, and received his Ph.D. from Marquette after his NFL playing days were over.

Going to college simply isn't the same for elite athletes as it is for typical students. Studies compete with football and myriad related activities for the student athlete's time, attention, and energy. Will Siegel, for instance, saw college merely as sidelight to sports: "To be very honest with you, I was just going there to play football. I wasn't a great student. I was an average student. . . . It was all football, and I had basketball and track, and I just enjoyed the athletic part of it. . . . I took all morning classes. I never cut class. I figured if you just attend classes, you are going to pass, and that is all I did, I just passed."[45] Others weren't as calculating; some were less conscientious. Many players simply give themselves over to football and fit studying in on the side. Still others pile on other "distractions." Tommy Jones, a veteran linebacker, for example, recalls, "I didn't focus on my classroom work, because I was too focused on the girls and the social life. . . . I struggled at [college]. I had to go to summer school just to be eligible the next year, because I was partying every Thursday, not going to study hall, and stuff like that."[46] Jones never got his degree.

Making the Grade

Colleges protect their investments. A five-year commitment to a football player at a major BCS school may be worth nearly $600,000 when all is said and done—and this doesn't include the costs of academic support programs, strength and conditioning, facilities, administration, athletic trainers, and myriad other sundry expenses.[47] Football programs can't afford academic eligibility problems, so they spend vast sums to promote classroom success. At the time most NFL retirees played their college ball, schools offered some form of academic assistance and special considerations. More recent retirees, however, had access to multimillion-dollar academic support facilities, tutors, study halls, technology, and more. According to the *New York Times*, in 2006, Division I schools spent $150 million on academic support for athletes. USC alone had an academic support budget of $1.5 million, while the University of Georgia spent $1.3 million for academic tutors for athletes—roughly the same amount the university spent on the campuswide tutoring program for its other 25,000 undergraduates.[48]

Academic support programs and facilities have now become part of the "facilities arms race" for attracting recruits.[49] For example, the University of North Carolina's academic support program is housed in the 150,000-square-foot Loudermilk Center for Excellence. The Student-Athlete Academic Support Center provides classrooms for teaching and tutoring, advanced computer technology, a writing lab, reading rooms, and office space.[50] At Michigan State, the Clara Bell Smith Student Athlete Academic Center—a two-story, 31,000-square-foot complex—serves student athletes and houses a 210-seat auditorium, a "hall of fame" gallery, two study halls, 60 computers, structured study areas, a student lounge, a conference room, four classrooms, tutoring rooms, a director's office, academic advisor offices, and a reception area. There's also the Student-Athlete Support Service offering an academic support program that assists student-athletes with the transition to college and continues that support throughout the athlete's collegiate career, providing academic counseling, tutorial programs, and career exploration, planning, and placement.[51] State-of-the-art academic support facilities are now de rigueur if a program is to compete in big time football.

"Majoring in Eligibility"

While academic support is a vital service, it tends to spoon-feed players their college education. Academic advisors design daily schedules and programs of study to fit both students' needs and the demands of their sport. Support staff members register athletes for classes, typically with priority registration arrangements. They monitor athlete's classroom attendance and performance, and enforce mandatory study hours. This was a mixed blessing for George Koonce:

ECU gave me my schedule with professors and times already chosen and a map to get to class. I had tutors and got help if I needed it. Football players had to be done with class by 2:00 p.m. If there was a class or lab that took place at 3:30, 5:30, or 6:30, you were not allowed to take it. . . . A professor once told me that a student should study about two to three hours outside of the classroom for each class hour. That meant I should have been devoting roughly 40 hours per week in and out of class. That was impossible. The coaches scheduled ten hours a week for study hall. I put roughly 20 to 25 hours per week into my academics. I put in at least 30 hours of training and game time each week, and my coaches encouraged me to do more hours of weight training and film study.[52]

Unlike many players at ECU, Koonce picked his own major. In discussions with various advisors, he recalled the work he did around his father's contracting business. He was interested in the financial aspect of construction and wanted to pursue the field professionally, so he declared a major in industrial technology and construction management. This pleased his advisors because, coincidentally, they were steering a large majority of the scholarship football players into this major. *"If you were a football player,"* recalls Koonce, *"there was probably a 70 percent chance that you would be in industrial technology."*[53]

While this worked out well for Koonce, in the bigger picture, this sort of academic career management may limit players' academic and career horizons. And bucking the system can annoy the coaches. Jim Harbaugh, San Francisco 49ers head coach and former NFL quarterback, recalls that football players at the University of Michigan were steered toward easy coursework to ensure their eligibility. Harbaugh was talked out of majoring in history because it would take too much of his time. "Michigan is a good school, and I got a good education there," says Harbaugh, "but the athletic department has ways to get borderline guys in and, when they're in, they steer them to courses in sports communications. They're adulated when they're playing, but when they get out, the people who adulated them won't hire them." Myron Rolle, who won a prestigious Rhodes Scholarship while playing at Florida State, recalls that his college coaches were concerned about him being a premed major because they feared it would distract him from football.[54]

Every campus has its reputedly easy courses and "jock" majors. Of course, these "gut" courses and majors vary widely from campus to campus, but athletic department advisors know where to find them. Players aren't prevented from pursuing their own courses of studies, but there are well-traversed paths down which players are steered. The University of Michigan appears to have changed since Jim Harbaugh's days, since, in 2008, 78 percent of UM football players declared majors in general studies compared with 1.6 percent of Michigan students overall. Around the same time, 68 percent of Texas A&M players were majoring in agricultural development (versus two percent of all undergraduates), while at the University of Texas, 41 percent of the football team was majoring in youth and community services, compared to 0.2 percent of all undergrads. Such "clustering" is widespread among FBS football programs. In 2008, *USA Today* found 79 FBS programs with clusters where more than 25 percent of the football team was in the same major and 28 programs with "extreme clusters" where more than 40 percent of a team shared the same major. The "jock" majors varied widely from school to school. There were many of the "usual suspects" (e.g., communication studies, criminal justice, sociology, recreation and leisure studies), but there was also notable clustering in generic nondisciplinary majors (e.g., general studies and university studies) as well as highly specific and esoteric-sounding programs such as apparel, housing, and resource management.[55]

There are two significant upshots of the special academic handling that college football players receive. On one hand, college football players are likely to get college degrees. On the other hand, even if they receive degrees, big-time college players often get empty educations.[56] They make it through school, staying academically eligible, but often find their degrees haven't prepared them for life after college. Many fall short of earning degrees before their eligibility runs out and discover that while they have accumulated considerable academic credits toward graduation, they are woefully short of fulfilling the specific requirements of an actual degree program. Even when they earn degrees, many of them can hardly be considered college educated because of the way they've avoided academic challenges. Along the way, as a matter of simply getting through college, many players cede control of their academic lives. It's part of the cost of majoring in eligibility.

Special Treatment

Academic support isn't the only special treatment afforded college football players. Indeed, the perceived "perks" of playing ball are legendary around any college campus with a major football program. Some things are obvious, especially to other students. For example, George Koonce lived in an athletic dorm at ECU, and his accommodations were probably better than those of most other students. But in comparison to some campus accommodations for college football players, Koonce was living in "affordable housing." For almost a half century, athletic dorms were the signature of serious and successful football programs. The NCAA, however, put an end to them in 1996. Why? In 1991, *Sports Illustrated* characterized athletic dorms as a "perverse combination of Plato's Retreat [a notorious New York swinger's club] . . . cocaine den . . . and munitions dump."[57] By the standards of the day, living quarters were luxurious, the amenities lavish, and rules of residence life were loosely interpreted and enforced.

Hoping to stem the excesses, the NCAA banned housing catering only to scholarship athletes, instituting a rule that requires that every dormitory floor housing scholarship athletes must be occupied by at least 50 percent non-athletes as well. In recent years, colleges have been finessing this regulation by re-creating athletic palaces, but allowing equal numbers of non-athletes to live there, too. The opulence of today's accommodations is astounding. In 2013, the University of Oklahoma opened the $75 million Headington Hall housing facility; the six-story, 230,000-square-foot building features an outdoor dining and grilling gazebo in its central courtyard, a 75-seat theater, a formal "living room" commons that includes a fireplace and oak paneling, a restaurant-style dining hall, a game room, and retail space that is expected to include a coffee shop, a convenience store, and a restaurant. Each residential floor also will have space devoted to individual or group study, a computer lab, a conference room, and an academic center. The residential rooms themselves will be more like hotel suites than dorm rooms. "We wanted to create a living and learning experience," said an OU administrator. "We know that students and student-athletes come to campus living away from home for the very first time. We wanted them to have the greatest possible start to their career from a living perspective."[58]

The concept of housing athletes together, but apart from other students, however, remains controversial. Those supporting athletic dorms argue that student athletes deserve excellent accommodations: they've "earned" them. Further, the dorms facilitate the use of both athletic and academic training facilities and resources. Finally, having players live together both fosters team cohesiveness and facilitates the supervision of young men living on their own for the first time. But others note major drawbacks, often pointing to aspects of the special culture it fosters—a culture that's both a boon and a blight. A cradle of camaraderie and a shelter from outside aggravation, the athletic dorm can also become an isolated hangout for bad habits. Separated from the general student population, athletes aren't well integrated into campus life. They stay to themselves, inhabiting virtual "islands of homogeneity," and sometimes fail to grow into well-rounded students. They miss out on the socialization that typifies the college experience. As early as the 1970s, the faculty athletics representative at Indiana University warned that "the student-athlete has become a specialized product of contemporary culture" and was in danger of being cut off from the larger life of campus.[59]

Even more insidiously, athletic dorm culture can spiral out of control, with dramatic implications. For example, during the 1980s, a time when many of today's NFL retirees attended college, a series of scandals rocked the athletic dorm scene. Perhaps the most notorious involved the athletic dorm at the University of Miami. In September 1986, 14 police units were summoned to Foster Hall because about 40 players were engaged in what police reports characterized as "a brawl" and others called a "riot in the football dorm." Seven times in 1985, police arrested Hurricane players at the dorm on charges ranging from trespassing to arson. "It was like being the caretaker of an Old West bordello," recalls Alan Beals, an academic counselor during that time. "Saturday nights were ugly. You'd see girls rolling around outside your window, fighting over [former wide receiver] Michael Irvin. [The players] would just trade around." University of Miami president Edward Foote eventually shut down the dorm, explaining: "Part of being a college student is learning how to manage the treasure of freedom. It's true, there is more control if you have them [football players] all in one place. But the point of education is not to control but rather to create an environment that is rich in the opportunity for personal growth. Part of that is to make mistakes, to stay up too late or to fail an examination. And to face the consequences."[60]

For better or worse, athletic dorms often become "athletic islands," isolated from much of student life.[61] While he doesn't lay all the blame on athletic dorms, George Koonce thinks that football diminished his college experience.

My social circles were limited. Just about all of my friends were teammates, not classmates or fraternity brothers. . . . One of my biggest regrets about being a student-athlete is that I did not get a chance to take part of all of the things a university has to offer. . . . I didn't have a balance.[62]

And the balance is further upset as players find their college life closely tethered to their training facilities. All the top football schools have shining new athletic complexes that provide meeting space, weight rooms, rehab centers, and recreational outlets. Indeed, the "arms race" for training facility superiority is positively nuclear. With multimillionaire donors such as financier T. Boone Pickens (Oklahoma State: $265–400 million) and Nike's Phil Knight (University of Oregon: $300 million) paying the way,[63] universities are building increasingly extravagant sports palaces to attract the best recruits and "nurture" superior players. The University of Oregon's Football Performance Center tops the list. With a cost conservatively estimated at $68 million, the 145,000-square-foot complex is a palace designed to satisfy nearly all of a young sportsman's dreams. Giant screen TVs, video games, lavish furnishings, locker rooms, training facilities, and more. It's enough to make a young man feel special.

Premium Perks

The NCAA boasts of a plethora of additional benefits beyond tuition, room, and board. The official list includes: degree completion and postgraduate scholarships, life skills training, and development grants. Among the primary financial benefits is the NCAA Catastrophic Injury Insurance Program to assist student-athletes who suffer catastrophic injuries while participating in an intercollegiate athletics activity. The NCAA also provides other insurance programs and also helps student-athletes with unmet financial needs through the Student Assistance Fund.[64]

Nevertheless, additional perks—many of them "off the books"—are widespread and legendary, if not systematically documented. These include direct financial payment to players by coaches, alumni, and boosters, financial enticements offered to recruits, money made by selling football awards and memorabilia, shelter from university and criminal justice sanctions, academic fraud to preserve players' eligibility, provision of prostitutes to players, and special incentives and "bounties" offered for game performance. Such transgressions at high-profile programs are too numerous to catalog, and have been going on for decades. Recently, for example, former players at Auburn University made a series of startling, yet all too familiar allegations: coaches were paying football players; payments were offered to players to forego entering the NFL draft; prospects were offered illegal recruiting enticements; players were commonly engaged in illicit drug use; players were sheltered in dealing with the criminal justice system; grades were inappropriately changed, and on and on.[65] Similarly, the University of Miami has been accused of illicit payments of hundreds of thousands of dollars, implicating 72 former Hurricane athletes.[66] At USC, a Land Rover and airline ticket were provided to a key football player.[67] Ohio State players were guilty of accepting improper benefits and selling awards (including Big Ten championship rings), gifts, and university apparel valued from $1,000 to $2,500.[68] Some of these "bonuses" are negligible and many are written off as the consequence of players merely trying to tap into the tremendous financial profits turned by big-time football, although all players are apprised from the start about NCAA regulations relating to financial benefits. But other rewards are far from trivial, occasionally approaching six-figure payoffs. In the 1970s and 1980s, for example, Southern Methodist University boosters maintained a $400,000 "slush fund" for paying athletes—with the knowledge and cooperation of coaches and the complicity of university presidents and members of the university Board of Governors, including a governor of the State of Texas. The situation got so out of hand that two players hijacked the entire slush fund without repercussion because coaches were afraid the players might expose the program to the media if they were punished.[69]

Such payouts have been around from the beginning of intercollegiate sports, and tales—both mythic and true—have long circulated regarding special treatment accorded campus football heroes.[70] While the magnitude of contemporary perks is often staggering, old-timers remember legendary LSU running back and former NFL star Billy Cannon making extra money by selling off entire *sections* of Tiger Stadium seats.[71] Clearly, rules and regulations didn't fully apply when you could run the ball like Billy Cannon. George Koonce recalls that they might even be bent for inside linebackers who seldom touched the ball.

Boosters were always around. They wanted to be involved. . . . After a pep rally, or the hotel on the road, they would try to get to know you. They had "Feed the Pirate" nights. A booster's family would take a player into their house for dinner. . . . Now and then I got some handshakes with some hundred-dollar bills. . . . I appreciated it, because I didn't have any money. So, I basically used it for gas or to get a sandwich. It's not like I was getting a lot of money to go to the mall or buy some jewelry.[72]

To be sure, Koonce was getting sandwich money, not Mercedes money, but special treatment filtered all the way down to a JC transfer linebacker. The point is not to belabor illicit gains by scholarship athletes. Rather it's to underscore the pervasive ways in which "being special" manifests itself in the lives of college players.

Certainly Special

"NFL Draft Day." They wait in the "Green Room" in New York or at home by the phone. It's a moment of defining truth, the moment when dreams are fulfilled or shattered. The elation and anguish is played out each spring on ESPN as top-rated players wait to see where they will be drafted—or *if* they will be drafted. Outcomes aside, however, the NFL draft culminates the process most players have pointed toward since early childhood.

"This is a dream come true," exclaimed Eric Fisher, the first pick in the 2013 draft. "I've worked for this all my life." "It's the best feeling of my entire life," said Luke Joeckel about being the second overall selection. "That's what America is all about," gushed Jon Gruden, ESPN analyst and former NFL coach. "A kid comes out of nowhere to become the number one draft pick in the NFL."[73] For the very few who are actually tapped on draft day, dreams have indeed come true. They have worked hard to get to that point as they arrive on the doorstep of their ultimate destination. On the road to the NFL, however, where else, metaphorically, has the lifelong pursuit of the dream taken these special players?

First and foremost, on the field, they've become accomplished athletes—the very best in (and on) their fields. They've forged their bodies and honed their skills. They've developed disciplined habits around their games and learned the mental aspects of the game. Off the field, compared to most of their peers, elite athletes have been surrounded by material luxury. They've lived in swank athletic dorms and eaten at sumptuous training tables. They sport a nearly endless supply of athletic garb and footwear. They study in electronically tricked-out facilities with tutors and advisors at their beck and call. If troubles arise, someone from the program is quick to intervene.[74]

At the same time, however, many players reach adulthood with limited experience in how to actually manage their own lives. Of course all children are cared for and guided by adults, but elite football players have been under heightened scrutiny and control since they were mere boys. Coaches, onlookers, and adult benefactors have guided their decisions on and off the field for years.[75] Teachers have known that many players need special consideration or their hopes for a better future will evaporate. Snoop Dogg lavishes junior players with attention and nicknames. Hall of fame coaches and college recruiters dangle enticements in front of 12-year-olds. Millionaire boosters want to be seen with 19-year-old linebackers. The college provides players with the finest dorms, but coaches tell them where to live and who to live with. Extravagant meals are prepared for them. They order from seemingly endless, but set menus, both literally and figuratively.

By the time elite players are knocking on the NFL's door, they've been treated as special *people* for most of their lives. Their self-images and self-esteem can't help but reflect the ways they have been perceived and treated. Elite players come to see themselves as others do—or at least as others say they do. It's a social psychological truism: when people treat you as special, you view yourself as special.[76]

The Dark Side of Special

But as they come to see themselves as special, players come to *expect* special treatment. To be fair, this isn't in every realm of life, nor on every occasion. But elite players routinely expect singular consideration within the context of their daily lives on campus—and maybe even back home. Mundane details aren't their concern. They have to "take care of business" as it relates to their athletic lives, but that business is carefully mapped out for them. If they fail to register for classes, someone will work things out, smoothing over any bumps along the way. Their material circumstances are taken care of. When you've lived four years in a luxurious athletic dorm, why should you expect less? Kids want your autograph. Coeds want to date you. And, at the end, the pros come knocking. By this time, expectations can run high—realistically or not.

The darker side of such expectations, however, is that elite athletes sometimes lose sight of conventions, rules, and regulations by which most everyone else abides. If rules don't always apply, they're easy to overlook or forget. Most of the time, it's minor stuff. If a player stays up late watching Letterman and his grades begin to slide, perhaps the athletic department can find ways for work to be made up and grades salvaged. But this, over time, may lead to chronic irresponsibility in the academic realm that can seriously jeopardize the chance of earning a degree.

Sometimes flaunting the rules leads elite players to run amok legally. Instances of property crime, assault, and sexual misconduct are unfortunately common. While public opinion certainly decries athletes' misbehavior, systematic evidence is equivocal regarding whether college athletes are more prone than other male students to legal transgressions.[77] But two aspects of this situation are clear. First, when student athletes run afoul of the law, and those situations come to light, the athletes are generally thrust under a bright spotlight.[78] At the same time, colleges (and especially athletic departments) are notorious for downplaying, mishandling, or even covering up student-athlete–related campus crime.[79] Serious offenses may never reach campus police officers or their off-campus counterparts because complaints are funneled directly to university or athletic department administrators. When violations are acknowledged—even serious ones such as sexual assault—they may be processed as "student conduct violations" rather than legal transgressions, thus allowing colleges to shelter student-athletes from public scrutiny under student privacy laws such as the Family Educational Rights and Privacy Act (FERPA).[80] If things get really bad, colleges may pull out all the legal stops. They (or their agents, alumni, or boosters) often provide athletes with the best legal defense available, as well as institutional resources and power that can help insure palatable resolutions to sticky legal situations.[81]

There's certainly an obligation on the part of colleges and athletic departments to protect the rights of their student-athletes. Nevertheless, bailing them out of legal jams (both literally and figuratively) condones, if not encourages, the sort of selfish, undisciplined, or antisocial behavior for which college players are becoming increasingly well known. Repeated instances of hooliganism at college powerhouses such as the University of Miami, campus sexual assaults, academic shenanigans, and illicit financial gains cast a spotlight on college players that's extremely unflattering. Helping athletes escape these encounters relatively unscathed contributes to feelings of entitlement and invulnerability.[82]

Relinquishing Responsibility and Control

William Rhoden is quite critical of how special treatment of young elite athletes shapes their lives and identities. He decries the effect of loading young athletes onto the conveyor belt that transports boys and young men into the mills of the "sports-industrial complex" where their talents are exploited while their selves are distorted.[83]

> The Conveyor Belt introduces young people to the worst ills of the contemporary sports-industrial complex while they are still young and impressionable. It's at the camps where many first learn about the gifted athlete's limitless entitlement. The better athletes learn that no wrong is too great to overlook, if not erase—that no jam is too severe to get out of. The Conveyor process makes a future star feel he is above the fray from an early age. Isolated on the Belt, the young athletes become accustomed to hearing "yes" all the time and having adults fawn over them and give them second and third chances because of the promise of their talents. The end result is often as evident on the crime blotter as in the sports section. No matter how focused and disciplined they are on the court [or field], young athletes are not given any restraints off the court [or field].[84]

But the process does more than condone bad behavior. With others treating them as special, allowing them to bend the rules, and bailing them out, elite athletes inadvertently cede control of their lives to others who help them capitalize on their talent. This has the debilitating effect of preventing the players from learning to manage their own affairs—to take care of the consequential details of their own lives. Star players are steered through life without having to actually look out for themselves. When they are constantly allowed to go to the head of the line, get special help with assignments and exams, have the academic "bar" set conveniently low, perks become expectations.

Taken to extremes, the process fosters a pernicious dependency, "infantilizing" young men who are ostensibly being educated and socialized into adulthood. Many elite football players—standing at the brink of adulthood—continue to be treated like children who are incapable of recognizing their own best interests or managing their own affairs.[85] At the end of the day—or, more precisely, at the end of their college careers—too many big-time football players are less prepared to venture into the real world than are their non-athlete counterparts. They have been academically and socially sheltered, so that even if they earn college degrees, they haven't acquired the academic and social skills, knowledge, aptitudes, attitudes, and sense of adult responsibility that usually constitute a college education.[86] Nevertheless, it's unfair to blame colleges for all players' educational shortfalls. After all, for many players, a college education isn't the ultimate objective. It's merely the "final audition" for the NFL dream.[87]

Restricted by the Dream

By the time players reach the threshold of their NFL dream, they are thoroughly committed to its fulfillment. Their reactions on draft day— "I've worked all my life to make this dream come true"—are equal parts cliché and reality. No one makes it to the NFL without talent, effort, and commitment—an all-consuming personal investment of body and self. Becoming a football player is all that matters.

This commitment requires sacrificing nearly everything in the name of football. Sociologists Patricia and Peter Adler contend that elite athletes submerse themselves so completely in their athletic roles that they lose sight of other interests, activities, and dimensions of their selves.[88] They live in the company of athletes, work in the company of athletes, and relax in the company of athletes. There lives are isolated sanctuaries from the rest of the world. As their social worlds and experiential focus narrow, they neglect or abandon other aspects of their identities, becoming totally engulfed in the athlete role. This "role-engulfment" sneaks up on players. They start out playing a game that's fun. They become enamored with the peripheral rewards that come to those who are good at the game. If they're successful, by the time they reach adulthood, they're swallowed up by the athletic role and have deemphasized all others. Their immersion is so complete that they become dependent on football to provide their sense of self identity and worth.

Role engulfment is not necessarily insidious. It's probably characteristic of most highly successful people, especially professionals. But it represents a trade-off, a commitment to specialization. It restricts one's circles, especially social networks. For elite athletes, this often involves a sort of encapsulation in a peer culture where members share norms, values, experiences, knowledge, myths, heroes, hopes and, of course, dreams.[89] Engulfment in football is necessary for elite players to achieve the dream. They incrementally modify, reduce, or bargain away other roles and commitments, as well as the attitudes, aptitudes, knowledge, and skills they comprise. As troubling as this sounds, however, it's merely a radical version of what nearly everyone experiences as they assume adult roles. We narrow and specialize. We embrace particular activities and attitudes and abandon others. Elite football players experience this to the extreme, at a relatively young age. The rewards can be superlative. The costs are sometimes subtle and they may not be apparent until much later in life.

Some argue that engulfment in football leaves elite players at the threshold of adulthood ill prepared to meet its challenges. Echoing many of William Rhoden's sentiments, Troy Vincent, former Pro Bowl defensive back and past president of the NFLPA, implies that the seeds of NFL retirees' problems have already been sown before players reach the pros. Troubles begin when players are told about their special brilliance while they're still in high school, especially when college recruiters come courting. Players are easily spoiled by the resources and luxuries of college life, the adulation of fans, and the perks of stardom. They've been overindulged by "enablers" for years; it's somebody else's job to take care of their problems. From here, suggests Vincent, it's a slippery slope to real troubles once the special treatment ends.[90]

As compelling as this argument may be, its implications and conclusions are too simple. Players' experiences before and during college are dramatically diverse. Not all players depart college entitled, irresponsible, uneducated, and spoiled. Michael Oriard may be atypical, but his path illustrates possibilities, contingencies, and options that confront most aspiring NFL players.[91] Oriard grew up in a white, middle-class family in Spokane, Washington. He was a star at Gonzaga Prep, a first-rate Jesuit high school. Valedictorian of his class, he graduate with a 4.0 GPA and scored 1460 on his SAT. He had several options coming out of high school, but loved football and wanted to play for Notre Dame. With no scholarship offer, Oriard nevertheless enrolled at South Bend as what might today be called an "invited walk-on." By his junior year, he worked his way into the starting lineup and as a senior was named team captain and second team All-America. He was drafted in the fifth round by the Chiefs.

Along the way, Oriard earned his degree in English and won a prestigious Danforth fellowship for graduate study in English literature. As extraordinary as Oriard may be, none of this came easy. Two years of football practice without actually playing in a game takes its toll. Football didn't hurt his studies, but it consumed virtually all his non-study time during the season and a considerable amount in the off season. As he earned playing time, on-field success, and recognition, any concerns he may have had about his engulfment in football began to fade.

But Oriard wasn't totally engulfed. He lived in regular student dorms and his friends were mainly non-athletes. By his own account, "The only difference between me and my engineering roommate was that I spent my weekday afternoons in football pads and cleated shoes."[92] Oriard also took his studies seriously. Starting out as a physics major, he eventually switched to English. Around the time Oriard was at Notre Dame, about 75 percent of the scholarship athletes in football were liberal arts or business majors; the other 25 percent were mostly engineering, pre-med, or prelaw.[93] All of the seniors on the football team in Oriard's class graduated in four years. His fellow starting offensive line mates had a 3.4 GPA. When he graduated, Oriard was not only in the NFL draft, but he was accepted into the Stanford University Ph.D. program in English literature. The Stanford graduate school is to English lit what the NFL is to football—the big leagues, to be sure.

In light of this experience, Oriard reflects on his career leading up to the NFL:

> I played football . . . without making a single academic sacrifice. My daily schedule during the season was a Spartan one . . . but it was manageable. It also . . . was aided by my lack of any social life in the all-male environment of ND. . . . I left Notre Dame in 1970 with the best education the university could offer me, as well as a full college experience.[94]

When Oriard speaks of "education," he implies something beyond what he learned in the classroom. Certainly, his scholastic experience was superb, but he was also "educated" by having to navigate student life with a minimum of outside management. While he concedes that life on the ND campus was isolated, he was never cut off from other students. He was caught up in the activities and traditions of Notre Dame in the same way as fellow students—not just fellow football players. He left college for the NFL in pursuit of *one* of his dreams, but he kept another intact when he also enrolled in graduate school.

I wondered how those two lives would mix. Should there be any conflict, graduate school would come first. I might play football for a few years, but teaching would be my lifelong profession. . . . Football offered the supreme challenge any player can face. Would I be good enough? As a kid I had dreamed of playing for the Los Angeles Rams. At twenty-two, I was less intoxicated by fantasies than I had been at eighteen, but I was fired by the realization that yet another dream might become a reality.[95]

Oriard went onto an "average" career in the NFL (three years with the Chiefs, plus a final half season in the CFL), and an exceptional career in English literature, earning his Ph.D. from Stanford, then working his way up to the rank of distinguished professor of American literature and culture at Oregon State University, where he also served as associate dean of the College of Liberal Arts until his recent retirement from academics. He published seven books and dozens of scholarly articles on his way to becoming, arguably, the country's foremost cultural historian of football.

Michael Oriard and George Koonce took different paths to the NFL. Koonce was a more accomplished football player, while Oriard was the better student. One is black, the other white. One grew up in modest financial circumstances; the other was more comfortably middle class. One went to public schools, the other to private, religious schools. While it's tempting to argue that the foundations for life success are determined in players' formative years, it's painting with too broad a brush to suggest—as have Troy Vincent and others—that players start down a slippery slope to ruin from the minute they encounter the myriad temptations and indulgences that come their way because of their special talents and special treatment. Oriard and Koonce aren't necessarily models of how to deal with life leading up to the NFL. Rather, they illustrate diverse adaptations to the disparate and varied contingencies of their early years. Generational differences, race, social class, economic circumstances, family background, geography, playing ability, and just plain good or bad fortune vary from player to player, from life to life. These sociological, psychological, cultural and economic factors can all make a difference in later life outcomes.

There clearly are some red flags, however, that signal possible potholes down the road. We would be injudicious, even foolish, to ignore them. At the same time, we shouldn't single out a few key factors, taken out of context, and blame them for players' later troubles. Perhaps seeds have been sown, as Vincent suggests, but ultimate outcomes are far from automatic. What we might learn from Koonce and Oriard is that players enhance later life outcomes by keeping options open as they pursue their dreams.

2

INSIDE "THE BUBBLE"

Man, we all lived in a bubble. . . . The team took care of everything. They had you scheduled all day, everyday. It was our lives. But I loved it. And the fans—everybody loved us. In Green Bay, we could do no wrong. Everyone wanted to do things for you. People just wanted to say hello and wish us well. Our meals were always "comped." I never had to park my car.[1]

NFL players live in a distinctive world of their own, a social sphere George Koonce calls "the bubble." It's an apt shorthand for saying that players are immersed in a cultural, structural, psychological, and experiential world that insulates them from many mundane aspects of everyday life. The NFL may be the most totally encompassing of professional sports institutions. It provides year-long training regimens, training camps away from all distractions, team facilities that cater to every need, and rules dictating behavior, comportment, and attire, both on and off the field. NFL players gladly hand over their lives because there's so much at stake: the dream, the money, the fame, the belonging. Life inside the bubble instills a powerful "NFL player ethos" that comprises a unique worldview, a set of habits and expectations, and way of life that can't be matched.

Of course, life in the bubble isn't uniform. Players differ and teams treat them accordingly. Conditions vary over time. Back in "the day," the NFL was less professionalized and certainly less lucrative, but the bubble was there, even if it wasn't totally encompassing. No description of a social world can be complete, so what follows is a brief sketch of life in the NFL, its culture, and the player ethos that constitute the bubble. It comes with a reminder: like all bubbles, this one is fragile. The average NFL career lasts only 3.5 years.

The Game

Any discussion of life after football needs to consider the nature of the game itself and how players feel about it. The vast majority of them loved the game. Will Siegel, who played for three teams in the 1950s and 1960s, captures a common sentiment:

> I enjoyed playing football so much . . . I would play right now if I was physically capable of doing it for the same money. I couldn't wait for training camp and most of the guys felt the same way. I just loved to play football. It was so much fun with the guys. I don't know how I could have done anything that I enjoyed more. It was amazing.[2]

The game appeals on diverse levels, providing an experiential allure that seemingly overshadows other sports. The *physical* dimension of the NFL game is obvious. Players are extraordinary athletes, combining a rare blend of size, strength, speed, and grace. When players engage one another in a "collision" sport, violence is both commonplace and spectacular. It's the visceral essence of the pure physicality of the NFL. Mike Singletary, a notoriously violent player for the Chicago Bears, shares what he *felt* from a good hit on running back Eric Dickerson: "I don't feel pain from a hit like that. What I feel is joy. Joy for the tackle. Joy for myself. Joy for the other man. You understand me; I understand you. It's football, it's middle-linebacking. It's just . . . good for everybody."[3]

But it's not merely the appeal of savage brutality. Rather, according to Michael Oriard, the "*tension* between the hit-or-be-hit side and the ballet side defines the essence of football: not the perfect pass or circus catch alone, nor the obliterating tackle, but the catch made despite the tackle."[4] It's the players' capacity to withstand violence and produce something exquisite from it. The challenge of playing hard and fast on the precipice of danger gives players a visceral, emotional high that's hard to duplicate.

For such a physical enterprise, football is also *intellectually demanding*. Coaching, tactics, game plans, and playbooks structure the game from beginning to end. Before each play, coaches electronically transmit complex instructions for how to execute the next maneuver on both offense and defense. Playbooks are literally hundred of pages. Players and coaches spend hours watching game film and planning strategy. Each play implicates multiple formations and alignments, personnel packages, assignments, and predesignated adjustments. As former Super Bowl–winning coach Brian Billick observes, the days of straightforward plays, strategies, and schemes are over: "'Brown Right 38' has given way to 'Shotgun Solo Right Close Z Left 2 Jet Rattle Y Drag.' Modern football is a complex mix of trickery and misdirection, of shifts and motion and disguises."[5] The universal use of the Wonderlic Cognitive Ability Test to evaluate players attests to the NFL's demand for intellect of a sort—a combination of general intelligence and football smarts.[6] Coaches demand functional intelligence and players have long acknowledged that playing smart is important. Phil Villapiano, formerly of the Oakland Raiders, observes that "God equals out the bodies. Someone's bigger, someone's quicker. . . . But the thing that makes you win is your brain."[7]

Football is also *social*, the ultimate team game. Of course most sports require collaboration, cooperation, concerted actions. Football, however, demands the conscious coordination of all 11 players on each and every play. Success depends on each player executing his own responsibilities so they mesh with those of his teammates. Each player knows his role, his assignments, and those of others as well. Teammates feel like integral parts of the "corporate" body that can thrive only if each part is in sync. They experience their individual contributions as vital cogs in a carefully designed, well-oiled machine. Understood in terms of any number of familiar organic metaphors, playing winning football is ultimately social. Everyone depends on everyone else.

The Money

While the game may be the main reason for playing and watching football, the money surely captivates most NFL players and fans. Salaries in professional sports continually astound the public: How can players make so much playing a kid's game? To be sure, the figures bandied about are enormous and players are acutely aware of their financial horizons. But the actual parameters of wealth in the NFL are poorly understood and frequently misrepresented. The financial dimension of players' lives demands close attention to separate mundane facts from sensationalized myths and fictions.

Any discussion of players' earnings needs to be placed in the context of the NFL's astronomical economy. It's the most lucrative sports league in the world. NFL teams are worth an average of $1.17 billion. By comparison, the world's top soccer teams have a mean value of $968 million. The average Major League Baseball team is worth $744 million and an NBA team is worth $509 million. The NFL's 15.4 percent annual operating margin exceeds that of any other sport. When we hear about players signing *multimillion*-dollar contracts, remember that they are being paid by *billionaire* owners.[8]

The average player salary in the NFL has been widely reported to a bit over $2 million for 2013.[9] While not every player approaches this amount, there's still a lot of money spread around. Star players, of course, and those who man key positions, command a disproportionate share of the salary pool. Early in 2013, Green Bay Packers quarterback Aaron Rodgers signed what is reputed to be the most lucrative contract in NFL history: $22 million a season for five years. That's $110 million total, added on to Rodgers' current $8.5 million per year contract. This topped a $20.1 million per year deal signed by Joe Flacco only two months before. Drew Brees reportedly makes $20 million per year, and Peyton Manning $19.2 million. Little brother Eli makes "only" $16.25 million a year. Across the board, quarterbacks in the NFL pull down nearly $4 million per season.[10] And these figures don't include endorsement money.

Estimates of endorsement income are unreliable, and they vary widely from year to year. Peyton Manning reportedly made $13 million from endorsements in 2012, while brother Eli took in about $8 million. Drew Brees of the Saints reportedly made nearly $8 million, while the Patriots' Tom Brady earned $4 million. Clearly, quarterbacks are the valued property—especially white, good-looking quarterbacks playing for successful teams. Other top players cash in big, but not nearly at this level (e.g., premier receiver Larry Fitzgerald, $1.5 million; top running back Adrian Peterson, $1 million). And occasionally the financial sun shines on lower-echelon players, who, because of their position, team, notoriety, good looks, or good fortune, command hefty endorsement fees (e.g., much-maligned quarterback Mark Sanchez—formerly with the New York Jets, now with the Philadelphia Eagles—makes $1 million). Endorsement money for most other NFL players pales in comparison. Top-flight players (Pro Bowlers and players with contracts in the league's top 100) may make between $200,000 and $1 million, but most NFL players are fortunate to pick up a few thousand here and there, mostly from local media advertising deals.[11] Players may also pick up "pocket money" by signing autographs and appearing at card and memorabilia shows and other special promotions, but these, too, generate substantially less income than most players make on their NFL contracts.

For the top players, the financial view is impressive. Even the "middle class"—those near the average—are sitting pretty. Financial circumstances for the players near the bottom of NFL rosters aren't quite as lucrative, but even there, compensation is generous by everyday standards. The 2011 collective bargaining agreement (CBA) between the NFL and NFLPA set minimum salary limits, based on length of service in the league, at the following figures for the 2013 season:[12]

Rookie	$405,000
1st year	$480,000
2nd year	$555,000
3rd year	$630,000
4th–6th	$715,000
7th–9th	$840,000
10th+	$940,000

While these minimum levels are a far cry from what elite players make, even the last rookie on the roster makes good money.

But before we're overly awed by these figures, we need to examine the structure of NFL contracts and salaries to better understand how monies are actually distributed. Things may not be as impressive as they seem. First of all, NFL players make *far less* than their counterparts in the NBA or MLB, even though NFL revenues far surpass their competitors'. In 2011, the average salary in the NBA was $5.15 million, while MLB players averaged $3.31 million for the same year.[13] Second, players' salaries vary widely according to position, time in the league, and other circumstances over which players have little control. NFL quarterbacks average nearly $4 million a season, and defensive ends $2.6 million. Average positional salaries drop off considerably from there: defensive tackles, wide receivers, linebackers, offensive linemen, and safeties average around $1.8 million, followed by cornerbacks, kickers, and punters ($1.7 million), running backs ($1.6 million), and tight ends ($1.4 million).[14] There is, of course, considerable variation within positions. Top-flight left tackles, for example, command far more than their offensive-line colleagues. In assessing salaries across the league, it's important to bear in mind that only a relative few players at key positions pull down astronomical salaries.

What Is an "Average" Salary?

To properly evaluate these salary figures, we also need to understand how "averages" are figured, and what these "averages" actually represent. The simple calculation of an arithmetic "mean" salary—the average most frequently reported—divides total player compensation by the total number of players. But determining the total compensation pool and the number of players who actually share it can be problematic. Each team has a 53-player roster, but more than 53 players occupy roster spots during any season, including players on injured reserve (IR), the practice squad, the physically unable to perform (PUP) list, suspended players, and players added to rosters for partial seasons. Thus, the first uncertainty is how many players are actually figured into an average. Secondly, each team has a 2013 salary cap of $123 million. Some of this will be considered "dead money"—money that has been paid or is contractually obligated to players no longer on the roster. So, it's not certain that the average salary for any particular year is based on the actual salary cap figure. But if we take the simplest scenario and divided the 2013 cap allotment by 53, we end up with a *mean* salary of $2.3 million per player. That, however, is notably higher than what *most* NFL players actually make.[15]

Statisticians routinely note that the mean is disproportionately influenced by extreme values in the distribution of values from which it is calculated. Toss Microsoft's Bill Gates into the calculation of the mean income of your neighborhood, and *everyone* living in the neighborhood becomes—*on average*—a multimillionaire, at least statistically speaking. In most measures of income or wealth, there's a lower limit below which one can't drop—zero—but the sky is the limit at the upper end. So, in the NFL, the highest values (Aaron Rodgers' and Joe Flacco's $20 million a year salaries) "pull up the average," so to speak. To take this into account, statisticians typically use a different average to summarize earnings—the "median." The median is the middle value in the entire distribution, when the values are arranged from highest to lowest. For the NFL, the median salary would be the middle salary among all players, which is currently estimated at around $770,000.[16] Half the players make more than this; half the players make less. Note that this average is well over a million dollars *less* than the mean that's usually reported.

Because the number of players actually included in the calculation of the median is also problematic, the reported $770,000 may also be misleading. A quick look at the Green Bay Packers' roster in October 2012 showed that 62 players were being paid at the time, including those on the practice squad and on IR, but not including players on the PUP list or already released. Using this base number (and not, say, the 53 players then on the active roster), the median Packers salary was approximately $640,000 at that time. This figure turns out to be very close to the average *minimum* base salary for a player who has been in the league for the overall career average of 3.5 years.[17] This may, in fact, be a good approximation of what players across the board actually make. Many players occupying roster spots make the minimum *or less* (given partial seasons on the roster). As many commentators have noted over the years, there's a very small "middle class" in the NFL; a relatively few stars make most of the money, while a large portion of the players make close to the minimum.[18]

In light of this, the typical player since 2010 might have made a bit over $2 million total football income if he'd played the average number of years in an NFL career. This amount would be somewhat greater if the player were on the active roster for the entire time and if he received signing bonuses or contracts for more than the minimum base salary.[19] Many starters would have made considerably more, but not many would have approached an average of $2 million per season (the purported NFL yearly average), or $7 million total for 3.5 years. Fringe players, those not on the roster for all games—those figuratively hanging on by their fingernails—might have made considerably less. Some estimates suggest that around 20 percent of players on NFL rosters make the league minimum salary for their entire tenure in the NFL.[20] While this is a lot of money to earn before the age of 26 or 27, it's a far cry from what the public often believes NFL players make.

Generational Differences

Today's NFL retirees span several historical eras and generations of players. A retiree who played before the 1990s probably didn't earn very much—certainly not what players make today. Several factors contribute to the generational differences. In the early 1960s, burgeoning TV contracts and competition from the upstart American Football League prompted a significant leap in players' salaries—especially for the stars. The competition provided by the short-lived United States Football League from 1983 to 1985 offered a similar salary bump, but again, top-echelon players reaped most of the benefits.[21] The most significant factor in advancing players' salaries, however, was the advent of unrestricted free agency in 1993. The NFLPA has struggled for decades over players' rights and benefits, winning incremental gains along the way. But the 1993 CBA that instituted unrestricted free agency opened the salary floodgates.[22]

Accounts of the historical progression of NFL salaries are both inconsistent and sketchy. There's no definitive record of average league salaries over the decades. Nevertheless, a brief informal history of NFL salaries provides a sense for the differing financial circumstances for players who have played and retired in different eras.

THE EARLY YEARS

In 1956, the minimum NFL salary was reported as $5,000.[23] In 1957, Paul Hornung, Notre Dame Heisman Trophy winner and the first pick in the 1957 draft, signed for $17,500 plus a $2,500 signing bonus. "That was more than many of the vets on the team were getting paid," recounts his teammate Jim Taylor. A second round choice himself in 1958, Taylor signed for $9,500 plus a $1,000 bonus.[24] Future Hall of Famer Willie Davis earned $6,800 a year playing for the Cleveland Browns in 1958. During his subsequent decade playing in Green Bay, Davis never made more than $50,000 a year.[25] Among the NFL's older retirees, Will Siegel remembers what it was like during the 1950s:

> We had to sign a paper [in 1959] that we wouldn't tell our teammates how much we made. Mason [a journeyman quarterback] made $8,500 and I made $8,000. My dad couldn't believe this. He said all the time he'd done in the steel mills and all that money he made in the tavern, and never made $8,000 a year.[26]

While financial circumstances were not flush in the early days, NFL players still made a decent, middle-class living. Siegel was the envy of his own hard-working father.

THE AFL ERA

With the American Football League's inaugural 1960 season, competition for players proved to be an instant bonanza for a few top-rated draft choices and a select group of veterans who were willing to jump leagues. Billy Cannon, the 1959 Heisman Trophy winner, signed a $100,000 contract to play for the Houston Oilers, twice the amount the NFL was willing to pay him and five times as much as Hornung made just three years prior. Five years later, Joe Namath signed with the New York Jets for $427,000, the highest amount ever paid to a collegiate football player.[27] With the bidding war in full swing, the next year Donny Anderson and Jim Grabowski signed with Green Bay for $600,000 and $400,000 respectively, and soon thereafter, the NFL agreed to merge with the AFL.[28]

While most of the benefits of the bidding war accrued to high-profile draft choices, players' salaries across the board edged upward during this era. By 1970, the average NFL salary was around $20,000. Michael Oriard, a second team All-America center at Notre Dame and fifth round draft choice of the Kansas City Chiefs, signed a three-year contract, totaling $55,000. Of course, this was actually a series of three one-year contracts for $15,000, $16,000, and $19,000, plus a $5,000 signing bonus.[29] The average player salary rose to approximately $30,000 by 1974. By then, there was a $12,000 rookie minimum and a $13,000 veteran minimum. A teamster of this era, Oriard notes, might make around $10,000 annually. By 1977, the average salary rose to $55,300, with a minimum of $14,500.[30] A decade later, second round draft choice Darryl Gatlin recalls playing his rookie year for a base salary of $125,000 when the highest-paid player on his team made $450,000.[31]

THE FREE AGENT ERA

The financial landscape changed dramatically when the 1993 CBA granted players the right to free agency under particular circumstances. The benefits were immediate and striking. The average unrestricted free agent signed for $1.04 million; restricted free agents averaged $780,000. Reggie White signed a four-year, $17 million contract. Whereas no KC Chief offensive lineman—even the All-Pros—made $50,000 in 1973, 25 years later, several offensive linemen across the league were making over

$6 million a year. By 2000, the minimum first-year salary had risen to $225,000 with a $525,000 minimum for six-year vets. The league average was $1.1 million. By 2005, the mean NFL salary had risen to $1.4 million; the median was $569,000.[32]

- - -

Clearly, compensation is much better today than it was for players who retired before the 1990s. Those players were often in financial situations similar to school teachers, auto workers, insurance salesmen, and shop keepers. Players lucky enough to come along after 1993, however, were often "millionaires"—at least in the sense that that they likely earned over a million dollars if they had average careers. While the financial parameters of the bubble were not nearly as opulent for old-timers, even those back in the day had it relatively good. But for NFL players since free agency, the bubble has become something of a Garden of Eden, snakes and all.

No Guarantees

Perhaps the most important factor affecting player compensation is the NFL's longstanding practice of not guaranteeing long-term contracts.[33] Unlike the NBA or MLB, the only fully assured money in NFL contracts comes from signing bonuses. A player may be released at any time, whereupon the player's contract terminates and the team and/or league has only limited financial obligations (e.g., severance benefits). In effect, multiyear NFL contracts are a series of one-year contracts. This means that many of the dollar figures thrown around when hyping a player's contract bear only a loose relationship to what the player may actually be paid.[34]

Looking at Aaron Rodgers' contract, which is touted as a five-year, $110 million deal, Rodgers is actually guaranteed only $40 million—the amount he will be paid in 2013 by way of salary and signing bonus. To illustrate what can become of non-guaranteed contracts, consider what happened to Nnamdi Asomugha. In 2011, the Philadelphia Eagles signed Asomugha to a five-year, $60 million contract, with only $25 million guaranteed through signing bonuses, special provisions, and his first-year salary.[35] Disappointed with Asomugha's performance, the Eagles released him in the spring of 2013, before the beginning of the 2013 season when Asomugha was scheduled to make $15 million. In all, Asomugha made less than half of the money that was written into his deal. In contrast, NBA and MLB contracts are almost fully guaranteed, meaning players will receive the amount indicated in their contracts, barring a relatively limited set of circumstances that could void them. Thus, when Alex Rodriguez signed his ten-year, $275 million contract with the New York Yankees in 2008, he was assured to receive every penny of the $275 million (except for the year he has been suspended for violating league drug policies). But should an NFL player suffer serious injury, he could be released and receive only a fraction of the remaining money on his contract.

Non-guaranteed contracts almost always work against players' financial interests. They give teams the option of releasing a player if they no longer think he is worth the money. Or they can use the threat of release to coerce players into financial concessions—to renegotiate their contracts. This happened twice to Packers linebacker A.J. Hawk. In 2006, Hawk—a first round draft choice—signed a six-year, $37.5 contract, making him, *on average*, one of the league's highest-paid linebackers. He became a solid starter, but failed to live up to the "big play" expectations the Packers held for him. From the team's standpoint, the $10 million Hawk was scheduled to receive in 2011 was excessive. Early in 2011, the team released Hawk, but resigned him three days later to a restructured contract with terms more favorable to the Packers ($33.75 million for an additional five years). Later, in 2013, with renewed threats to release Hawk, the Packers again convinced him to renegotiate his contract, getting him to forego $10 million for the 2013 season and accept a restructuring that will pay him $10.6 million over the final three years of his contract, compared with the $17.85 million originally stipulated in his 2011 contract. Thus, regardless of specific details, a player's long-term contract frequently overstates its actual value.[36]

Structure and Control

We got a playbook for on the field, but they gave us one for off the field too.[37]

NFL teams manage their investments carefully. They leave little to chance when it comes to maximizing player performance, subjecting players to highly regimented, rigidly structured working conditions that belie the public's perception of NFL players' lavish, freewheeling lives. It's a continuation of the pattern established in college where players increasingly cede control of their lives to the football enterprise.

But, once in the NFL, players now have money in their pockets—typically more than they've ever seen in their lives—and a small measure of time that's actually their own. They're "not in Kansas anymore," both literally and figuratively,[38] but unlike their college days, they've got plenty of cash to spend and more opportunities to spend it. Younger players begin to exercise adult freedoms and discretion, and, while teams want their organizations staffed by mature, responsible individuals, they also believe that winning requires full commitment, round-the-clock discipline, and the subordination of individuality. Thus, the NFL is vigilant in structuring players' lives, even as players try to "stretch their wings."

Both sides agree that excellence on the field demands full commitment off it. To that end, preparation and training consume almost all of players' time in-season, and much of it during the off season. It may not be 24/7 for 12 months a year, but it comes close, as George Koonce recalls:

In season, players went to work at the stadium around 7:15 a.m. for the first meeting and worked until around 5:00 p.m. They saw doctors and trainers, participated in strength and conditioning activities, studied film, reviewed their playbook, then they practiced from 11:00 to 11:45 on the field, and then ate lunch at noon. The second practice started at 1:45 and would go until 3:45, after which we would shower, then study practice film to watch what we did in practice so we could make corrections. Film study lasted an hour or a little longer. If you were injured, you had to fit in treatment and rehab somewhere, sometime before or after meetings and practice.[39]

There's little time left outside the team's jurisdiction. Players typically get Tuesdays off, but many of them show up for injury treatment, light workouts, and film study anyway. While details change from player to player, team to team, and generation to generation, the story remains largely the same. It may not have been true 50 years ago, but today the NFL is a full-time job.[40]

This is true of the ever-shortening off season as well. Training camp starts in July and preseason games begin in August. The regular season runs from September to January, and the postseason can extend well into February. That leaves four months of off season that are nevertheless filled with informal weightlifting and fitness regimens, injury rehabilitation, workouts and rehab at the team's training facilities, "voluntary" organized team activities (OTAs) that all but a few veterans attend, and mandatory "mini-camps." "Organization" is a hallmark of the NFL, so there's little flexibility. Schedules are crafted, posted, and enforced. Even seemingly informal activities like meals and conversations with representatives of the media are timed down to the minute. Koonce recalls the schedule for a typical day during an *off-season* mini-camp:

6:15 a.m.	Shuttle departs to facility
7:00 a.m.	Breakfast
8:00 a.m.	Team meeting
10:15 a.m.	Break; prepare for workout
10:30 a.m.	Weight workout
12:15 p.m.	Lunch
12:45 p.m.	Media access
1:15 p.m.	Team meeting

1:30 p.m.	Special teams meeting
2:15 p.m.	Position meeting
3:30 p.m.	Break; prepare for practice
3:50 p.m.	Shuttle departs for practice field
4:00 p.m.	On-field practice
5:30 p.m.	Practice ends
6:15 p.m.	Dinner; player development lectures
7:00 p.m.	Dinner concludes
7:15 p.m.	Shuttle returns to hotel

A training camp day might be similarly structured, except it would generally include a second practice session. And, of course, there are curfews—in your room and lights out—every night. Being absent, late, or inattentive, missing curfew, forgetting a playbook, having unauthorized female "guests" in team quarters, and a litany of other offenses are subject to hefty fines.[41]

While this schedule seems packed from dawn to dusk, note that it doesn't include injury treatment, rehab, routine taping, tape removal, showering, or the myriad other things that grab a few minutes here and there. On top of this, nearly all players put in additional hours of individual film study. This isn't formally mandated, but without it, a player isn't around very long.[42] In addition, many players spend time with the media, and teams often encourage players to participate in promotional activities and charitable work "after hours" or on the occasional off day. As Andrew Brandt, former player agent, Packers vice president, and league consultant, suggests, NFL players' lives are thoroughly organized by the game: "Team meetings, position meetings, practices, spring practices, lifting and running sessions, team meals, bus rides, flights, team prayers, etc. The player's job is to show up and perform; the team takes care of the rest."[43]

When the team "takes care of the rest," it doesn't stop at the gates of the playing field or even the locker room doors. Among professional sports, the NFL is notorious for its desire to control every aspect of its domain.[44]

Emphasizing the benevolent side of control, teams pile on what they often refer to as "player assistance." This impressed Brandt: "It always struck me how many resources we [the Packers] had for our players. When players entered Lambeau Field, staff was there to coach them, treat them, feed them, train them, counsel them, etc. And their lockers were meticulously prepared for them according to the daily schedule, with practice, workout or game gear cleanly laid out."[45] But this is only part of the story. The Packers, like other NFL organizations, have a director of player development (the "PD"), a position held by George Koonce while he and Brandt were both in the Packers' front office. While player development and assistance are presumably in a player's best interest, team activities along these lines can also be perniciously intrusive.

Most PDs are former players. Koonce took the position with Green Bay six years after he left the game, seven after his last appearance as a Packer. PDs' responsibilities vary by team. Generally, they include helping players acclimate to and manage their roles as NFL players, both on and off the field. This might involve help with mundane logistics such as orienting new players to the area, finding an apartment to rent or a house to buy, hiring a nanny to help with child care, or doing background checks on players' potential employees. But the assistance can also be more specialized, such as helping players make career decisions, seek internships, finish college, or find professional representation or investment counseling. Sometimes the PD's counseling extends into psychological and emotional realms as he tries to help players with personal problems.

The PD's biggest responsibility is helping first-year or new players make the transition into the NFL by organizing programs and teaching basic life skills, such as managing a biweekly paycheck and balancing a checkbook. Increasingly, PDs are involved in guiding older players in planning their transition out of the game. And, of course, along the way, PDs advise players regarding their expected contributions to their teammates, the community, and team chemistry. Some PDs view themselves as mentors to their players, making themselves available to talk about football, everyday life, or anything else that might be on their minds. They try to impart insights from their own experience. "For me, I have to realize I was a young guy at one time," offers Redskins director of player development Phillip Daniels. "I can't tell guys not to go out to the club, but I always tell them how to go out. I mean, nothing good happens after 12 o'clock. If the club closes at two, leave at 12."[46]

The aim of this assistance is ostensibly to help players and their families address the practical challenges and pressures of daily life, while minimizing distractions. They help players focus on their jobs, keep their lives in order, and stay out of trouble. They even provide chapel services and bible study groups to cater to players' spiritual lives. But sometimes this special handling comes perilously close to babysitting players. Teams provide drivers and rides for players who go out on the town. They arrange and monitor drug and alcohol rehabilitation stints, check up on players' aftercare, probation and parole status, and even check in with players' parents to make sure that players' lives are on track.[47] Viewed in the most positive light, these measures are ways in which teams look out for players' best interests. Skeptics, however, note that these activities resemble their insidious cousins, surveillance and subjugation.[48]

Regarded in these more pernicious terms, player assistance and development are subtle extensions of what sports journalist Mike Freeman calls the NFL's "irrational desire to control everything around them, every player, every member of the franchise, every reporter, every blade of grass."[49]

No detail is too small or insignificant. Most NFL teams have strict dress codes for road games, when players are traveling through hotels and airports. Often, players are required to wear suits or sports coats and ties. The code may even extend to requiring black dress socks. Rules for home games might be slightly more relaxed, but still call for "professional appearance": no T-shirts, flip-flops, or jeans.[50] A dress code even shows up in the NFL rule book and on the field, specifying in great detail how players must dress on the field before and during games, including helmets, jerseys, socks, shoes, colors, materials, styles, and logos.

Players are fined thousands of dollars if they violate any rules.[51] The NFL employs official inspectors—known as the "Uniform Police" or "Clothes Nazis"—to inspect players during pregame warm-ups and notify players of violations for which they could be fined.[52] If socks aren't pulled up to the correct height, or the color of taped ankles isn't up to code, it costs the players money.

While it overstates matters to imply that the NFL is a "police state," player assistance and pervasive control are two sides of the same coin. Player development requires monitoring and managing players' actions and behavior. The entailed surveillance inevitably implicates power and control over players' lives.[53] While this undoubtedly has positive ramifications for the quality of the game on the field, its effects on players' lives are decidedly more mixed. It contributes to a rigidly structured, all-encompassing bubble.

Extraordinary Treatment

The bubble comes fully equipped with benefits and perks. It's more of the exceptional treatment players have received since they were teens, but being special in the NFL is a substantial upgrade. The most obvious difference is that perks in the NFL can be "above board." There's no need for a booster to surreptitiously slip players hundred-dollar bills in a handshake. Indeed, the teams themselves provide for almost everything imaginable related to playing the game. Off the field and outside the game, fans and followers show their appreciation any way they'd like.

"I'm Spoiled and I Love It"

With geopolitical tensions running high over the Berlin Crisis of 1961, President Kennedy ordered a buildup of the U.S. armed forces, called National Guard and reserve forces to active duty, and doubled the military draft quota. Among others, Green Bay Packers Ray Nitschke, Boyd Dowler, and Paul Hornung were ordered to report for active duty. Almost immediately, Senator Alexander Wiley from Wisconsin requested that the Department of Defense defer Hornung and Nitschke until the end of the season. Widespread public outcry scotched that proposal, so the players all reported. Through the regular season, however, all three were granted weekend passes allowing Nitschke and Dowler to play in every game and Hornung in all but two. The Packers rolled to the NFL's Western Division championship and were set to face the New York Giants in the title game in late December. Hornung was scheduled to begin a six-day leave beginning the Tuesday after the championship game, but when he asked for the leave to be moved up a few days, his captain refused. Hornung immediately called Coach Vince Lombardi and explained the situation. This was apparently the final straw for Lombardi. He told Hornung, "Let me make a phone call, and I'll call you back in 20 minutes." A few minutes later, Lombardi was back on the line: "I think your captain is about ready to get a phone call that will get you off to play." Lombardi had called President Kennedy, and Hornung was soon on his way to Green Bay to play the Giants.[54]

Very few NFL players get presidential favors, but most of them get special handling. Baltimore Colts linebacker Mike Curtis once proclaimed: "I haven't held a job in my life. I play a game for a living. I'm spoiled and I love it."[55] Most players would agree. Inside teams' training facilities, players have lavish creature comforts. Off the field, teams supply special perks for players and their families, such as movie tickets, guest passes to Disneyland, golf club memberships, and the like. Outside the team's realm, NFL players get assorted "freebies" or other tokens of generosity. Players seldom need reservations to be immediately seated in a restaurant. Many get their meals and drinks "on the house." Special deals on automobiles, jewelry, and clothing constantly beckon. Family members take advantage, too. Says one former player's wife, "Some NFL women have a virtual Rolodex of hook-ups. They talk about dropping the 'Eagle bomb' or the 'Forty-Niner bomb' during conversations with merchants in hopes of getting a lower price."[56] The bubble indeed has its privileges.

Adulation and Adoration

For some players, there's nothing more gratifying than the respect and adulation of others. Fans are eager to oblige. They recognize players and want their autographs. They go to outlandish lengths simply to be in a player's presence, to grab a piece of greatness. Today, even though nearly 15 years have passed since he last donned a Packers uniform, when George Koonce walks the streets of Green Bay, the neighborhood reverberates with chants of "Kooooonce, Kooooonce." Bart Starr or Donald Driver can literally stop traffic. Of course Green Bay is a small town, where unabashed hero worship abounds. But it's not just a small-town phenomenon; it's a prominent feature of most players' everyday lives. High-profile players are recognized thousands of miles from home, even outside the U.S.[57]

And it's not just rabid fans or autograph hounds. There's little that hasn't already been said about the "adoration" and "affection" that women shower upon NFL players. Most football biographies and autobiographies have a section, if not an entire chapter, devoted to players' "romantic" escapades. It's seldom a problem for players to find willing female partners. The 1990s Dallas Cowboys may have set the pace. Many of the players on those teams were constantly on the lookout for sexual liaisons. Safety James Washington boasted that many of the players were "addicted" to sex and pursued every opportunity—of which there were plenty. Placekicker Lin Elliott chimed in: "Being a Cowboy—the women came easy. I was a slightly out-of shape balding guy who wore glasses, but the star on the helmet works magic. If I had practiced kicking footballs as hard as I worked chasing girls and drinking beers, I'd have had a 15-year career." All-Pro receiver Michael Irvin topped them all, reportedly ushering a dozen women to his room over a four-day span just before Super Bowl XXVII.[58]

Shannon O'Toole, wife of former NFL player and current coach John Morton, says players are constantly hounded by "starstruck groupies."[59] Most wives agree that these women eagerly pursue players, who don't have to be nice or charming to curry their favor. Groupies show up just about any place NFL players congregate: bars, autograph signings, hotels on the road, even the players' private parking lots. Reggie White once complained that women even showed up at the funeral of teammate Jerome Brown: "I saw a lot of women in short sexy dresses who looked more like they were going to a cocktail party than a funeral . . . they were there to pick up guys."[60]

Above the Law

The NFL is a bastion of rules and regulations, but when players run amok, teams and sympathetic others are generally quick to intervene. Teams routinely fine and discipline wayward players, but monetary penalties typically amount to "chump change" for many of today's players who cash six-figure biweekly paychecks. In December 2010, the NFL fined Brett Favre $50,000 for his involvement in an alleged "sexting" scandal (Favre apparently sent lewd text messages and photos to a former Jets game hostess).[61] With a base salary of $11.6 million, Favre reportedly made about $10,000 per minute of game time in 2010, so he could pay off the fine in five minutes.[62]

Enforcing the rules is important, but a team seldom suspends or releases a player who flaunts team policy—although threats abound and players nevertheless worry. Teams actively monitor their players, but disciplinary measures are typically tempered by the need to keep players on the field. Stories of the "Renegade Raiders" in their heyday under Al Davis or of Paul Hornung's and Max McGee's extracurricular escapades with Vince Lombardi's Packers seldom end with anything other than a good laugh at the players' (or coaches') expense. Even when legal transgressions are involved, there's no shortage of reports of players getting special treatment by the law. Incidents stemming from drug use and drinking are too numerous to chronicle. George Koonce remembers his brushes with the law during times when he was "imprudent" in his use of alcohol.

I'd get people to drive me when I'd go out drinking. I had a cousin who would drive me to wherever. I had trainers or friends drive me. I even had police officers drive me home. They'd say, "George, have you had anything to drink?" And I say, "Yeah, I had a few tonight." And they would say, "Jump in [the police car] and I'll take you home." I was protected a lot. A lot of players were.

While there's no systematic evidence to support the claim that NFL players are more crime- or violence-prone than others sharing their demographic profile, serious repercussions are rare for those who might run afoul of the law, especially when drugs or domestic violence are involved.[63] Drug violations are "taken care of" without arrest. Even seemingly egregious incidents—especially those involving violence against women—are often overlooked. According to Mike Freeman, many NFL players are nearly oblivious to the possible repercussions of their actions, from both the NFL and the criminal justice system. They know that doing jail time is unlikely because most victims of domestic violence don't prosecute their abusers, and even if they do, "most players are wealthy enough to hire a top-notch attorney who can work the system to keep them free." Describing a number of high profile cases involving NFL players with multiple arrests for violence against women, Freeman argues that "players, especially the highly talented ones, also understand that no matter what they do, short of a murder conviction, there will always be a job waiting for them in football. They've learned. They have watched this scenario play itself out a hundred times. . . . Teams and the court system make embarrassing compromises so a player can take the field despite accusations of abuse."[64] Shannon O'Toole concurs: "An abuser in the NFL does not have to think as hard about the consequences of his actions if he's caught." Putting it bluntly, she contends that some players are "too famous for their own good."[65]

But not all offenses can be swept under the nearest carpet, so teams sometimes let the legal system run its course, for example, in homicide cases involving Ray Lewis, Rae Carruth, and Aaron Hernandez. But teams are at the ready with legal assistance and public relations advice, and are typically willing to welcome players back into the fold once legal matters are resolved. The Green Bay Packers, for instance, reinstated defensive lineman Johnny Jolly to their roster after over five years of involvement with drug-related offenses and the criminal justice system. Since 2008, Jolly has been arrested three times and convicted for possession of codeine with intent to distribute, placed in a pretrial diversion program (which he violated), placed on probation (which he violated), and sentenced to six years in prison, six months of which he served before being placed on "shock probation" in May 2012. Along the way, the NFL indefinitely suspended Jolly in 2010, then reinstated him in February 2013.[66] Coach Mike McCarthy welcomed Jolly, generally known as a good guy and productive player, with open arms: "It's great to have him back."[67] The point here is not to belabor Jolly's drug addiction and unlawful behavior, but rather to underscore the extent to which the NFL is willing to forgive what goes on outside the lines *if a player has something to contribute on the field.* It's quite a different story for marginal players, or for those who are perceived as salary cap liabilities. For them, any annoyance to the team may result in being cut on the spot.[68]

Isolation and Dependency

All the special attention works to isolate many players from the normal social transactions of everyday life. George Koonce remembers his early days in the NFL:

I didn't go out much. I didn't go out until my fourth or fifth year because I was trying to get my game up to where the other guys were. I wasn't in any social circle. I just saw the players and the coaches. . . . I didn't have any transportation, and they [the team] provided all the meals for us. So, I wasn't really integrated into the city yet.[69]

To be sure, Green Bay itself is as isolated as it gets in the NFL. When Koonce first arrived, he wasn't certain if he was in Michigan or

Wisconsin. He didn't know where Milwaukee was. He was surprised to find that there were virtually no African Americans in Green Bay, and later to learn that there *was* a substantial black population in Milwaukee. In the 1990s, as part of rebuilding the Packers into a popular free agent "destination" franchise, the team brought in soul food from Milwaukee caterers and barbers from Milwaukee to cut African American players' hair. Again, however, these thoughtful gestures represent two sides of the special treatment coin. Players received valued perks, but, at the same time, their dependency on the team deepened.

Isolation, however, isn't necessarily a problem from the team's point of view. To help players "focus" and minimize "distractions," teams separate them from the rest of the world for training camps, mini-camps, road trips, and even nights before home games. Nearly every minute is accounted for. Wives and family members are barred from team hotels and other living quarters.[70] Almost every player remembers being separated from loved ones for holidays, even Christmas Eve.[71] And any time players are together, outsiders are generally banned, except for controlled access by the media. As former Chief Michael Oriard puts it, "Insiders and outsiders were clearly defined: the insiders included us players and perhaps the coaches and a few proven others; the outsiders comprised the rest of mankind. . . . The center of our world, the locker room, was closed to most outsiders."[72]

Wives of NFL players agree. Shannon O'Toole calls NFL players and coaches "drive-by husbands," underscoring players' transient presence around the house during the season.[73] Many NFL couples see very little of each other, and many face serious personal and emotional barriers. Wives are not only physically barred from team quarters, but they are distinctly excluded from the locker room culture that dominates players' existence. Players are typically tight-lipped about matters at work, maintaining emotional distance regarding interpersonal difficulties on the team, insecurities about playing time and roster status, and the severity of their injuries. By remaining stoic and trying not to complain to their wives, they compound their isolation. They might share nearly any and all details of their lives with teammates inside the locker room, but they find it difficult to strike up or sustain friendships outside.[74]

Some of this is purely circumstantial; players' outside contacts are limited. For example, one NFL wife reveals, "I have got really, really good friends that my husband has never met. There are people in our neighborhood that will walk by and wave and he doesn't know who they are. He'll look at me and say, 'Who is that?'"[75] But players are also wary of making friends; they're suspicious of exploitative newcomers on the scene. Distance grows, even between longtime friends, the longer players inhabit the bubble. As one veteran admits, "People's perceptions got— were altered, and it was just very difficult to be around people that I loved because they just saw me—they treated me differently instead of treating me like [his name]."[76]

A significant upshot of this social isolation is players' loss of identity and self-determination. As William Rhoden suggests, NFL players surrender personal autonomy and responsibility in exchange for extravagance and entitlement. As Andrew Brandt put it, players are "cocooned" inside the team sphere, with limited contact with "reality."[77] Isolated and habituated to hearing yes, they lose touch with restraints that guide everyday life. They become accustomed to being shepherded through the system without having to look out for themselves.[78] With their own complicity, players end up in a world of their own, sometimes treated like children who are unable to fend for themselves or who can't be trusted. Says one NFL owner, "It is like being the father of 32 children, some of whom are not potty-trained."[79]

Full-Time Wives and Managed Lives

While wives and girlfriend are excluded from vast regions of players' lives, they are simultaneously in charge of nearly all of the mundane details of players' everyday existence apart from the team. According to one NFL wife, this is especially true in the early years: "My husband told me before we got married that my life was going to be totally different. I'd need to just bear with him for the next five to six years, when life would pretty much be about him. If I could just bear with him, afterwards we would be fine because he was going to do his part."[80]

NFL wives assume all household and childcare responsibilities. While they have financial resources to pay for outside help, they are neverthe-less *solely* responsible for running the household: paying bills, making financial investments, shopping, carpooling kids, attending school func-tions, doing routine home and car maintenance (NFL wives are warned to become familiar with a wrench and screwdriver), and otherwise shel-tering players from the "trivial" demands of daily life. While this sounds like the traditional American household division of labor, it is exagger-ated by "the-game-is-first-at-all-cost" mentality that leads both partners to shield the player from *any* distractions at *all* cost. Of course this is impossible, but it's the expectation for many NFL households. O'Toole tells a story of a pregnant NFL wife who phoned her husband at the team facility to tell him that she was sick to her stomach and vomiting uncon-trollably. Her OB/GYN told her to go to the hospital immediately for an examination and intravenous fluids. Hearing the story, her husband asked, "So how are you going to get there?"[81]

Outside the household, many wives assume the role of unofficial manager and agent, dealing with the myriad demands on their celebrity husbands. Wives may keep up with players' fan mail, forge autographs on pictures and other football-related items, maintain players' personal appearance calendars, and order special nutritional and rehabilitation supplements that players might need to stay in shape and cope with injuries. They manage and entertain the parade of visitors who come to attend games, and arrange for their tickets. According to both players and wives, the demand for tickets is staggering, especially in light of the fact that players generally get two free tickets to each game. They may purchase others, but at face value, which can cost hundreds of dollars. Moreover, they may have to go outside the organization to acquire tickets for their "extras," which can cost significantly more and take considerable time to track them down. Run-ins with family and friends are common because players (more precisely, their wives) don't have endless supplies of tickets and hospitality. But all this falls outside the players' purview. It's the wives' territory and they deal with the hassles and grief.

Being married to an unofficial manager and agent certainly benefits NFL players—although the cost to marital relationships is sometimes high.[82] Many players recognize the practical advantages. Still others believe that being married improves their chances of making the team. As George Koonce recalls, "*Coaches feel like if you're married, you got a family, you're more responsible.*"[83] It's a sign of maturity and stability. "Uncoupled" players often look for the next best thing. Many let their agents take over life-management tasks: putting players on living allowances, managing spending and investments, arranging for insurance, leasing houses—most of the duties NFL wives assume.[84] Others rely on friends and family. Pals from home, brothers, cousins, even mothers, may join players at their in-season residences. Sometimes the "extras" turn into entourages or "posses." While some of them are just looking for a free ride, it's clear that there's also an instrumental dimension to such living arrangements. It's not all extravagance, ego, and sycophantic hangers-on. Friends and family take on the life management functions otherwise performed by wives.

The NFL Player Ethos

Life in the bubble both constitutes and cultivates an NFL player ethos that provides meaning to players' experience.[85] An ethos is the distinctive character, disposition, spirit, and attitude that typify a social group. It reflects the on-field values promoted around the league—for example, teamwork, mutual respect, commitment, integrity, and excellence—but it's far from comprehensive, and it is certainly not a coherent, consistent set of tenets or strictures. Often inarticulate, it's a sometimes impassioned way of expressing what it means to be an NFL player.[86]

The player ethos incorporates several related components noted in the sports literature, including general societal values such as success, achievement, and cooperation that both underpin and are highlighted by most organized sports.[87] The "sporting ethos" typically refers to cultural attitudes regarding sportsmanship and competition.[88] The "sports ethic" is a related term used to denote a set of norms or standards that define what it means to be an athlete and to successfully claim an identity as an athlete. One prominent rendition of the sports ethic holds that (1) athletes make sacrifices and are totally dedicated to "the game"; (2) athletes strive for distinction; (3) athletes accept risk and play through pain; and (4) athletes accept no limits in pursuit of success.[89] The player ethos encompasses these tenets, but it uniquely reflects the NFL experience. It's an encompassing set of expectations, orientations, and values concerning life and identity in relation to and *beyond* the NFL game.

The titles of recent books about the NFL offer a revealing glimpse of the NFL ethos: *Bloody Sunday; In the Trenches; The Ones Who Hit the Hardest; Blood, Sweat and Chalk; The Fire Within; Next Man Up; Coming Back Strong; Never Give Up on Your Dream; Where Men Win Glory; Boys Will Be Boys: The Glory Days and the Party Nights of the Dallas Cowboys Dynasty; Badasses; Football Hero; More than a Game.* Taken together, these titles adumbrate diverse components of the player ethos, which NFL players almost universally appreciate, value, and embody.

While players may not explicitly specify this credo, it permeates most accounts of their NFL lives. At times it's been called a "code" by which players live.[90] This analytic treatment of subcultural imperatives appears in myriad descriptions of other insulated communities, the prison convict code or the code of the street in impoverished urban ghettos, for example.[91] Applied to NFL players, however, the imagery is far too deterministic, implying a set of rules or guidelines that govern individuals' actions. It's also too simplistic, suggesting that players merely learn the rules—both formal and unspoken—then follow them. The ethos is more of an implicit accountability structure to which players refer when interpreting their own and others' behavior. As such, it doesn't so much determine actions as it helps players constitute the meaning of their experience.[92] The following are some of the key tenets of the player ethos, many of which are closely interrelated. There are additional elements that might be included, but these are the foundational principles.

INSIDE "THE BUBBLE" * 73

Commitment, Competition, and Excitement

Players are expected to commit themselves fully to the game. One of the game's most popular, yet banal, assertions is a variation on "We have to give 110 percent." If a player isn't giving more than 100 percent—which, of course, is literally impossible—he's probably considered a loser. But the commitment to *winning* is even more celebrated. "Winning isn't everything. It's the only thing." Being supremely competitive is a hallmark of the NFL. Longtime NFL media analyst Rich Eisen claims that the league's players are the most prideful athletes he's encountered: "They don't like to lose. At anything. To a man, when an NFL player walks on that field, he believes his opponents are trying to take food off his table and money out of his pockets, which means they are going after his wives and kids and maybe his momma too. That's how badly they want to win."[93]

The spirit of competition spills over into nearly all aspects of NFL life. Says former player and coach Herman Edwards, "These guys compete at everything. That is why they are successful." Former NFL lineman Leon Searcy confirms this: "I competed just as hard off the field as I did on the field."[94] Every team has its player who is known to be a "sore loser," who needs to come out on top, no matter *what the game*—going all out to win at card games, dominoes, or ping-pong in the locker room, betting $2,000 that he can do more pushups than a group of other players, betting $10,000 on golf games, spending huge sums of money on jewelry, houses, cars, and women. "It is always competitive when it comes to spending," offers former receiver Andre Rison. "You see your teammate and he has a big chain on, and it's bigger than yours. And so you sit there and say, OK, I'm going to go buy the new 911 Porsche and pull that up to practice and see how he likes that."[95] T.J. Ward of the Cleveland Browns refers to this sort of off-field competition as "stunting." "It means to show off. 'I have more than you so I'm going to stunt. I got this car. I got this jewelry. I got this girl.' Anything that kinda makes somebody jealous." Ward suggests that this sort of competition is pervasive, extending so far as players competing with one another over who has the most and biggest firearms.[96]

This all adds up to an exhilaration that's hard to match. One former player says he got "goose bumps and the rush of adrenaline" just anticipating a game. Another described a game as "three hours of complete euphoria."[97] Michael Oriard claims that for some, the excitement's as addictive as any drug.[98] Football, he says, is "life with the volume turned up . . . 500 watts per channel and a massive subwoofer."[99] Regardless of description, a powerful visceral rush accompanies competing in the NFL. "I hit [opponent] really hard. I mean, I destroyed him. That got the adrenaline flowing. . . . I felt like the superhero Colossus from the X-Men."[100] Pursuing sheer exhilaration, both on and off the field, is central to the player ethos.

Toughness, Injury, Masculinity, and Respect

Football is controlled violence, played with a "take no prisoners attitude."[101] Perhaps the most common and sincere way players laud one another is to acknowledge their toughness, their willingness to confront violence and not back down. All-time greats Walter Payton and Emmitt Smith, for example, were relatively small men whose greatness is generally attributed to their courage, toughness, and sheer will power.[102] Brett Favre is forgiven his myriad interceptions and indiscretions because he is considered perhaps the toughest, most fearless competitor the game has ever seen. On the other hand, when players want to disparage an opponent, they're likely to challenge his toughness—say he's weak or soft. Even if a player is less than a sterling performer, he can hold his head high if he's considered tough.

Toughness and masculinity go hand in hand in most men's sports, but they're magnified in the NFL.[103] One former NFL cornerback says it plainly:

> Every day your manhood is being challenged. [Football is] a very masculine-based world. . . . And you have to live up to that. . . . If you're ever seen as a coward, then you're pretty much not going to fit in. . . . So you got to

prove every day or every weekend on Sunday at one o'clock or whenever that you're a man. . . . I think that is unique to our profession.[104]

The NFL ethos constantly holds players accountable to "be a man." Masculinity is virtually compulsory.[105] Of course this is often couched in terms of toughness and competitiveness, but it is also a matter of attitude and demeanor, on and off the field. For example, coarse, brutish behavior is commonplace during most team activities and profanity is widely considered the official language of the NFL.[106] Sexuality is frequently implicated. According to Mike Freeman, "Calling a player gay is worse than calling him weak or even gutless."[107] To be sure, there are plenty of positive attributes in the NFL's masculine ethos, including courage, tenacity, loyalty, and brotherhood, but the ethos also narrows the range of acceptable behaviors to a manly profile that's exaggerated into a sort of "macho" hypermasculinity.

Being a man is crucial to winning respect in the harsh and competitive NFL world. It's among the very first things that come to mind when players talk about the essence of the game. There's a culture of toughness and respect around the NFL that's reminiscent of the code of the street and culture of respect that permeates the hard lives of violent inner-city neighborhoods. It's hard won and deeply cherished.[108]

The violence of the NFL game makes serious injury routine. It's simply a way of life, something to be feared, but also accepted. Certainly, players don't want to injure other players. There's an unwritten rule: "Don't mess with a man's livelihood." Inflicting pain with a big hit, however, is another matter. And accepting pain and injury stoically is a necessity. George Koonce reflects on his experience:

Guys used to say, "You can't make the club in the tub." Early on, I was afraid to miss a day of practice, so I never missed a single practice or took a day off, even if I was hurt. We were all eager to perform, so guys would often deny the severity of their injuries. It's one thing to be injured and another thing to be hurt. An injury is something like a broken leg, when a guy can't play. But if he's only hurt, he can play through the pain. You just suck it up, get an injection, take pain medication, do whatever you have to do to play the game. Being hurt is just part of the game.[109]

The unspoken message is clear: if you're off the field due to injury, someone else will replace you. Players often conceal their injuries from coaches and trainers, "suck it up," and find a way to play.

"Livin' Large"

Players and the NFL game seem larger than life. For decades, image and reality have fed off of one another, creating a colorful mythology about players' excessive penchants and proclivities. For some players, "livin' large" is a lifestyle, a full-time commitment. It's pursuing a life that's as fast, reckless, and oversized as the bodies that play the game. It's reveling in gargantuan appetites and enormous excesses: fun, food, drinking, clothes, jewelry, women, among myriad other pursuits. It's pushing life to the fullest.[110] Extravagance is the byword. For Michael Irvin, it's a dozen women. For Andre Rison, it's "making it rain. We're talking about throwing money up, and watching it come down like rain drops . . . going to a strip club and just throw your money all up in the air. . . . We have moved far beyond raining to snowing. Instead of $5 bills, now you are flicking $100 bills." Leon Searcy fills in some details: "I'm in the car with another football player, and I bought me some jewelry, about $50,000 worth, and this guy wrote a check in the car, with the jewelry guy behind us, for like $250,000. . . . If you looked good, played good, they paid good. That was our philosophy."[111] As a corollary to excitement, livin' large can take off-field thrill seeking to decadent heights, perhaps involving gambling, firearms, or drugs.[112]

Livin' large is more than simply the pursuit of extravagance. It's also an attitude toward one's self in relation to norms and conventions that takes "stunting" or "stylin'" to outrageous heights. It's trying to assume mythic status, to stand outside the rules and customs that typically tame social behavior. Livin' large, players may adopt outsized, even outrageous personas, if not personalities. Casual talk and behavior may push the boundaries of civility, typically exaggerating the hypermasculine ethos that permeates NFL environs. Livin' large isn't necessarily malicious, but it is intentionally conspicuous. It often inscribes its signature by way of flamboyant nicknames: "Hollywood," "Neon Deion," "Broadway Joe," "Prime Time," "Cadillac." There's plenty of space for livin' large inside the bubble.

Locker Room Culture

Nowhere is fellowship or camaraderie deeper than in the locker room. Indeed, the locker room becomes a home away from home. As former defensive tackle Mike Golic puts it, "You are with your teammates more than you are with your family."[113] "In that locker room," recalls Tommy Jones, "we did everything. Hung out. Played dominoes. And then you think about the misery, the times of the wins, the losses with those guys. That is something that can never be replaced."[114] Locker room culture magnifies aspects of the family atmosphere, with a decidedly masculine twist. The locker room is the home of bravado, obscene language and crude behavior, horseplay, hijinks, pranks, and practical jokes, accounts of which can make legends of otherwise nondescript players.[115]

For most players, the locker room is sacred ground. To appropriate a now-popular adage, "What happens here stays here." Signs to that effect have hung in NFL locker rooms for decades.[116] Locker room privacy is sacrosanct. It's the inner sanctum where family matters stay in the family. Upholding traditional family values, however, is another matter. Remember that profanity is the language of choice in the locker room and that "macho" may not be a strong enough term to describe the locker room's ambiance. Says the wife of one NFL player, "I never let [our kids] go there. It's an adult male place. . . . They were just out there cussing and grunting and tying to kill each other. I don't want my boys around that."[117]

According to the player ethos, nothing in the locker room is divulged, but everything is shared. And honesty among players is the coin of the realm. According to Hall of Famer Jesse Dampeer, "You don't lie [to teammates] . . . so there is an aura of truth about the locker room."[118] Players will disclose legal transgressions, marital infidelity, even betrayals of the team, with the full expectation that the discussion goes no farther. It's a sacred trust that transcends other obligations. And that trust extends to the expectation for teammates to "have your back," to stand up—even cover up—for you if the need arises. Ultimately, the locker room is a state of mind more than a physical locale.

Locker room culture is also shaped by the fact that, in recent decades, the NFL has been populated mainly by African American players. The 2013 Racial and Gender Report Card indicates that in 2012 about 66 percent of NFL players were African American and about 30 percent were white. The percentages have hovered in this range since 1990. About 15 percent of head coaches have been African American over this time, and the percentage of African American assistant coaches has been in the vicinity of 30 percent.[119] This means that African Americans numerically dominate the locker room, and have for decades. In many respects, the NFL locker room turns American racial distributions upside down. Outside of football and basketball, there's hardly an American social institution where whites find themselves in the minority. This has notable cultural implications.[120] African Americans are integral to team leadership. They comprise most of the star players. African American preferences (to the extent that such things might be linked to race) in music, attire, and cuisine shape the contours of the locker room. "Black style"[121] sets many trends.

Culturally, this may be foreign territory for many whites, although players of all races become accustomed to this brand of "diversity" as they move up the ranks of elite competition. By and large, players and former players say that race is "not an issue" in the NFL. They frequently proclaim that the league is far ahead of the rest of American society when it comes to race relations. As African American Hall of Famer Chris Carter notes, "The NFL is the least racist environment I've ever been in."[122] Players routinely say that everyone's treated the same in a game where only talent and commitment matter, although concerns about racial "stacking" at certain positions still linger.

That's not to say that the NFL is color blind. Racialized talk in locker room is commonplace. While racial slurs are usually bandied about in a light-hearted manner by members of the same race, players admit to hearing and using them in earnest from time to time. And old stereotypes die hard. Some still consider African Americans to be intellectual liabilities at certain positions and whites to be insufficiently athletic for others. Former wide receiver David Jordan, for example, recalls that African American defensive backs and receivers never gave him due respect because he was a "white guy playing a black position." No one believed he was fast enough, even though he was an Olympic-caliber athlete. By his account, Jordan made the best of the situation and eventually won the respect and friendship of many of his African American teammates.[123]

Nevertheless, players claim that racial animus is rare. They cite plenty of cross-race friendships, although locker rooms tend to be racially segregated. In large part, this is due to players being assigned lockers according to position groupings, which tend to divide along racial lines. The "white" sections of the locker room, for example, may be composed of offensive linemen, quarterbacks, and kickers.[124] And, as with other groups, like tends to attract like, so that white players tend to hang with whites, and African Americans tend to stick together. The groupings aren't exclusionary, and multiracial groups and activities are common. The upshot of the NFL's racial composition is a work environment that is nearly unique among highly paid professionals.

Contradiction and Paradox

The NFL player ethos is rife with paradox. Often romanticized, it's a powerful set of orientations that sometimes confronts players with deep contradictions. Frequently, for example, commitment to winning—to giving one's all for the team—collides with the propensity for livin' large. Sometimes this makes for amusing anecdotes. Green Bay Packer Max McGee stays out on the town all night before Super Bowl I, shows up on game day severely hung over, then turns in a sparkling performance: seven receptions for 138 yards and two touchdowns. He becomes a legend. The Oakland Raiders of the 1970s and the Dallas Cowboys of the 1990s party their way to multiple Super Bowl victories. No harm, no foul.

But there are just as many instances where one tenet of the ethos prevails to the detriment of another. Recently, for example, separate media stories emerged about Green Bay Packers linemen T.J. Lang and Evan Dietrich-Smith. Both narratives featured the theme of unheralded players coming to Green Bay, persevering, and working their way into starting jobs on the offensive line. But in both cases, the march to success was waylaid by bouts of livin' large. Both players, so the stories go, took to extravagant eating, drinking, and staying out late. They grew complacent and out of shape. But each got a "wake-up call" in time to turn their off-field behavior—and their on-field games—around.[125] These tales are uplifting because commitment trumps livin' large, giving credence to the more "upstanding" aspects of the player ethos. Again, in the end, no harm, no foul.

But consider the unfortunate case of Eugene Robinson at Super Bowl XXXIII. On the day before the game, Robinson—the Atlanta Falcons' Pro Bowl safety and spiritual leader—was awarded the Bart Starr Award from the Christian group Athletes in Action for his "high moral character." That night he was arrested for soliciting oral sex from an undercover police officer posing as a prostitute. Robinson spent the night in jail but arrived at the stadium in time for the game. He played, but gave up an 80-yard touchdown reception early in the game and later missed a tackle that led to a long run to the Atlanta 10-yard line. The Falcons lost the game 34–19. Later, a teammate defended Robinson: "Guys had been going there all week. It's just that Eugene was the only one who got caught." Said another former teammate, "All the guys like to get their cocks sucked the night before a game."[126] The comments were made partly in jest, and with considerable bravado, typical of locker room culture. But more emblematic of the player ethos is Robinson's teammates' willingness to stand by him when he let them down on the biggest day of their football lives. In the end, it's a clash between competing values of commitment and winning versus those of livin' large and locker room culture. Loyalty at times supersedes commitment to excellence. The NFL players' world, like the world of sports more generally, is fraught with contradictions.[127]

The Greedy Institution

Some players say football's appeal results from its on-field authenticity.[128] There are unambiguous ways of determining success and failure, winners and losers. The game provides clear opportunities to prove one's self physically, to show one's strength of mind and character, and to contribute to the common enterprise. Each play demands teamwork and individuality, finesse and toughness, brains and brawn. Other players emphasize the game's excitement, camaraderie, or extrinsic rewards. Regardless of their reasons, it's hard to find an ex-player who didn't love the game or who regrets giving himself so wholeheartedly.

But the NFL is a "greedy institution."[129] Its demands are voracious, gnawing at players' minds, bodies, and souls. It claims players' exclusive and undivided loyalty, clamoring for their unwavering commitment. The NFL pressures players to abandon competing interests. It insists that players go "all in" if they're going to succeed. In effect, the NFL ravenously devours the men who play its game in order to create the players that make the league successful. You're either inside the bubble or you're out.

Like other greedy institutions, the NFL gets its way because it is also immensely rewarding.[130] Providing material incentives beyond most dreams, the league effectively steers players away from outside options. For most players, it's the only game in town. The NFL doesn't have to be overtly coercive. Rather, it infiltrates all aspects of players' lives so that they view everything through the NFL prism. The game's priorities become their own. Separate spheres of interest dissolve. Not only is the NFL greedy, it's "omnivorous"—indiscriminately all-consuming. It wants more than just 60 minutes on Sundays. It insists on players' lives.

3

THE END

What does it mean, to go out on your own terms? There is no perfect exit.[1]

Why is it so hard for players who've earned millions of dollars, who've been battered and broken, to walk away while they still can? Why don't they simply sit back and enjoy the well-deserved fruits of their talent and labor? Why can't players simply leave the bubble and get on with their lives? Former All-Pro Michael Strahan offers a possible explanation:

> That's the tough thing about professional athletes. . . . It's over and you are in your mid-thirties. . . . You wake up one morning and they tell you you're not doing something that you're used to doing for your entire life. What's your next step? That's the biggest challenge, I think, for most professional athletes.[2]

It's a shocking scenario, fraught with change, uncertainty, and anxiety. For many players, "the end" is traumatic because of how it *begins*, with the immediate, shocking displacement Strahan so eloquently describes. Although many former players endorse this explanation, if we look closely at what actually happens to most players, Strahan is slightly off the mark. The end is seldom so straightforward, not nearly as dramatic. It's unlike almost any other retirement. In fact, the term "retirement" seldom describes the end of an NFL career because players often don't realize that their careers are over. They don't retire; they get fired, and they may not even know it.

That's what George Koonce discovered. He played in the NFL for nine years, a starting middle linebacker with the Green Bay Packers from 1992 through his last game with the Seattle Seahawks in 2000. He was a defensive stalwart for two Super Bowl teams. He signed two multiyear, multimillion-dollar contracts. His career was three times longer than the average NFL player's. But when he reached the end, it wasn't how Michael Strahan suggests.

At the age of 31, Koonce started 15 games for the 1999 Packers. In week ten, he injured his shoulder. Team physicians told him it would require surgery but he probably couldn't further aggravate the injury. He could take pain-killing injections and play out the rest of the season or he could immediately go on injured reserve, have the surgery, begin rehab, and start preparing for next season. The Packers were going through a rough season: major coaching changes, up-and-down play, a good possibility of missing the playoffs. Koonce wanted to play—for the team, for his pride, and yes, for the money. He had recently signed a long-term contract and wanted to show the Packers that he was worth their investment. So he played. He took painkilling shots before every game and sometimes at halftime, and played for the rest of the season.

After the final game, Koonce did the normal season-ending exit interviews with coaches and the team medical staff. They scheduled him for surgery, which he had about a month later in February 2000. Shortly thereafter, Koonce's agent called to tell him that the Packers wanted him to "renegotiate" his contract. Before the 1999 season, Koonce had signed a four-year, $10.75 million pact that was considered quite lucrative for a middle linebacker. Now the Packers were asking him to restructure the deal—a euphemism for a pay cut. The team was contractually obliged to pay Koonce his negotiated salary for the upcoming years, if he remained on the roster. But remember: NFL contracts aren't guaranteed. If a player is released, his contract is void. A request to restructure a contract usually carries the implied threat that if the player doesn't agree to decreased compensation, he'll be released, and there will be *no* compensation. Koonce and his agent opted for the downscaled contract. This wasn't the first time he'd been asked to renegotiate a deal. The Packers had cut his salary under similar circumstances in 1997 after he underwent surgery for a torn ACL.

About three weeks later, Koonce got another call from his agent: "On March 15, the Packers are going to release you." Suddenly, Koonce wasn't a Packer. *"When I got the phone call I was using the Packers' facilities for my rehab and treatment. I was getting ready for next season. When I got the phone call I was no longer allowed to use the facilities. So I went back to North Carolina."*[3] Injured, without a job, virtually without a home, Koonce never considered retiring. He headed back to ECU, where, as a courtesy to a valued alum, the athletic department allowed him to use their training facilities and trainers.

Koonce had been close with his agent; they spoke almost daily for nine years. They were fellow ECU alums, friends as well as business associates. He said he would put out the word across the NFL that Koonce was now available. Koonce also contacted his former teammate Johnny Holland, a Seattle Seahawks coach at the time: *"I reached out to Johnny and he knew my situation that I had been released from the Packers. . . . I asked him to put in a word with Ted Thompson [Seattle director of player personnel] and Coach Holmgren [head coach and general manger of the Seahawks]."* Then, for months, Koonce and his agent waited.

I didn't hear anything. The only concrete conversation or information that I got was from my friend Johnny. He said he was going to talk to Ted Thompson, and he was going to give a message to Coach Holmgren. Coach Holmgren called me in June and asked me if I wanted to be a part of their organization. Coach Holmgren said, "George, I'm going to give you the veteran's minimum."

Koonce had played for Mike Holmgren in Green Bay before Holmgren departed for Seattle after the 1998 season, taking the reins of the Seahawks as both coach and general manager. He took several members of the Packers' organization with him, including Thompson and Holland. For a short time, the Seattle organization was jokingly called "Green Bay Northwest." But it was still the NFL, and Koonce signed a one-year contract for the veteran's minimum salary of around $600,000. It was a considerable pay cut, even from his restructured Packers contract.

Regardless, it was a roster spot and Seattle assured Koonce that he was part of their plans.

Koonce started all 16 games for Seattle in 2000. He was second on the team in tackles. On December 3, in a 30–10 throttling of the Atlanta Falcons, he returned an interception 27 yards for a touchdown. Apparently, Seattle's minimal investment paid off. After the final game—a 42–23 loss at home to Buffalo—Koonce went through the year-end exit interviews and packed to return to North Carolina where he would work out in the off season. He knew he'd played on a one-year contract, and that there were no guarantees for next season. Like everyone else in the league, Koonce knew that "N-F-L means not for long."[4] But as he left town, no one suggested that his days in Seattle were numbered. He figured he'd be back for at least one more year.

There was nothing mentioned about me not coming back. It was more like, "It was a very disappointing year for everyone. You know the record [6–10]. George, you played well." I didn't really know what was going to happen, so I was in constant contact with my agent trying to get clarity. In retrospect, nobody was honest with me, letting me know my career was done.

Koonce had been living in an executive condo in Seattle—a temporary, short-term rental—so he had little more than a couple of suitcases as he departed from the Seattle airport. Back in North Carolina, he waited on word from his agent. January passed. Nothing. Trepidation crept in: "*For the life of me I couldn't believe that I could go from starting 16 games and being second on the team in tackles to completely out of the National Football League. I thought that it might be, 'George, you'll have to take a backup role.' But in my case that didn't happen.*" Months passed. His agent said he'd put out feelers across the NFL, but nobody called. Finally, Koonce reached out once again to his friend Johnny Holland:

"Johnny, what's going on in Seattle?" He said, "George, I think we're going to go with a guy named Levon Kirkland [who had recently been released by the

Pittsburgh Steelers]." I said, "Really?" I had trouble believing what I was hear-
ing. Johnny said, "George, I can't really figure it out. I thought you had a really
good year for us." . . . Officially, I didn't hear any of this from Seattle. If I didn't
know Johnny, I wouldn't have had any explanation.

Seattle was out of the picture—suddenly, but, in retrospect, not surprisingly. There were incentives built into Koonce's 2000 Seattle contract stating that if he played 75 percent of the defensive snaps from scrimmage he would be paid an additional $300,000—increasing his salary for the year by about 50 percent. As the 6–10 season wore on, however, and the organization realized they were out of the playoff chase, his playing time declined. He found himself more and more on the sidelines, even though there was no drop-off in his on-field productivity. In the end, he didn't hit his incentive goals. Maybe this was a message Koonce had ignored. Looking back on the 2000 season, he now admits that subtle signs of depression were creeping into his life. He began to wonder if each trip to an away game would be his last time to play in that particular stadium.

By May 2001, at age 32, Koonce was still out of a job, but not out of hope. He religiously continued his training, working out four or five days a week under the supervision of the ECU training staff: *"I'd schedule my day around when I could work with the strength and conditioning coach at East Carolina. When he wasn't training student athletes, he was taking me through a regimen to get me ready for the upcoming season."* A season that never came.

The NFL draft passed. Spring and summer mini-camps came and went. Training camps were about to open in July. No job offers. Nothing.

I'm asking my agent, "What's going on?" I talk to the [Cleveland] Browns, I talk
to the [Kansas City] Chiefs. They're like, "If someone goes down, we'll bring you
right in." That goes on for the whole season, that type of conversation. I'm still
training, working out. On Sundays I watch the Packers' games. All this time, all
my agent says to me is, "George, you need to stay ready." Nobody called. I kept

saying, "I can play. I can go back to the stats, and with the right opportunity I can do that again."

And there was no paycheck coming in. Koonce was on his own, living on savings, working out, staying ready. 2001. 2002. Nobody called. Not even his agent. In January 2002, Koonce met his wife-to-be, Tunisia. In their early conversations, they talked about his career, his plans. *"I told her I was getting ready for next season."* But by now, there were more than just traces of depression:

I didn't realize everything that was going on at the time, all the drinking, trying to hide and mask the pain. I wasn't doing cocaine or anything like that but I was drinking. . . . I was very depressed. The only time I wasn't depressed was when I was doing something football-related.

Koonce was in a real-life limbo. For him, his career wasn't over; he hadn't retired. But Tunisia forced Koonce to confront some harsh realities. *"She said, 'George, that's great that you want to stay in shape and you want to play, you want to hook on with a team. But how about you add some other things during your day, like going to school? Maybe get a job.'"*

Initially, Koonce resisted. He had a job: getting ready for next season. But Tunisia planted the notion, and Koonce trusted her judgment.

One day, jokingly, I said, "I need a job, these bills keep coming in." She said, "Well, George, you have a job." I said, "What's that?" She said, "You own over 100 apartments. [Over the years, Koonce had invested in rental properties.] Why are you having a management company run those? You can do it yourself." I said, "I got to work out. I need to be ready. I can't do that and do all my workouts and all that stuff." She said, "George, you need to think about that." Then, when the season came around in 2002, I said, "Tunisia can you help me? I want to run those apartments." She said, "I have a letter all ready. It's a letter to send to the management company. I read your contract with them. You can terminate it with 30 days' notice. There is an apartment open at the complex. You need to turn that into an office." I said, "OK." And that's how it all got started. Later, she kind of took me by the hand and said, "George you need to sign up for these [college] classes."

But there was no fairytale ending to Koonce's career crisis. Managing his apartments and going back to school for his master's degree, Koonce continued to work out, continued to stay ready. Midway through the 2002 NFL season, Tunisia finally confronted him. "George, you're done. It's all over." That's when Koonce didn't speak to Tunisia for a couple of weeks. Then came the car crash a few months later. Slowly, George Koonce began to redefine himself. His old identity didn't surrender easily. His NFL dreams didn't die overnight. It was the end of 2003 before Koonce began to think of himself as something other than an NFL player.

Perhaps he finally became an "ex-player" in November, when Tunisia persuaded him to apply for a job in the ECU athletic department.

I did the interview. I thought I'd done well and they offered me the job. For $36,000, but I was disappointed. Tunisia was waiting for me as I walked across campus and she asked me about the interview. I said it went OK, and she asked if I got the job. I said, "Yeah, they offered me the job but for only $36,000. I told them I would have to think about it." Tunisia said to me, "How much they going to pay you?" I said, "$36,000." She said, "How much you going to make if you don't take the job?" I said, "Nothing." She said, "Do you know how much people make in the real world?" I said, "No." She said, "Turn your ass around and go right back there and sign that contract." I did, and that's probably when I really truly knew I was never going to play again.

Koonce's story may not typify all NFL players, but it's a more common scenario than the one Michael Strahan describes. The end seldom comes suddenly, cleanly, in unambiguous terms. It's more like removing a Band-Aid slowly than suddenly ripping it off—an agonizingly drawn-out pain.

Uncertainty

Official NFL retirements garner a lot of attention, perhaps because they're so rare. Occasionally, a player decides enough is enough and formally announces his retirement. Everyone remembers that Hall of Famer Barry Sanders walked way from the game suddenly, apparently of his own volition, even though he was within striking distance of several cherished NFL rushing records. John Elway and Ray Lewis famously announced their retirements, then took flight on the wings of Super Bowl victories. Others go out with less fanfare, but with finality nonetheless. Hakeem Chapman, a veteran from the 1960s and 1970s, talks about calling it quits:

> I was playing with the [Team 1], and they traded me to [Team 2] just to get rid of me, because I was making more money than the quarterback. So, I went to [Team 2] . . . and I was making more than their starting quarterback. . . . I was released, but everybody wanted me to play, and I said I don't want to play anymore. I might get hurt. So, that's how I left it. . . . They offered me a bigger contract in [Team 3] to come up there and play. No way, José! I was finished![5]

Clean breaks like this are exceptions to the rule.[6]

Injury makes the decision for many players. Some injuries are life altering, as was the case for former Lion Mike Utley, who was hurt on a routine tackle in 1991 that left him paralyzed from the chest down. Injuries dramatically ended the careers of Joe Theismann, Sterling Sharpe, Michael Irvin, and dozens more. For many others, however, injury starts the player down a painful, tortuous slope, effectively terminating a career, even as the player tries to prolong it. Hundreds of players try to "bounce back" but find their physical skills so compromised that they slide to the bottom of rosters, and eventually into football oblivion. Former running back Gary Ellerson, who found himself out of a job in the 1980s, was one of them:

When I was released by the Detroit Lions, I tried to hook on with the Indianapolis Colts, only to flunk my physical. . . . The flight home was truly a low point in my life. I remember sitting around for almost a year, rehabbing my knee, and hoping that some NFL team would still give me a chance. It never happened.[7]

Even barring injury, many players don't realize that their playing days are over until well after the fact. In recent years only about a quarter of retirees indicate that they called it quits without trying to sign on with another team after being released.[8] Countless players cling to any prospect of playing again, trying to catch on with team after team. Some call this "running laps"—the perennial rite of players signing with teams to fill out rosters for training camps, being cut during preseason, then re-signing when spots open up due to injury or players' failure to perform.[9] Some players are signed and cut a half dozen times or more before they finally throw in the towel. In a 35-month span from 2001 to 2004, for example, long snapper Mike Solwold was signed and released seven times before his career was over. [10]

Under the circumstances, it's no wonder the end is blurred. Teams and coaches willingly nurture whatever optimism persists. Keeping players' hopes alive keeps them in the pool of potential roster replacements when spots inevitably open up. Rarely will a coach tell a player: "That's it. You don't have what it takes. You're washed up. You're through." Listen as former Ravens coach Brian Billick informs players they've been released.

[To Javin Hunter:] You showed me you can do this [play cornerback in the NFL]. We have injuries, we might very well call you back. [To Ron Johnson:] You have the ability to play in this league, Ron. You need to think about why you're sitting here right now. You've never embraced the idea of special teams. Look at someone like Harold Morrow. You have more ability than he does, but he's in the league because he's embraced the idea of being a special teams player. You need to do that with your mind, your body, and your soul. You do that, you can still play in this league.[11]

Jacksonville Jaguars general manager David Caldwell underscores that it's just a matter of circumstances: "You're a great player. We just can't see you fitting the system. You'll get a shot on another team." "Fitting" often means fitting under the salary cap. Veteran players with higher minimum salaries know that they cost a team more than equally talented but less experienced players. Someone, they maintain, will be willing to pay the price for talent *and* experience.[12]

With coaches being less than candid and agents and well-wishers offering encouragement, players grimly grasp at faint prospects. Most careers don't end with a celebratory bang, they fizzle away. The NFL is seldom "Here today, gone tomorrow." Instead, leaving the game is often an excruciating, unceremonious erosion of possibility and hope, a process fraught with ambiguity that compounds the anguish at the end.[13]

Fired, Not Retired

Most NFL players simply don't leave their profession in the same way other professionals "retire" from their jobs. Indeed, the term "retirement" suggests that players move through a voluntary, anticipatable transition out of one role and into another. It's an image of stepping back in order to take it easy, to "kick back." It's typically seen as a well deserved, coveted respite from the previous grind, something everyone looks forward to with more or less positive, if not eager, anticipation.[14] But not for most NFL players. "It's involuntary retirement," says former defensive tackle Mike Golic.[15]

In fact, many former players forswear the term "retirement," even though it's a handy way of warding off the stigma of being cut or released. As former Bear and Packer Stanley Davis put it, "I didn't retire. They just quit calling me to come back. I don't know too many guys that played this game that voluntarily [quit]."[16] Another recent retiree puts a sharper point on it: "I didn't have no choice. I was fired and there was nothing I could do about it."[17]

Given this scenario, it might make better sense of ex-players' experience if we view them as terminated employees, military personnel receiving "general military discharges," or even "dumped partners" in divorce proceedings. Only 40 percent of older retirees (over age 50) and 27 percent of younger "retirees" (age 30–49) report leaving the NFL voluntarily.[18] This means that roughly two thirds say they got fired. In light of what we know about the experiential uncertainty of the end of playing days, and given the face-saving quality of saying one "retired," versus admitting to being "cut" or "fired," it's safe to say that a relatively small minority of players leave the game happily of their own accord.

These inglorious endings often leave ex-players without the exit strategies, routines, and rituals that generally wrap up careers and insulate retirees from the sting and stigma of losing their jobs. After the fact, a player may call the end of his career a retirement to save face or provide a sense of "closure," but they're usually unhappy with the outcome.[19] But just as we caution against the use of the retirement metaphor, we don't want to press the "fired" imagery too far, either. While many players are actually evicted from their jobs, their departure is usually open-ended (remember, "Stay ready!"). And not all players feel displaced "with prejudice," as the term "fired" might imply. But the imagery of "fired not retired" does help account for the anguish, turmoil, and depression that doesn't seem to accompany the orderly culmination of other careers.[20]

The end of any type of career might be conceptualized in terms of "role transition." As a role, an NFL career is a set of normative behavior patterns associated with playing the game. It's an attitudinal and behavioral script for NFL players.[21] Retirement is a form of role *exit*. Sociologist H.R.F. Ebaugh has explored the complexities of "becoming an ex-" and draws some fascinating comparisons among various career exits. Nearly everyone is an "ex-" of one sort or another at some point in life—an ex-student, an ex-soldier, an ex-husband or ex-wife; we all experience role exit. Several factors make the immediate transition from one role to the next more or less challenging. Ebaugh's research shows that it matters whether the transition is intentional and voluntary, as opposed to coerced. Controlling one's destiny is important in determining how people respond to life changes. So is navigating the experience alone or in a cohort of "exes." Graduating from college with an entire class is an entirely different exit experience from retiring as a college teacher after 30 years on the job. Whether the change is irrevocable is also key as transitions can be more daunting if there's no going back. Finally, the importance or centrality of the identity left behind makes a big difference in how "exes" feel about leaving.[22]

Typical retirements often spark apprehension, but generally not to the extent that we hear from former players. Consider, for example, how an ex-minister recounts leaving the clergy: "It felt a little scary. I would be a liar if I didn't say I had some fear because there's always apprehension."[23] It's a familiar refrain, but it lacks the gravity of ex-players' laments. Most "exes" admit to initially feeling "at loose ends" or "ungrounded," but the feeling isn't as encompassing or persistent as with NFL players. In a high-profile scenario in 1981, President Reagan fired air traffic controllers for striking. Accounts of the incident reveal that those fired "experienced feelings of anger, resentment, and self-pity. . . . The majority of ex-air traffic controllers also felt sad and depressed that they were no longer able to practice a career for which they had trained long, hard hours and which most of them enjoyed."[24] This scenario would ring true for many "retired" players. They're more like auto workers who are told not to report for work anymore than the auto company executive who gets a retirement party, laudatory speeches, and a gold watch. Players don't even get a pink slip and end up sitting alone by the phone, awaiting the ultimate confirmation that no one wants them. That's a hard way to go. George Koonce recalls feeling *like a part of me had died. I didn't know where to turn.*[25] It's a version of what some have called the "social death" at the end of athletic careers.[26]

While NFL player transitions appear qualitatively different from most career transitions or role exits, they do resemble transitions from other elite athletic careers. The literature on sports retirements is generally more conceptual than empirical, but it points to a constellation of inter-related psychosocial factors that offer some suggestive insights into the end of NFL careers.[27] First, this literature notes that a career in professional sport is much shorter than most other careers. It's a "compressed career"[28] that ends abruptly, due to injury, declining skills, age, or simply being "deselected."[29] This, of course, directly implicates the degree to which retirement is voluntary, accidental, or coerced.[30] Perception of control over the end of one's career is often associated with the quality of adaptation to the sport-career transition.[31] While empirical evidence is slim, more general research in clinical, social, and physiological psychology suggests that perceived control is highly correlated with optimal human functioning. In the few studies on athletes, the tendency seems to hold.[32]

Perhaps most importantly in terms of psychological impact, sports researchers suggest that the identity implications of retirement for elite athletes have profound effects on how they feel about their lives after retirement. For athletes whose identities and self-worth are overly invested in their status as sports stars, the end of a career may set off a cascade of negative outcomes. When self-esteem is tethered to athletic excellence, the end of the athlete role can pose major social and psychological challenges. Some elite athletes are so invested in their sport that they become one-dimensional at the expense of other domains of their lives. The loss of the structure of competitive athletics, social support, and the attention that surrounds their careers may result in psychosocial problems, although there is some empirical evidence that elite athletes are not especially prone to such "adjustment difficulties."[33] Sports sociologist Jay Coakley tries to locate all this in a broader social context by suggesting that the greatest challenges confront athletes whose sports careers may have limited their social sphere to other athletes and inhibited the development of personal characteristics, life skills, and interpersonal dexterity that non-athletes generally acquire.[34] This sounds suspiciously like life in the NFL bubble.

The Terms of Disengagement

NFL players and "exes" frequently grumble that "you never leave on your own terms."[35] While this is typically a figure of speech, there's an important literal component that provides crucial insight into players' mindsets as their careers end. Players often replace the terms "cut" or "released" with the word "deselection." It's used in both scholarly and vernacular parlance, ostensibly to neutralize the negative connotations associated with being "fired" from the NFL. But it's not "just semantics." It's important to the way players think and feel about themselves and their careers.

More and more frequently, players who are out of the game, or who are contemplating retirement, arrange to sign one-day contracts with the teams of their choice in order to "retire as a 49er," or whatever the team may be. It's ostensibly a move to bolster the players' identity as a member of "his" team.[36] But there's more at stake with this symbolic gesture. As they move beyond their prime playing days, many players bounce around through trades, free agency, or deselection. They lose control of their football fates, as the end sneaks up on them. Many, like George Koonce, never announce their retirement, they just fade away.[37]

When it finally becomes apparent that one's playing days are truly over, some players reassert control by staging "retroactive retirements." This symbolic ritual recasts the uncertainty of the players' departure from the league with the finality of a ceremonial "retirement," with all the attendant positive associations. It's a way of repairing damaged identity and lost esteem that accompany a career that simply fizzles out. The growth of the "Sign and Retire Club"—whose membership now includes such stars as Donovan McNabb, Tim Brown, Jerry Rice, and Emmitt Smith[38]—suggests a desire among players to take control and establish, if only for themselves, that they left the game on "their own terms." It's a way of publicly proclaiming that they were "*retired* not fired." As they interpretively reconstruct the ends of their careers, players once again become valued members of the "families" to which they once belonged. Ultimately, the gambit may help players deal with the disillusionment, frustration, anger, and shame they experienced during their less than voluntary exits from the NFL. By revising the last chapter in their career stories, they rewrite the terms of their disengagement, at least symbolically allowing themselves to go out on their own terms.

Thrown for a Loss

There's typically some remorse—a bit of sorrow—at the end of any career; teachers, accountants, and engineers are usually a little sad to see it end, even as they look forward to retirement. But it's different for many NFL players, who typically feel profound loss. George Koonce recalls that a released player *"is a dead man walking. That is what they called you."*[39] Will Siegel recalls the feeling when he was cut: "It was like losing your best friend, and that is you."[40] Stanley Davis, a former teammate of Koonce's, put it even more dramatically: "I lost the love of my life. . . . Everything you ever dreamed about, everything you've ever driven yourself for, is taken."[41]

Former New York Giant Tiki Barber was virtually paralyzed with despair when he retired: "I couldn't figure out what to do next. . . . It was strange to not have people telling me what to do because that was all I'd ever known. All of a sudden there was a malaise taking over me."[42] For former offensive tackle Roman Oben, it took six months for the pain to set in. In July, when he would normally be packing for training camp, "I just started tearing up. . . . This is the rest of your life. . . . What the heck am I going to do? What can I put into my life that gave me the same passion?"[43] Players often feel like they're sinking ships. There's nothing they can do about it and they're going down alone. As Koonce recalls, *"I was totally numb. It took me to a dark and lonely place. I was embarrassed to talk with friends in the league."*[44]

Many players *feel* cast aside and abandoned, no matter how ready they are for retirement. So they shelter and subdue their feelings, often in self-imposed isolation. They'd like to "tough it out," as they've always done, and that means swallowing their emotions and sheltering their masculine pride. Leaving the game puts their identities at stake—especially their *masculine* identities. In a sense, when they can't be football players, it's hard to be the *men* they once were.[45] It's not just their jobs that disappear. So do the foundations of masculine identity and the camaraderie that underpin their character. Without the bubble and its locker room culture, players lose the primary sources of who they are as men, as warriors or gladiators, and they are left at a loss, feeling unfulfilled and empty. The loss is painful and depressing. As Koonce recalls, "*I was in denial. I lost confidence and I was out of my element when that call never came. I felt like I had nobody to talk to who understood what I was going through. When you leave the NFL, you are basically on your own.*"[46]

Adrift without the Dream

Without football, many players find themselves at loose ends. Tiki Barber turned on the TV, watching an endless cycle of reruns: "You've been replaced on the field and you've been replaced in people's minds. That's when you start getting depressed."[47] For him, each set of DVDs was another way to avoid dealing with the uselessness he felt now that he was out of football. But escape isn't the only motive. Ex-players frequently say they took time to "decompress" after a lifetime of physical and mental duress. It's not uncommon for them to "take a break"—a year or two to "unwind" or "heal up." Recalls an eight-year veteran cornerback, "I gave myself about three, four, or five months just to kind of, you know, make the transition. . . . I've been playing football—I've been doing this for about twenty-five years, you know, so I just wanted to give myself some time."[48] A fellow defensive back from the same era chimes in: "I kind of felt I need to go ahead and give my body rest anyway. . . . I said, 'You know, I need to take some time off.' I took about a year, year and a half off where I really didn't do anything other than just letting my body recover from years and years of just pounding."[49] (Both players had suffered chronic injuries during their playing days.) Players also reinvolve themselves with their families after years of being drive-by husbands and fathers. "I was able to spend time with family, my wife, my kids . . . really enjoy life because I started at the age of eight, and played football every year. . . . You're always trying something to train your body and to be the best you can be."[50]

But sometimes the temporary hiatus grows from a "break" into a life-style. For some, this is financially feasible, for others it's an invitation to disaster. Brandon Gold played nine years for three teams in the NFL, appeared in two Super Bowls, and made it to the Pro Bowl once as a special teams player. His was a solid, if not spectacular career. He was in the comfortable middle of the NFL financial pack. Age and injury cost him his blazing speed, and his career ended more with a whimper than a bang:

> I finished in 2003. I stayed at home. I read the Bible. I read a lot of spiri-tual books. I had some money in the bank, so it enabled me to just relax a little bit and try to figure out what to do . . . and then I bought a house. It appreciated like crazy, because it was before the economic meltdown, so that enabled me to live a couple of years almost making what I was making in the NFL. . . . It bought me more time. And then, when I saw the realty market, [my family and friends] explained to me that the real estate market was crashing. I sold my house, so it enabled me not to go bankrupt, but I still don't know what I want to do.[51]

Gold had financial resources, good advisors, family support, but only vague aspirations. He didn't do much with his first years out of football. He was bogged down, in a quagmire. He stayed in top physical shape, even if he knew he would never play again, but he didn't get seriously involved in anything else. He didn't have a "real" job for years. In a sense, Gold's inertia might be traced back to the NFL dream he described in Chapter 1.

> I wanted to be an NFL player. . . . I played nine years, and then when it was really over, I had no idea what to do, because that is what I wanted to

do my whole life. All of my dreams were I wanted to go to the Pro Bowl. I wanted to go to the Super Bowl. But then all of a sudden one day, I realized that was awesome, but now you have to live another whole life. I kind of felt like I had to become a completely new life, because that life [football] is over, not in a bad way, but you did it, and now what happens?[52]

Gold may seem aimless, but he's far from debilitated. He leads a life many would envy. He's worked as a personal trainer at a fitness center. He's coached high school football. He's spent a lot of time on the beach in the Caribbean. If he's drifting without the laserlike focus of his football days, the NFL dream doesn't *haunt* him. But he has retreated from the world in which he once was a commanding force. He's lost his goals, and there's no powerful ethos to hold him accountable. After 20 years under the spell of football, Gold wonders where to turn and what to do. Like so many others, with his dream in the rearview mirror, Gold no longer has a destination.

Moving On

It's easy to focus on the travails players face when football's over, but we shouldn't overlook success stories. Many players navigate the end of their careers without a hitch. There are countless attorneys (e.g., Brad Culpepper, Kellen Winslow, Larry Williams) and several MDs (e.g., Steven Brooks, Patrick O'Neill, James Kovach [who also has a law degree]) among NFL alumni, who moved more or less seamlessly from one career to another. Others hitched small businesses to the NFL wagon and successfully rode their notoriety immediately from one venue to another. As one ex-player noted, "A lot of guys got their shit together right away."[53]

But why do some drift while others move forward? Sports sociologist Jay Coakley suggests that retirement for elite athletes is not an inevitable source of stress or trouble. He outlines social structural factors that variably influence the transition out of sport.[54] As previously noted, Coakley suggests that players deeply entrenched in the bubble—those with limited real world experience and few outside associates—may have trouble dealing with retirement. Coakley also suggests that the likelihood of retirement problems increases for athletes who don't cultivate alternatives in their lives. The unique circumstances of NFL players and their "greedy" institution heightens this challenge.[55]

Of course, many players actually capitalize on their unique NFL backgrounds to propel them toward post-football goals. For some, it's just a matter of jump-starting their lives: "The first month or two when you're not working is OK. After that . . . 'Man I gotta do something, I'm bored. Sitting around the house watching *SportsCenter* gets old.'"[56] So what did this former Carolina Panthers linebacker do? He got off the couch and went to dental school. The intelligence and initiative that made him an NFL stalwart translated well into his next professional enterprise. Another former player recalls how he got his life rolling: "I said . . . I'm not comfortable with the couch, so let me go see what Plan B is. I've got a degree. What do I want to do? . . . I got a guy that's in my close circle that owns a mortgage company, and I went to work for him. I got my license and all that stuff." Within two weeks, he was on the job.[57]

Some argue that players from the "old school" were more apt to get on with their lives immediately because they didn't have enough money to sit back and take stock. It's likely that financial necessity was a more significant motivator "back in the day," but it's probably simplistic to say that old-timers simply got on with their lives out of financial necessity. Many had plans and purpose. Consider the path taken by James Sutton, an All-Pro defensive back from the 1970s:

> Football wasn't going to last forever, and I made a point to graduate from college. I got a degree in education, so I knew I could always teach. I always said a person without a goal is a person without a vision, but in sports, you always have to have something to fall back on, because I think it is like one out of every 450,000 high school football players are going to make it into the pros. . . . Well the transition wasn't that hard because during the off season, I taught school. . . . I was what they called a long-term sub. . . . I did that for 17 years. . . . I was not teaching school for the money.

Because they are the lowest paid salary jobs that have the most influence on a kid. . . . They can mold, shape, and develop kids in any shape, fashion, or form, so I enjoyed teaching. I had a calling all my life to work with kids, and so it was one of the ways that I could actually give back, and make a little money. . . . It was a transition that wasn't that hard. It felt strange the first year until I hit myself in the head and said, "Hey you are no longer a football player. Let it go. It's time to move on."[58]

No Perfect Exit

Was George Koonce right when he said there was no perfect exit? An occasional player disagrees. When asked why he retired at age 29, while seemingly on top of his game, legendary running back Jim Brown replied:

> Football is one part of your life. After nine years, I wanted to do other things. I had prepared myself. I graduated from Syracuse University in four years. I went to the service as an ROTC second lieutenant. I worked for Pepsi Cola for nine years when I played and I knew I wanted to go into a high-profile profession, so I got into movies. So, it was not hard at all for me to leave at 29 years old, MVP of the league, and the last two years of my career we played for the championship. Now, why would I stay there and keep getting hit when I could be with Raquel Welch, Stella Sevens, and Jacqueline Bisset?[59]

Brown's story, however, is an exception to the rule. There's a long list of players who return to the game after leaving or being forced out. Brett Favre, Junior Seau, and Reggie White come immediately to mind. Their struggles to hang on underscore the extent to which players don't want to be evicted from the bubble. They're desperate to leave on their own terms, even if they embarrass themselves in the process. Brett Favre's ongoing retirement soap opera—with repeated retirement announcements, coy courtships with new teams, and triumphant returns—shows a man trying to postpone the inevitable while working fervently to leave when, where, and how he wanted. It's as if Favre was trying to simultaneously "retire" while he was still livin' large from the seat of his tractor in Kiln, Mississippi, continuing to be larger than life, even as NFL life slipped away.

Some players are more graceful as they exit the stage. Donald Driver, longtime Packers favorite and teammate of Favre's, retired after the 2012 season. The team held a dignified and moving press conference which turned into a national media event. Driver was widely praised for both his sterling career and his poised exit. In June 2013, Driver hosted his annual charity fund-raising softball game. Over 9,000 people—the equivalent of nearly half the population of the town of Grand Chute, Wisconsin, where the event was held—cheered Driver for 25 minutes as a Green Bay street was named after him. The mutual love and respect was moving. And yet, that very afternoon, Driver, perhaps unwittingly, hinted at a lingering pipe dream. "I'd be in shape," he ventured. "At the end of the day, if they called, I'd be willing to play. If not, I'm done." Was Driver channeling Brett Favre? The perfect exit, it seems, still had an escape hatch.[60]

4

A LIFETIME OF HURT

Retired NFL Players Endure a Lifetime of Hurt
—*Washington Post*[1]

No aspect of players' football lives is more debilitating, controversial, or paradoxical than injuries and their consequences. The media strike a frightening chorus: "The NFL is killing its players and the league doesn't care."[2] "Most pro football players face a future of disability and pain."[3] "Retired NFL players experience living hell."[4] At the same time, other sources proclaim—as *Sports Illustrated* put it—"NFL players, in general, live *longer*" than their American male peers, and there's evidence that they're in better health than their non-player counterparts in many respects.[5] Even more strikingly, we read that "former NFL players . . . are overwhelmingly happy they played in the league, including more than 85 percent of players who suffered at least five major NFL injuries."[6] Player after player culminates his story of NFL mayhem with the same surprising refrain: "I'd do it all over again in a heartbeat!"[7]

In recent years, the NFL has undertaken massive rule changes to curb violent hits and combat disabling injury, yet players overwhelmingly say the league is going too far.[8] "I understand that they want the sport to be safer," laments All-Pro safety Troy Polamalu. "But eventually you're going to start to take away from the essence of this game and it's not really going to be the football that we all love."[9] In spite of all they know about the prospects of disabling injury, players say they don't want to be protected. It's a tough man's game, and they want it that way.

No doubt, football is violent and dangerous; that's part of its appeal. But it's also part of the enduring mark it leaves on players. NFL Sundays— but also practices and workouts—clearly jeopardize players' health. There were more than 30,000 injuries in the NFL from 2002 through 2011, including nearly 4,500 in 2011 alone.[10] That's more than two per active player. While some of these are fleeting, and recovery is complete, there's hardly a player who leaves the game without painful reminders of his violent past. Ninety-three percent of former players missed at least one game due to a major injury, and over half report suffering three or more *major* injuries during their NFL careers. Eighty-six percent report that they underwent orthopedic surgery as a result of a football injury.[11] A substantial majority of ex-players said that injury played some role in ending their careers.[12]

If the surgical scars aren't reminder enough, nine out of ten former players wake up each day to nagging aches and pains that they attribute to football. About eight in ten report that the pain lasts most of the day. Among younger retirees aged 30 to 49, one third say their work lives are limited in some way by the aftereffects of injury. Retired players are much less likely than their age peers in the general population to rate their health as excellent or good, and nearly 30 percent of NFL retirees rate their health as only "fair" or "poor."[13] Even though mortality rates among former players are lower than the general population, in many other respects, it's a grim picture. Many former NFL players are damaged goods.

The Concussion Crisis
In August 2013, the NFL reached an out-of-court settlement with over 4,500 former NFL players who sought damages stemming from disabilities brought on by head injuries suffered while playing in the league. The players alleged that the NFL had willfully concealed information, circulated significant misinformation, and obstructed research indicating that players put themselves at severe risk of chronic brain disease by playing pro football. The NFL agreed to pay up to $765 million to fund medical exams, concussion-related disability compensation, and a program of medical research into brain injuries. Payouts would extend over 20 years, with 50 percent coming in the first three. The agreement

explicitly states that the settlement in no way represents an admission by the NFL of liability or a concession that the plaintiffs' injuries were caused by football.

The settlement actually extends beyond those players who filed suit, and covers all 18,000 of the league's retired players, quadrupling the number eligible to receive compensation. Players can opt out of the settlement, thus declining compensation but retaining their right to pursue further legal action. All retired players or their families are eligible for compensation if they can show severe cognitive injury or impairment related to NFL football, but players who died before 2006 (and their families) will be excluded from benefits. The settlement caps payments at $3 million per individual for dementia, $4 million for chronic traumatic encephalopathy (CTE), and $5 million for Lou Gehrig's disease (ALS), Parkinson's disease, Alzheimer's disease, or another severe cognitive impairment. At the time of the provisional settlement, there appeared to be at least 300 cases of former players who would qualify in the highest compensation categories.[14]

While the NFL admitted no legal liability, the settlement is a tacit admission that the NFL has actively prevented players from knowing the full extent to which they were inviting chronic brain disease by playing in the NFL—information vital to making informed decisions about their long-term physical and mental health.[15] The NFL's shameful complicity in suppressing information about the consequences of concussions and its attempts to thwart scientific research into concussions and their aftermath were further unmasked by media exposés such as the 2013 book *League of Denial* and an accompanying PBS *Frontline* documentary of the same title.[16] There's little question that brain injury is a much more serious problem than the NFL has wanted to admit.

Momentarily setting aside the controversy over concussion research at the heart of the lawsuit, what's most remarkable in this scenario is the sheer number of former players claiming significant brain damage from playing in the NFL. More than 4,500 *living* players maintain that they have symptoms of football-related brain damage. That's nearly a quarter of all living NFL alumni. A 2013 *Washington Post* survey found that around 90 percent of former players indicate that they suffered at least one concussion while they were playing. Of those who did, two thirds say they still experience symptoms.[17] The NFL Player Care study—commissioned by the NFL itself—asked alumni respondents if they had ever been "diagnosed with dementia, Alzheimer's disease, or other memory-related disease." While relatively few reported such diagnoses, comparisons with age peers in the general male population are shocking. Older retirees (50 and older) are five times more likely to report such diagnoses (6.1% to 1.2%), while younger alums (30–49) are 19 times more likely (1.9% to 0.1%).[18] Moreover, neurodegenerative mortality among a 1959 through 1988 cohort of NFL players was three times higher than that of the general population, and the mortality rate for this cohort due to Alzheimer's disease or ALS was four times higher.[19] While these data don't say that football wreaks havoc on *all* players, they clearly suggest that former NFL players are dramatically more likely than the average man on the street to suffer from long-term brain damage.

Every NFL player has his "bell rung." These shots to the head are likely to cause concussions. They leave players momentarily stunned, disoriented, "seeing stars," feeling woozy. The most pronounced symptoms may pass in a few minutes, but headaches, impaired vision, memory loss, or cognitive "fuzziness" may persist. Nevertheless, most players simply "play through" the symptoms, getting back into action as soon as they can.

The medical definition of a concussion is a bit more ominous. It's a brain injury caused by a force transmitted to the head that results in a collision between the brain and the skull that surrounds it. When someone takes a jolt to the head, the brain bangs around inside the skull case. The collision sets off organic, neurological, and chemical reactions that alter the brain and disrupt its functions. There's a wide range of possible symptoms: loss of consciousness, memory loss, slowed reaction times, cognitive impairment, drowsiness, headaches, irritability, and emotional fluctuations. Some people even go temporarily blind. Most of these symptoms, however, resolve spontaneously.[20]

No two concussions are alike. Some are more serious than others, and some may persist for days, if not weeks. NFL players have "shook off" the effects of concussions since the game began. There are countless stories of players having their bells rung, but playing on, not knowing what they were doing, and remembering nothing afterwards. In one memorable instance, Cowboys quarterback Troy Aikman was "dinged"—kneed in the head—during the January 24, 1994, NFC championship game. Aikman had played well and the Cowboys beat the 49ers, but Aikman ended up in the hospital with a concussion. He couldn't remember *anything* about the game.[21] Steve Young, a contemporary of Aikman's and a fellow Hall of Famer, was once asked about how many concussions he suffered. His reply: "You mean official ones? . . . An official one is when you're knocked out and carted off the field. But I get dinged all the time and just continue to play. We might dumb down the playbook a little bit, but I couldn't count those."[22] Jim Otto, Hall of Fame center from the AFL and NFL, probably took as many hits to the head as anyone.

> I've had over 20 concussions myself. . . . There were so many times that I would walk off the field and my eyes would be crossed. Did you ever have that happen to you? Get hit in the head so hard your eyes were crossed? You sit there. It's strange; it's really strange. Or what about if you had amnesia for two days? When you looked at your wife and you didn't know who she was, like, who's this chick? And you couldn't remember. You got hit in the head, and you had amnesia.[23]

Eventually, Aikman, Young, Otto, and hundreds of others whose bells have been rung snap out of it—more or less. For generations, that meant that they were good to go. But part of the recent concussion controversy has centered on exactly what happens over the long run when the brain is jarred enough to produce concussion symptoms.

By his own count, Mike Webster, Hall of Fame center for the Pittsburgh Steelers and Kansas City Chiefs from 1974 to 1990, played in 300 games, going back to high school, without missing a single game. He reckoned he'd shown up for 890 of a possible 900 practices in the NFL. He'd knocked heads literally tens of thousands of times in the "pit" of the offensive line. Within a few short years of his retirement, Webster's every-day aches and pains became severe. He battled hand and foot afflictions. His teeth began to fall out. In addition to physical deterioration, many friends and associates noted that there was something wrong inside his head. He couldn't sleep. He became paranoid and behaved erratically. His speech was scattered and disjointed. His memory failed repeatedly. He lost his balance. He took on a vacant look—no emotion, no affect. His cognitive functioning slipped. He was "beat up" and "discombobulated," according to his doctor. Ultimately, Webster became socially dysfunctional. He couldn't hold a job or live normally in the company of others. His family couldn't cope with his erratic behavior and his wife divorced him. He simply wasn't the man they had loved and grown up with. He came to rely upon Ritalin to maintain momentary focus, but eventually abused the drug and began forging dozens of prescriptions. His life became the horror story of an unbalanced, erratic transient.

Finally, Webster, with the assistance of a team of friends, doctors, and attorneys, filed for NFL disability benefits, presenting testimony from four physicians to establish that Webster had disabling brain damage due to his play in the league. The NFL, however, dragged its feet. The Retirement Plan Disability Board insisted on a fifth handpicked "independent" neurologist. When he agreed with Webster's doctors, the NFL finally granted Webster "total and permanent" disability benefits. The league's explanation for the decision included an extraordinary admission: "[Webster's] disability is the result of head injuries suffered as a football player with the Pittsburgh Steelers and the Kansas City Chiefs." This concession would become even more significant when subsequent concussion litigation arose.[24]

Webster's story, however, doesn't end with the disability board. Three years later, his maladies caught up with him, and he died, ultimately from heart problems, at age 52. During a routine autopsy, however, the forensic pathologist, Bennet Omalu, noted that the death certificate indicated that Webster had suffered from "depression secondary to postconcussion syndrome." Not a football fan himself, Omalu recalled media stories of football great Mike Webster's erratic behavior and tragic demise, and realized that this was the very same Webster on his examination table. The body was ravaged beyond belief, but when Omalu examined Webster's brain, it looked completely normal, a startling anomaly. Curious, Omalu got permission to study Webster's brain. His findings set off a torrent of questions, followed by a flood of research that eventually morphed into a major controversy.[25]

Beneath the surface, Mike Webster's brain was anything but normal. He had a serious pathology that's come to be known as CTE. The condition is a progressive degenerative disease found in athletes (and others) with a history of repetitive brain trauma. This might include symptomatic concussions as well as asymptomatic subconcussive blows to the head. The head trauma triggers progressive degeneration of the brain tissue—the scientific literature often refers to this as a pathologic "cascade." The pathology includes the build-up of an abnormal substance called "tau," a protein that enables the brain to function, but that can also strangle it if the tau congeals into clumps called "neurofibrillary tangles." These tangles can choke neurons inside the brain, causing a wide variety of problems. The changes in brain chemistry associated with CTE may begin months, years, or even decades after the last brain trauma.[26]

CTE is insidious. It may lead to memory loss, confusion, impaired judgment, impulse control problems, aggression, depression, cognitive impairment, and, eventually, progressive dementia.[27] As the disease progresses, symptoms become more severe and broader in scope. Memories fail. Victims can't concentrate or focus their attention. The brain's executive functioning declines; victims' organizing capacity fails, they can't plan things out, they exhibit poor judgment, and multitasking suffers. Sometimes speaking becomes disjointed or difficult. Victims become uncharacteristically irritable, impulsive, or aggressive. Some become completely apathetic at times, in complete contrast to other outbursts of aggressive behavior. Others suffer from depression, paranoia, even suicidal tendencies. Instrumental activities are compromised so that routines of everyday life become impossible. Ultimately, full-blown dementia may set in. While CTE may have symptoms similar to Alzheimer's disease and other neurodegenerative conditions, its organic presentation is different. Equally important, whereas Alzheimer's disease and other dementias appear later in life, CTE shows up in relatively young people.[28] Mike Webster was only 52, and the interior of his brain was laced with tangles of tau.

Given the statistical evidence of widespread aftereffects of head injuries, how likely is it that former NFL players are actually suffering the ravages of CTE? Clearly, all of them aren't symptomatic. But most have had concussions and thousands claimed some sort of brain damage in the 2013 law suit. For years, the NFL steadfastly denied that concussions were common, or that they had any lasting health consequences. Moreover, the league completely rejected the notion that head injuries sustained playing in the NFL *caused* lasting brain damage or disease. These denials were at the heart of the former players' lawsuit. The NFL, they argued, had been deceptive by denying the harmful effects of head injuries and suppressing information about the dangers of playing in the league. Without all available information, the suit argued, players could not make intelligent, informed decisions about the risks they were taking.

Late in 2013, award-winning journalists Mark Fainaru-Wada and Steve Fainaru pulled back the curtain on the NFL's deception in a relentless account of how, for decades, league officials manipulated information about the incidence, prevalence, and consequences of concussions in the NFL. *League of Denial* vividly details how the NFL misrepresented data, conducted questionable research, and attempted to suppress and discredit research others were doing on concussions and their aftermath. Along the way, the NFL compromised the professional peer review process to get its own research published in scientific journals, exerted illegitimate influence to suppress other scientists' research findings, and attacked the work and character of legitimate researchers who produced findings contrary to the NFL party line.[29]

The NFL was covering up a mounting body of evidence that Mike Webster's case was far from unique. In a staggering series of tragedies, former NFL players Andre Waters, John Grimsley, Terry Long, Dave Duerson, Ray Easterling, and Junior Seau committed suicide. Tom McHale died of a drug overdose. Justin Strzelczyk was killed in a car crash after leading police on a 37-mile high-speed chase. Each man had exhibited striking behavior and mood changes leading up to his death. Autopsies showed they *all* had CTE. In the past few years, autopsy after autopsy of the brains of former players have shown signs of CTE. By the fall of 2013, Boston University researcher Dr. Ann McKee had examined the brains of 46 deceased former NFL players. Forty-five of them had CTE.[30]

While there's a notable sampling bias in the collection of the cases studied—brains tend to be donated for study by families of deceased players who were suspected of having brain disease—the consistency of these findings is compelling. Moreover, not a single case of CTE has been found that wasn't preceded by some sort of brain trauma.[31] Does this mean that all NFL players have or will get CTE? No. Does it mean that every player who suffers a concussion will develop CTE? Again, the answer is probably no. It's nearly impossible to establish a certain causal link between suffering a concussion and developing CTE. Given the evidence currently available, it's also difficult to establish the likelihood that a former player, or a player who suffered a concussion, will develop CTE. The incidence and prevalence of the disease are still unknown. But some scientists—such as Ann McKee, who has probably examined more postmortem cases of CTE than anyone—are willing to speculate:

> The incidence and prevalence [of CTE], we won't know those until we have a way to detect it in living people. Then we can look at thousands of people who play these sports, and really come up with an incidence and a prevalence. . . . We have over 70 [deceased] football players with this disease, from all levels, and we've done that in five years. I just don't think we could do that with a rare disorder. I just don't think it's possible. Even if we were selecting

for families that thought that the individual had the disease, we have an enormously high hit rate. . . . So I think the incidence and prevalence have to be a lot higher than people realize. And I also think that given the worst of circumstances, if you take a single year, and you look at all the NFL deaths in a single year, and that's your denominator, and on the numerator you put all the cases that we've had with CTE of NFL players, assuming that we got the only cases of CTE of NFL players ever, anywhere, it's about 10 percent. Ten percent of NFL players get CTE. Well, that's a huge percentage, if you ask me. And that's the lowest it can be.[32]

The conservative estimate that ten percent of former NFL players might have CTE, accompanied with the dramatic autopsy evidence, casts the NFL cover-up in an even more unflattering light. It squarely implicates the league in the documented tragedies of players with CTE who've violently taken their own lives. It raises the possibility that other violent incidents—for example, the case of former Kansas City Chiefs tackle Jim Tyrer, who murdered his wife, then killed himself—may have resulted from football-related brain disease.[33] Equally important, the research suggests that the NFL may be liable for damages to thousands of former players who develop CTE and who may someday suffer the debilitating aftershocks of the hits they took in the NFL. This corroborates the league's tacit admission in the lawsuit settlement and its on-the-record acknowledgment that Mike Webster's disability was "the result of head injuries suffered as a football player" in the NFL. A telling pronouncement came late in 2009, in the wake of congressional hearings on the NFL's concussion crisis, when Greg Aiello, the league's communications director, quietly confessed, "It's quite obvious from the medical research that's been done that concussions can lead to long-term problems." This is the only time anyone from the NFL has publicly acknowledged a connection between football and brain disease.[34]

In the shadow of this mountain of damning evidence, the concussion lawsuit settlement between players and the NFL has generated considerable conjecture. On one hand, $765 million dollars is a hefty sum. On the other hand, spread across a possible 4,500 claimants, it amounts to a relatively small average individual payout ($17,000). An expanded number of claimants further dilutes the settlement pool. Why, then, did the two sides settle so quickly?

From the NFL's point of view, the $765 million payout pales in comparison to possible damages that might be awarded should the league lose the case in court. That amount could rise into the billions.[35] While $765 million is nothing to scoff at, the NFL is a multibillion-dollar industry that can absorb the financial hit. Perhaps more importantly, by settling the case out of court and signing an agreement that doesn't admit liability for players' head injuries, the NFL dodges the prospect of establishing legal precedent that could be cited in future litigation, which might cost the league even more.

Then why didn't the players press their advantage? Certainty is the key factor. Coupled with the immediate needs of many currently disabled players, a guaranteed payout is appealing. No court case is a sure thing, and even in victory, the amount of an eventual award is uncertain. It could be enormous, but it might also fall short of expectations. Should the players lose, they might not get a cent, and hundreds of players could find themselves in dire straits, with no help whatsoever. The NFL has the resources to effectively oppose the litigation and drag out the process for years, if not decades. For players with pressing medical and financial problems, a huge payoff ten years down the road isn't very promising. They and their families might not last that long.

Most crucially, despite the mounting scientific evidence and swelling public support, establishing the NFL's liability in court is a difficult proposition. The case would shape up much like class action suits against the tobacco industry, where, for years, epidemiological evidence wasn't sufficient to establish legal liability. In order to win a judgment, the players would need to prove that the NFL knowingly placed players in harm's way—that the league knew that playing NFL football caused chronic, debilitating brain damage and that the players were kept ignorant of the imminent danger.

The initial challenge would be to establish that players didn't know that football could cause brain damage. This is a major hurdle, because *everyone* knows that football is a violent game, fraught with danger. The second key issue would be establishing a direct causal link between injuries incurred on an NFL playing field and brain damage. It's virtually certain that playing football leads to widespread concussions. There is also convincing scientific evidence that multiple instances of brain trauma—especially repeated concussions, but also repeated subconcussive events—are associated with chronic brain disease.[36] But this evidence is probabilistic, not experimental. That is, it can be established that NFL players as a group are *likely* to suffer concussions. And players suffering concussions are *likely*, as a group, to develop brain disease. But court decisions don't hinge on probabilities. Cases are adjudicated based on clear, if not certain, causal connections between individual circumstances and individual outcomes. Here's where the players' case becomes difficult.

In defending their case, the NFL would argue that a player needed to establish the direct link between an injury incurred *in the NFL* and the subsequent development of brain disease. They would require players to provide documentation of brain injuries while playing in the NFL, and while such documentation is increasingly available, prior to 2000, almost none existed. Data currently at hand is unsystematic and often anecdotal. Team and player medical records are often inconclusive about the number, timing, and extent of player injuries. Players themselves are complicit in this shadowy documentation because they are notorious for not letting team officials know they're hurt. They get their "bells rung," shake it off, and get back on the field, even if they can't see clearly or remember where they are or what they're doing. Retrospective accounts of unreported concussions are not compelling legal evidence.

Even if a history of NFL-related concussions could be established, the defense would demand that claimants prove those injuries directly resulted in debilitating brain disease. Again, the evidence is largely probabilistic. It doesn't establish the *certainty* of causality, an argument that would surely be front and center in any litigation. For example, all neuropathologically confirmed cases of CTE have a history of brain trauma, but not all individuals with exposure to brain trauma develop CTE.[37] Players may be *likely* to suffer brain disease, but to win a court case, a player must establish that specific injuries directly caused his own *specific* debilitating outcomes.

Players would also be required to rule out other possible causes of brain disease. This, too, is difficult. The NFL would argue that everyone—concussions or not—has some probability of eventually developing brain disease. The onus would be on the player to prove that other factors that might reasonably cause brain diseases—for example, heredity, routine lifestyle choices, normal aging, and myriad other alternate explanations for players' current conditions—were not involved. Even more daunting, from the players' perspective, is the prospect of ruling out other *non-NFL* head injuries as the cause of current medical problems. This is virtually impossible. Nearly every NFL player has participated in four to ten years of organized football *before* reaching the NFL, including hundreds of games and thousands of practices. The NFL would argue that this participation almost certainly contributed to current medical conditions, thus absolving the league from liability for the present state of affairs. What's more, since recent scientific evidence suggests that initial concussions render players more susceptible to subsequent brain trauma, the league could argue that concussions experienced in high school and/or college were the precipitating cause of brain disease—that players already had "pre-existing conditions" *before* they reached the NFL. Players would be required to demonstrate that this was not plausibly the case. Proving that an elite high school and college player never had his bell rung is a tall order.

Given the challenges faced by both parties to the litigation, the settlement represents a compromise based on the perceived risks and rewards for both sides. The NFL limits damage and heads off catastrophic precedents. The players take home a guaranteed payoff without having to prove a problematic case that might involve years of litigation. Those gravely in need will get help almost immediately. The compromise cost the NFL $765 million. The players forfeit the possibility of a multibillion-dollar payday. Both sides can claim public relations victories. The NFL hasn't admitted responsibility for player injuries. The league can say it is simply doing what's right by taking care of its players and former players. For their part, the players can point to the tacit admission of guilt by the NFL and the quick and substantial payout to players who really need the help.

Reaction to the settlement has been decidedly mixed. The feedback is complicated by players' defiant attitude toward injury itself. For many of them, injury is just a "part of the game" that has to be accepted. Jim Otto obviously deserves considerable help from the NFL for the injuries he's suffered. He's more than willing to talk about the steep price he paid for his career. But he's adamant about accepting responsibility for his fate. He doesn't want the NFL's help or its money.

> Nobody is giving me any special help. And over here these guys [the players filing suit] are wanting the world. They're suing everybody for a lot of money, which I don't like because that's going to hurt football in high school, Little League and in [the] pros. . . . They're going to cost so much money that the owners and high schools won't be able to afford the insurance for the game and stuff like that. I'm against all that. Let's play football.

Asked about the evidence that former players are suffering the debilitating effects of concussions and CTE, Otto responds:

> Well, I'm trying in my mind not to relate that to my situation, you know. . . . I don't want to believe that that's what's happened. . . . Those are the battle scars of a gladiator. The gladiator goes until he can't go anymore. And that's what I'm doing. . . . I don't want to make excuses . . . I knew about concussions.[38]

Otto isn't alone in stoically accepting his fate, but others are equally adamant that the players settled for far too little. "$765 million?" asks former Minnesota Viking Brent Boyd, one of the original plaintiffs in the lawsuit. "The breakdown is $1.2 million over 20 years per team. What is that, a third of the average salary? There is no penalty there. It's pocket change."[39] Boyd has a point. In the broader scheme of things, the NFL stands to make somewhere between $200 billion and $500 billion over the 20 years during which the league will dispense the $765 million settlement award.[40] Viewed in this context, it is, indeed, pocket change.

In January 2014, Judge Anita Brody raised precisely this issue when she denied preliminary legal approval of the settlement. Brody's central concern was that not all retired NFL players who ultimately receive a qualifying diagnosis (or their families) will be adequately paid under the current plan. She also objected to a lack of data in support of the settlement's economic assumptions. In July 2014, the NFL agreed to remove a $675 million cap on compensatory claims for players with neurological symptoms, and Brody granted preliminary approval.[41]

But it's not only about the money. Like many other players, former NFLPA president and Pro Bowl center Kevin Mawae is disappointed that the NFL hasn't admitted culpability. "[Fans] see $765 million and they think it's a windfall for the players. It's great for . . . the guys that would fall in the category of needing immediate help," he says. "But it's $700 million worth of hush money that they will never have to be accountable for." Anticipating future litigation, Mawae argues that the NFL hasn't had to disclose damaging information it has withheld for years. He calls the settlement a "pittance," a relative "drop in the bucket." "The league won," he laments.[42] Former Packer Dorsey Levins, another plaintiff, also wanted an admission of liability, but acknowledges the need for immediate help: "When a guy [with symptoms of CTE] calls me and says, 'I've called the NFL five times. I can't get a response. My head hurts all the time. And if I can't get help, I'm going to take care of it [end his life].' I couldn't sleep. What do you say to a guy like that?"[43]

In the larger health picture, where do former players stand in the wake of all this? Many are suffering the aftereffects of hits to the head. Some are enduring the ravages of CTE. There's some financial relief on the way, but it's not as much as it appears at first glance. Some players may receive several million dollars, but the average payout is going to be far less. Perhaps the most chilling insight to come out of the concussion crisis is the realization for players that many of them may be looking down a very bleak road to a future of mental decline and disability. They wonder if it's already happening. Upon hearing of Junior Seau's suicide and the speculation that it was CTE induced, Steve Young pleaded with his friend and former teammate Gary Plummer. "Please, bro, tell me there's more to it than just the concussions, tell me that please."[44] Every former player who's had his bell rung is probably asking the same thing.

The Battle Scars of a Gladiator

In the fourth quarter of game six of the Green Bay Packers' 2013 season, tight end Jermichael Finley caught a pass over the middle and was leveled by a perfectly legal hit by the safety coming over to help out in coverage. He couldn't get up.

> My eyes were wide open. I was very conscious, but I could not move. I looked my teammate Andrew Quarless directly in the eye and whispered, "Help me, Q. I can't move; I can't breathe." The scariest moment was seeing the fear in Q's eyes. I knew something was wrong, but his reaction verified it. That really shook me up. I actually had feeling in my legs, but I couldn't feel much else. . . . I was a little panicked, I couldn't breathe.[45]

Finley survived the incident, apparently dodging a life-threatening injury. He was able to walk and move his arms within a few hours. He'd avoided a serious spinal cord injury—no fractures, no herniated disks. Just a bruised spinal cord. While his career is in serious jeopardy, Finley is far more fortunate than Darryl Stingley, Mike Utley, or Dennis Byrd, who all ended up permanently paralyzed from similar blows.

Unfortunately, dramatic injuries are a way of life in the NFL. They don't call them "Bloody Sundays" for nothing. Head injuries aren't the only grave concern. Painful acute injuries to every conceivable part of the body put hundreds of players on the disabled list each year. Surgery is routine for most players. Pain's a part of the game plan. And it doesn't stop when players get out of the game. As Jim Otto put it, injuries are the battle scars of the NFL gladiator. At age 45, George Koonce has his fair share of scars:

My back has been bothering me. My lower back. It's excruciating. I can barely get dressed in the morning. I had seven surgeries when I played. I had both shoulders redone and my right wrist and my knee. I tore my ACL right before the Super Bowl and they had to go in two other times to fix things up after it was reconstructed. I'm not complaining, but I have pain in my joints all the time. My shoulders, my back, my knees. I can only raise my arm so far. I was fortunate to play nine years in the NFL, but now I'm feeling the effects of it. But I'm in better shape than lots of guys.

Koonce's story is all too common. "I hurt like hell every morning when I wake up," says former linebacker Darryl Talley, now age 52.[46] Fifty-one-year-old former wide receiver Jamaal McDaniels can't even make it to the morning: "My whole body hurts. I wake up in the middle of the night in pain. . . . All my joints just start aching. After all that pounding . . . over time, it adds up."[47] Even relatively young retirees report aches and pains far worse and more often than their age peers in the general population. Eighty percent of NFL retirees aged 30 to 49 report severe pain lasting most of the day.[48]

The ultimate gladiator, Jim Otto, may be the "poster boy" for the NFL's walking wounded—although there were times when he literally couldn't walk. Not only did he suffer a host of concussions, but the rest of his body was beaten to a pulp along the way. It's the other lasting injuries, not the hits to the head, that plague him the most these days. He's had 74 football-related surgeries. He's had multiple joint replacements: his right knee six times, his left knee twice. His body is riddled with arthritis, and he has debilitating back and neck problems. He's fought off three life-threatening bouts of infection in his artificial joints. During one six-month span, he didn't have his right knee joint because he had to wait for an infection to clear up before another artificial knee could be installed. Eventually, the leg was amputated. Once Otto nearly died on the operating table and he's had heart surgery to deal with the many infections that ravaged his legs. Now 75 years old, Otto has been fitted with a $40,000 carbon fiber leg with a microprocessor knee that's decorated with a Raiders logo. Otto remains remarkably upbeat about his situation, making light of his limitations and near disasters. He jokes about once falling down in the Raiders office complex and not being able to get up for hours until someone eventually found him. Despite being severely handicapped, Otto says he wouldn't change a thing if given the opportunity to do it over again.[49]

How does this happen to so many players? Couldn't they see it coming? Couldn't they have sat out a few more games or retired a year or two sooner? Perhaps, but most players simply consider pain and injury as part of the job—something they accept and endure. Like so many others, George Koonce took great pride in playing through pain.

Week eight against the Detroit Lions, I hurt my shoulder. Tore it up pretty bad. I couldn't even raise my arm. The doctor said it would require surgery. The team said I could opt out and go on IR right now, or keep playing. Doctor Reynolds [a pseudonym for the team physician and orthopedic surgeon] said, "George, you can't make it any worse. You can get injections before the game and you should be fine." It was a no-brainer to play because I wanted to be a part of the team. I wanted to help the team win. I played through a lot of pain. I got shots before every game and during halftime for eight weeks. It was my decision, but you know that everybody wants you to play. Some guys had agents who might tell them, "You need to take care of yourself, you need to get healthy and see another specialist." But I never opted out or got a second opinion, and I was probably operated on five times during my stay in Green Bay. You hear about sucking it up for the team? That's what we did. Sometimes the guys might talk about a player who is on the injured list and doesn't seem to be hurt that bad. It depends on the person. If it was a Reggie White, a Leroy Butler, a George Koonce, the

*guys know no matter if their name is on that injury list, no matter what might
be hurt, those guys are going to play.*[50]

Koonce's willingness to play hurt highlights a clichéd but powerful maxim of the NFL: There's a big difference between being *hurt* and being *injured*. Koonce heard it from coaches, teammates, and team officials:

*Everybody knows that it's one thing to be hurt and another thing to be injured.
We're all hurt, almost all the time. Now, if a player is injured—like with a broken
leg—he can't play. But if he is hurt—muscle pulls, cuts and bruises, broken fingers, that sort of thing—he can play through the pain.*[51]

Despite the official party line stressing player well-being, players know they are expected to "suck it up" and play. They're lauded for their strength, loyalty, bravery, and recuperative powers when they bounce back in short order, but they're under great scrutiny while they're on the sidelines. Everyone expects them back, sooner rather than later. All-Pro tight end and noted "tough guy" Rob Gronkowski, for example, broke his forearm in a game November 18, 2012. He rushed back into action for the Patriots' December 30 game with Miami to catch two passes, one for a touchdown. Two weeks later, he refractured the arm in a playoff game versus Houston, ending his season. Before the 2013 season, Gronkowski underwent four surgical procedures on his forearm, plus another on his back. By all appearances, Gronkowski was *injured*, yet willing to tough it out. But when he wasn't in the opening day lineup in September 2013, controversy swirled, with the media constantly questioning the timing of his return. By October, there were widespread reports of teammates asking why Gronkowski wasn't playing on Sundays. While the Patriots' organization repeated that Gronkowski would return to the lineup when he was medically cleared for action, the atmosphere around the situation clearly implied that many in and around the Patriots' camp thought Gronkowski was dragging his feet and hurting his team by not playing. The point is not whether Gronkowski was indeed too injured to play, but that he was under tremendous pressure to accelerate his return—even in light of his extensive injuries and the calamitous result of his earlier attempt to come back "too soon."[52]

Under these circumstances, players don't need to be forced back onto the field. They force *themselves*. Suffering from a serious back injury, Joe Jacoby, a 13-year veteran lineman, recalls collapsing in pain in his bathroom at home. He couldn't get up. Committed to playing through pain, however, he returned to the lineup that week, only to find himself spending three days in a hospital, in traction, shot up with cortisone. "I wanted to keep playing, even though I was hurting. I felt like I was letting down the team," recalls Jacoby. "You've been brought up that way since high school. It's ingrained in you. I had a wife. I had a family. A business I was starting. But I kept hearing those little things in the back of my mind: You're letting your team down."[53]

Players aren't naïve about the game's dangers. They know what they're doing. "Seventy times a game you run into a human being as big as you are. They say that's like a traffic accident," says Curt Marsh.[54] Hakeem Chapman enriches the analogy: "You ever been in a head-on car crash? It sends a shock down your whole body. Well, I played a dozen games for 14 years and practiced hundreds of times. Not all my hits were head-on crashes, but there were plenty of those. The others were just like getting sideswiped. But they all smack you around. So I been in 14 years full of car crashes. That was my job. [Sarcastically:] Great job!"[55] "What is that?" asks Marsh. "Fourteen hundred traffic accidents a year?" It can add up to a 20,000-car-crash career.

Much of the long-term damage from football seems to sneak up slowly and incrementally. "The cumulative effect of what you did for a living is really not shown until age 40 to 45," says Bruce Laird, 62, who played safety in the NFL for a dozen years. "Guys try to stay active, play golf, tennis, work out. But all of sudden, you're around 45, you start waking up going, 'Man, my shoulder, my hip, my knee.' Then seriously by 50 to 55, it's constant pain everywhere. I can't stand very long. I can't walk very far. My neck is compressed. Arthritis is killing your shoulders. Everything."[56]

Today, Joe Jacoby has trouble walking on damaged ankles, but that's the only exercise his body will tolerate. "Some days the back gets unbearable," he says. "[The pain is] really deep in the lower back and goes down to my left buttock and hamstring. Sometimes it gets so bad it hurts my nuts. There's pain down my left leg now. My left foot has been numb for two months. The bone's pressing on the nerve. Too many years of abuse."[57] In 1996, linebacker Tommy Jones took a solid hit and went down with a "stinger"—a common injury in the NFL. It's usually a fleeting neurological injury, a "pinched nerve" in the neck that sends sharp burning or stinging pain, numbness, and weakness down the arms. All players get them at one time or another. Fifteen years later, the stingers caught up with him and he ended up having disk fusion surgery. His entire left side is now atrophied. Pain spreads across his upper body. He can't lift anything with his left arm. His torso is like that of a man 20 years older. He's virtually disabled at age 42.[58]

Perhaps the most cogent commentary on the long-term health consequences of football is that former players are "old before their time." Even those who left the game in relatively good health end up suffering from bodily deterioration relatively early in life. Brandon Gold was known as a fitness "freak" during his playing days. Indeed, he still is. Working out constantly, he was "ripped." *Muscle and Fitness* magazine named him "the best physique in pro football." Now, at age 42, after nine years in the NFL, Gold wakes up in pain, sometimes hardly able to move. Seeking an explanation for the pain, his doctors put him through a full-body MRI. "What kind of car accident were you in?" they asked, not knowing of Gold's football career.[59] It was eye-opening for Gold, who works as a personal trainer, with a clientele that includes quite a few "seniors." "I'm able to help a lot of 60- or 70-year-old people, because literally, I completely understand how they feel with injuries and how they recover because . . . I kind of have the same kind of issues. So it is a joke with them about how I am going to feel when I am 60, but it is kind of scary saying that." "I'm 40 years old, going on 65," echoes Roman Oben, an ex-lineman. "God knows what I'll feel like when I'm actually 65 years old."[60]

Collateral Consequences

It's not just the aches and pains. Physical difficulties often translate into functional disabilities. NFL alums are notably more likely than their age peers in the general population to have difficulty climbing stairs; standing for long periods of time; stooping, bending, or kneeling; reaching above their heads; grasping small objects; lifting and carrying ten pounds; and pushing or pulling large objects. This is particularly true of younger alums (30–49 years old) who are up to five times as likely to have these problems as their non-playing counterparts.[61]

Functional disability often restricts former players' ability to earn a living. Not many players are financially set for life; they still need sources of income. But 15 percent of younger NFL alums report that they are unable to work as a result of football-related disabilities. This compares to six percent of similarly aged men in the general population who claim they are unable to work.[62] NFL retirees are also far more likely than their age peers to report limitations on their ability to work.[63] That's where Tommy Jones, now 43 years old, finds himself. His neck injuries and their aftermath have made everyday tasks so painful that it's a challenge to find a job that his body will allow him to pursue.

> Right now, I wouldn't be able to have a job where I had to lift a lot. I even have a problem with the job that I'm in now [enrollment advisor for an online university]. It requires me to sit in front of the computer, calling students all day, leaning, switching between different program screens, typing, leaning forward a lot. . . . Now, after the surgery, the pain has intensified in a different area, and now I still can't sit down for more than like an hour at a time. I have to stand up and walk around. So, it is affecting me being able to sit down for periods of time without my shoulder and arm going numb and having sharp nerve pain in my back.[64]

There are hundreds of others in the same boat, relatively young men unable to sit or stand for more than an hour at a time, literally hobbled in their attempts to hold down routine jobs.

This spells financial disaster for some former players, but some may get relief from the NFL concussion settlement. Flying quietly under the radar, however, is another remedy thousands of former players are seeking through the State of California worker's compensation law. Under California statutes, players who played as few as one game in the state are allowed to pursue injury-related disability claims. Claimants are evaluated by doctors and, if they're judged to be disabled, they may receive financial compensation as well as medical-care benefits. Most players who stick around the league for several years eventually play a game in California, so the state has become the "disability venue of choice" for retired athletes in recent years, with thousands of former NFL players filing claims.

By some estimates, former NFL players could recoup as much as $1 billion by way of nearly 4,000 workers' compensation claims pending in California. Hundreds of players have been awarded disability benefits by going through the entire hearings process, but it's clear that players are taking a "fast track" similar to that pursued in the concussion settlement: take substantial, quick settlements while foregoing more lucrative pay-offs that would involve extended time and possible litigation. If a player presents a legitimate case for football-related injury and subsequent disability, he's entitled to a cash disability award plus an award of lifetime medical care related to the injury. Cases are adjudicated by an administrative judge, not a jury. Winning cases have typically resulted in permanent disability awards ranging from $40,000 to $100,000, paid over six years, plus the lifetime medical-care award. The vast majority of former NFL claimants, however, opt for cash settlements between $150,000 and $250,000, but without the medical insurance. That means trading lifetime medical care for more money right now. While the settlements are substantial, realistically, the up-front money won't cover the expenses associated with the long-term medical and surgical needs of many former players.[65] For some, it's a hard choice. It's not easy to forego a six-figure cash settlement when there are bills to pay, but a knee replacement in today's medical market can cost between $23,000 and $70,000. A hip can run anywhere from $10,000 to $150,000, with most hospitals charging in the $50,000 to $100,000 range.[66] As a result of his football injuries and 13 subsequent major surgeries, Dave Pear, for example, has run up medical bills in excess of $600,000.[67]

Like aches and pains, the financial consequences of NFL injuries may be slow to emerge, but they can be devastating. "Vested" players are currently covered by NFL insurance for five years after retirement (see Appendix 2 for a summary of retirement benefits), but that short window doesn't accommodate the sorts of problems and expenses that emerge several years after retirement. Non-vested players get no NFL health care coverage (and there are probably more former players who were never vested than those who are currently covered).[68] On top of that, many players can't purchase adequate insurance because of "pre-existing conditions." In general, vested former players are a bit better off than men in the general population. Ninety-two percent of vested ex-players aged 50 to 64 have health insurance, compared to 85 percent of all men in that age range. Ninety-one percent of younger ex-players (30–49) are insured, verses 78 percent of their age peers in the general population. The difference, according to the NFL Player Care study, is likely to be due to former players purchasing their own privately administered insurance.[69]

The long-term financial ramifications of football injuries aren't the only lifestyle changers. While a notable percentage of them end up at least partially disabled, for some players, the disability really is "total." About four percent of ex-players report needing help from others to deal with personal care needs such as eating, bathing, or dressing themselves (about twice the rate of the comparable general population). Around seven percent need help with everyday household chores, conducting business, shopping, and getting around town (again about twice the rate of non-NFL peers). Perhaps most chillingly, former players are over five times more likely than other men their age to suffer from dementia.[70] For some, encroaching dependency is mainly the result of more or less typical aging. But for others, deteriorating bodies and brains wreak havoc on lives of much younger men, as well as the lives of their families and loved ones. Some of the stories are heartrending.

In 2012, *Sports Illustrated* published a cover story titled "The Other Half of the Story."[71] It presented a moving saga of wives and loved ones who endure the burden of caring for players who've suffered severe injuries—primarily head trauma—and the pain of watching the men they love slip away. It's a painful account of once fit, powerful, and mentally vibrant men in the ostensible primes of their lives losing control of their bodies, memories, and mental faculties. It's a chilling portrait of descent into dependency: grown men needing to be treated like children. But it's also the depressing story of what NFL *families* lose to the ravages of injury. Not only do they lose their men, but they give up their own lives and freedom. Wives and girlfriends must monitor their men at every turn; watch them so they don't wander off and get lost; call the police to search the neighborhoods when they do; keep their loved ones out of the bathroom where they might mistake a razor for a toothbrush; help them with the most basic of hygiene and toilet needs. As former players' conditions render them more and more childlike, wives become progressively like mothers of infants, setting aside their jobs, social circles, and personal time to tend to their men. The toll on *their* lives is almost as great as the price paid by their injured players.

Drug abuse is another collateral consequence of injury. Sometimes players turn to drugs for respite from the pain. Given their injuries, it's not surprising that former NFL players have long histories of heavy over-the-counter and prescription drug use. It's hard to find a player who hasn't relied on painkillers of one sort or another. Players pop over-the-counter analgesics such as acetaminophen and ibuprofen like candy. Under the supervision of medical personnel, they frequently use more potent painkillers—opioids which include morphine, codeine, hydrocodone (Vicodin), and oxycodone (Percocet). Some players and former players report excessively self-medicating, sometimes with legitimate prescriptions, sometimes without. Often such drug use begins as treatment for pain due to injury, but escalates into escapist, if not recreational, drug use, and even addiction.[72] It's almost inevitable, according to former linebacker Keith McCants: "They are going to shoot you up with morphine after the game, give you cortisone during the game, whatever it takes to get you back out there on the field. And that is with each and every NFL team. So when an athlete ends up on drugs, they don't ask him why or how did they do it. They know damn well how it happened."[73]

Mark Schlereth, former offensive lineman and veteran of over two dozen major surgeries, is well known for his willingness to tolerate pain and persevere through injury. His approach to pain management was simple, yet comprehensive. "I've done it all," he says. "I would strap a dog turd to it if I thought that would make me feel better. I'd do whatever I have to do. Have I had Toradol shots? Yes. Have I abused anti-inflammatories? Yes. Have I used painkillers? Yes. Have I got shot up with painkillers and Xylocaine and different things to numb areas so I can play? Yes."[74] Reliance upon—indeed, the abuse of—painkillers has at least two significant ramifications for life after football. First, it increases the likelihood of players damaging their already compromised bodies by masking signals that more harm is being done. Toradol is just the latest in a long line of painkillers used to "shoot them up and get them back on the field." It is a non-steroidal, non-narcotic anti-inflammatory drug often used to manage postoperative pain. While it isn't addictive, the drug is considered dangerous enough that it's banned in some European countries. Kidney damage and gastrointestinal bleeding are possible side effects, while as an anticoagulant, it may also exacerbate the effects of concussions. But its primary danger for NFL players lies in its ability to deaden feeling, inhibiting a player's ability to sense pain and injury. A player can hurt himself and not even notice.

A recent *Washington Post* study found that 50 percent of players who retired in the 1990s or later reported using Toradol during their playing days. About 70 percent of players who got out of the game after 2000 said they used the drug. The *Post* reports that in 2000, 28 of 30 teams used Toradol injections on game days, averaging 15 pregame injections per team. The drug works fast; an intramuscular injection can quell pain within ten minutes. And it lasts for a full game, with a half life of over six hours. As former defensive end Tyoka Jackson puts it, "Once you get your first one, you realize, wow, you can play pretty pain-free for the entire game. . . . Whatever's ailing you, you don't feel."[75] Nearly 80 percent of former players using Toradol said they took the drug as a masking agent, intended to dull the pain they *expected* to feel during games. They used the drug to manage *anticipated* pain, not necessarily to deal with something that already hurt.[76] Either way, those using Toradol could injure, or reinjure, themselves and not realize it until well after the fact. Perhaps this is how so many players survived their 20,000-car-crash careers. But it may also be part of the reason they were in those crashes in the first place.

Whether or not drug abuse is inevitable, reliance upon pain medication can become habitual if not addictive. NFL players use painkillers at a much higher rate than the general population, according to research conducted at the Washington University School of Medicine in St. Louis. The study found that seven percent of the former players were currently using painkilling opioid drugs. That's more than four times the rate of opioid use in the general population. More than half of players used opioids during their NFL careers, and 71 percent reported "misusing" the drugs. That is, they used the medication for a different reason or in a different way than it was prescribed, or they may have painkillers that were prescribed for someone else. Fifteen percent of those who misused opioids during their careers continued to misuse after they retired, according to the study. One retired player reported taking up to 1,000 Vicodin tablets per month. Another said he might take 100 pills per day and spend more than $1,000 per week on painkillers.[77] While there is no systematic evidence that former NFL players are more frequently involved in illicit drug use than members of the general population, strong medication— often with perception altering properties—is a way of life of many players long after their playing days are done.

Players may also try to mask pain through alcohol use. While there's no certain causal linkage, former players are 10–15 percentage points more likely to have ever been drinkers or to currently drink than are their non-playing counterparts. Rates of heavy and binge drinking, however, are only slightly higher among former players than among the general population. Only about ten percent of former players include themselves in these categories, although self-reports of heavy drinking show rates among former players to be twice those of non-players.[78]

Taken together, the collateral consequences of injury add up to a depressing picture—literally. About one in four former players has either been diagnosed with depression or experienced major depressive symptoms. On a battery of lifetime depression screening measures, former players consistently report symptoms at higher levels than their age peers in the general population. While they are no more likely to report symptoms "at the current time," former players are more likely than age peers to have experienced a wide variety of problems, across the board, with the greatest discrepancies coming among men aged 30–49.[79] Players who have at least three concussions are three times more likely to become clinically depressed later in life than are players without concussions. And players with at least three concussions are five times more likely to be diagnosed with early signs of dementia.[80] Given the prevalence of head injuries, that adds up to a lot of depressed ex-players. [81]

Pain and the Sports Ethic

Most former players live with chronic pain, yet they stoically embrace their fate. They feel it, acknowledge it, accept it. They wear their surgical scars as badges of honor, seldom regretting the sacrifices they've made and the pain they bear. A mere glimpse into a recent Green Bay Packers Alumni Weekend is telling. Health concerns dominate nearly every conversation among veterans from as far back as the 1950s to those who recently retired.[82] We heard numerous variations on the following exchange:

> "How you doin', man? Haven't seen you in a while."
> "I'm OK, doin' well, doin' fine. The knee's holding up. I may not get it replaced for another year or two."

"That's great man, because if you can make it to 40, you might not have to get it done again when you're 60."

"How's the shoulder?"

"It's fine—long as I don't have to get nothin' off the top shelf." [He laughs.]

"I hear Michael got his hip done. About time. Last time I saw him, he couldn't walk. Had to cancel on that golf thing this summer."

"Well, great to see you. It's been too long. We gotta talk."

"Right, man. I got your cell. I really miss it, miss the game. Wish we could all do it again."

These players are more typical than Mike Webster or Jim Otto, living with the nagging reminder of chronic pain that dwell side by side with their fond memories of the game that hurt them. This peculiar ambivalence is not a brand of mixed feelings, uncertainty, confusion, or demoralization. Rather, it's the steadfast, open-eyed affirmation of players' powerful, deep-seated positive *and* negative feelings toward the game's violence. They are genuinely pulled in opposite directions. Players aren't lying, boasting, or dissembling when they claim at the same time that football has ruptured their lives but they would do it all over again without qualm.

The paradox isn't simply the upshot of psychological denial. By the time any player reaches college-level competition, he's probably been injured severely enough to warrant medical attention. An occasional player may entertain the hope that *he* will escape serious injury, even as others go down all around him. But this, too, is rare. Every NFL player expects to be both hurt and injured as part of the normal course of events. If there's any denial, it's in relation to the probability of bouncing back from injury. Knowing that injury is inevitable, most players believe that *when* they are injured, *they* will be able to overcome the pain and damage to get back on the field, even if they've seen hundreds of other careers end on IR. The bottom line: players know that life after football is certainly going to include chronic pain.

Why, then, do they gladly accept it? Why do they insist on jeopardizing their own health and safety at a time when the NFL is trying to legislate and officiate some of the danger out of football? The answer implicates achievement, toughness, respect, pride, and the pursuit of the dream—all aspects of the hypermasculine NFL player ethos. Consider how this plays out in a relatively nondescript on-field encounter during a midseason 2013 game between the Ravens and Steelers—two traditionally tough, physical teams. Their games have long been touted as "wars" between organizations committed to beating up and intimidating opponents. There's more at stake in a Ravens–Steelers game than wins and losses. Of course, these games get a lot of fan and media attention. In this particular instance, the media spotlight focused momentarily on a single play that was touted on the *Mike and Mike* TV and radio show as the most impressive play of the NFL weekend.

The play? Ravens running back Ray Rice broke off a run down the sidelines into the secondary, where a Steelers defensive back drew a bead on him. The DB had the angle and momentum to deliver a solid hit to knock Rice out of bounds. But this is 2013, and for weeks, if not years, the NFL has warned players about situations just like this. As a result of rule changes and zealous enforcement, tacklers are now having second thoughts about delivering a blow. A defender can't target the head and neck. Clothesline tackles are strictly forbidden. A tackler can't lead with his helmet or shoulder in the vicinity of the head. But he can't go low, either, because knees and ankles are protected. He can't grab the shoulder pads or helmet and fling his man to the ground. He can't launch himself at the opposition, leaving his feet to zero in like a guided missile. He can't touch a player once he's out of bounds. If he runs through a sideline tackle, he's going to get flagged. All of these draw penalties, maybe fines or suspensions.

So here comes Rice down the sideline and the DB pulls up, almost imperceptibly. He's not avoiding the tackle, not shunning contact. He simply raises his center of gravity and prepares to shove Rice out of bounds with his hands and arms. No harm, no foul—literally. But Rice has other intentions. Rather than veer out of bounds, minimizing contact without ceding yardage, Rice lowers his shoulders and drives squarely into the DB's chest, knocking him head over heels. Rice ends up out of bounds on his feet, the play's over, and nobody's hurt. But talk show host Mike Greenberg is enthusiastically proclaiming on America's most widely heard sports talk show that Ray Rice has just made the most remarkable play of the weekend by "lowering the boom" on the onrushing defender and "dishing out the punishment" instead of absorbing it.[83]

Why is this scenario significant? Did it change the course of the game? No, the Steelers didn't "back down" and eventually won. Did Rice pick up extra yardage, stealing a first down through his aggressive play? Maybe a yard or so. The impact of this particular play was minimal. But the description of the play speaks volumes about perceptions of toughness, safety, and commitment in the NFL. Greenberg said it all. Everyone loves the big hit, safety be damned. Ray Rice was the better man because he dished out the punishment instead of taking it. Hearing the reaction to the play, the next time a DB draws a bead on a running back along the sidelines, what are the chances that he risks the penalty in order to deliver the crushing blow—or more importantly, to avoid the appearance that he doesn't want to "dish out the punishment"? For all the media uproar about player safety, it's moments like this that broadcast the paramount value of toughness in the NFL. The fans want it, the media tout it, and the players live it. Who wants to be that guy who's knocked on his ass because he wasn't willing to risk a 15-yard penalty in order to "lay out" the opponent? In the bigger picture, avoiding injury takes second place to delivering the big hit, even when the big hit is clearly under fire.

In the NFL, nobody can afford to back down. Gary Plummer, a linebacker for 15 years in the 1980s and 1990s, pulls no punches:

> There is nothing more revered in football than being a tough guy. I encouraged others to be tough guys. I did some horrendously stupid things in my career—like having surgery on Tuesday and playing on Sunday twice. . . . The coaches have euphemisms. They'll say: "You know, that guy has to

learn the difference between pain and injury." Or: "He has to learn the difference between college and professional football." What he's saying is the guy's a pussy and he needs to get tough or he's not going to be on the team. It's very, very clear.[84]

Football is a tough man's game, with the accent on masculinity. As legendary linebacker Ray Lewis puts it, players "have to be respected as men before anything else."[85] Mike Greenberg doesn't put it in these terms, but clearly he loves the tough guy, the better *man*. By implication, the defensive back that plays within the rules and puts safety first—but is knocked on his butt—is "soft." He backed down.

While toughness is its own reward, it's also precious currency in professional football. NFL players are living their life-long dream—a violent, exciting, exaggerated version of the "American Dream" where anything seems possible if one is willing to make the sacrifice. Their bodies are part of that sacrifice. Former players lament the game's violence and its aftereffects so rarely because they've knowingly and willingly paid the price to achieve the dream. And they're constantly praised by nearly everyone who watches the game. Despite their zeal in displaying the grotesque physical dangers of football, the media are equally fanatical in glorifying the "big hit."

Players thrive in this complex cultural milieu that valorizes violence and pain.[86] It's an element of the "sport ethic" that drives players to ignore, if not invite, the challenges of pain and injury. Players are expected—and expect themselves—to endure pain and danger without backing down. It's part of a general "culture of risk" whereby players repeatedly lay their bodies on the line in the pursuit of victory. A player demonstrates he's a bona fide NFL player by subjecting his body to danger and pain, thereby establishing his worthiness. Embracing violence and injury is a way of demonstrating one's "love of the game."[87]

But the stance vis-à-vis injury isn't simply cultural. Players don't put their bodies on the line just to satisfy psychological urges or to prove they are "real men"; they do it to keep their jobs. Seventeen hundred players hold roster spots in the NFL. The difference in ability between about half of them and hundreds of aspiring NFL players is pretty scant. Rosters (and millions of dollars) are made by playing through pain. Remember: "You can't make the club in the tub." Seahawks cornerback Richard Sherman, for example, has played through the disorientation and pain of a concussion and insists that he did the right thing. In his 2011 rookie season, Sherman got his "bell rung" early in the first quarter of a game with the Cincinnati Bengals. "I couldn't see," recalls Sherman. "The concussion blurred my vision and I played the next two quarters half blind, but there was no way I was coming off the field with so much at stake. It paid off." As his head cleared in the third quarter, Sherman came up with the first interception of his career. A fifth round draft choice, Sherman wasn't an established starter at the time, but parlayed that playing time and interception into a spot on an All-Rookie team and, later, All-Pro accolades. He's gone from a fringe player to a star, and stands to make millions of dollars. It would be hard to convince Sherman—a Stanford graduate—that the risk wasn't worth the reward.

> All of us NFL players . . . chose this profession. Concussions are going to happen to cornerbacks who go low and lead with their shoulders, wide receivers who duck into contact, safeties who tackle high and linemen who run into somebody on every single play. Sometimes players get knocked out and their concussions make news, but more often it's a scenario like mine, where the player walks away from a hit and plays woozy or blind. Sometimes I can tell when a guy is concussed during a game—he can't remember things or he keeps asking the same questions over and over—but I'm not going to take his health into my hands and tell anybody, because playing with injuries is a risk that guys are willing to take. . . . Today, we're fully educating guys on the risks and we're still playing. We have not hidden from the facts.[88]

The next time he suffers a concussion? Sherman says he plans to "get back up and pretend like nothing happened."

Mark Schlereth's motivations were different, but no less compelling. He risked his health for respect.

> I played for the other 52 guys in the locker room. . . . I laid it on the line for those guys. . . . I never have one time looked back on my career and had regret. I got everything and more that I could possibly get out of my body . . . and I have the respect of every guy I ever played with and every guy who ever coached me and every guy I who ever played against.[89]

Remember Jermichael Finley, prone and paralyzed, unable to breathe in the aftermath of a jarring tackle? As frightened as he was at the moment, Finley remains committed to the sports ethic. A week after his injury, only a few days out of the hospital, he was eager to get back on the field:

> Of course I plan to play football again. This is what I love to do. . . . There is no better feeling in the world than making the "Lambeau Leap" into the stands, and I fully intend on having that surreal feeling again soon. . . . I've worked my entire life to do what I do on that football field. . . . The one thing no one can question about me is how hard I work to be a great football player. I want this. I need this. It's everything to me.[90]

Mark Schlereth offers a final benediction on players' commitment to the sports ethic:

> No matter how battered and bruised, I never lost sight of the fact that I was living out my childhood dream. And dreams are not granted or given—they come with a price. No matter what your goal, you're bound to face adversity, and it's during that adversity, when you find out what you're made of.[91]

5

"ALL THAT DOUGH: WHERE DID IT GO?"

I was absolutely living the good life. . . .When my first contract was up, if my
football career had ended at that moment, I wouldn't have had any money at all.
I spent everything I had.
—Chris McAlister, former Ravens cornerback and tenth overall draft choice
in 1999[1]

Chris McAlister's saga is all too familiar. In 2009, he was cut with two
years left on his seven-year, $55 million contract. Things went downhill
ever since. Having squandered about $50 million, McAlister is living at
home with his parents: "I have been unemployed since 2009. I have no
income . . . I live in my parent's home. My parents provide me with my
basic living expenses as I do not have the funds to do so." He also owes
multiple child support payments.[2]

Dozens of media accounts portray former NFL players as down and
out after extravagantly spending the fortunes they made in the game. It's
accepted wisdom that NFL players and alumni are both rich and irresponsible. The master narratives: "Blowing money!" and "Going broke!"
Sadly, too many of the stories are true. Nevertheless, and despite the
sensational headlines, most former NFL players are doing fine; we just
don't hear about them. "Warren Sapp Is Broke!" is simply more intrigu-
ing than "Not Broke: How NFL Players Stay Financially Stable after the
Game Ends," even though the modest everyday prosperity of life after
football is far more common than most people realize.[3] For example, NFL
alumni report higher annual incomes than their age peers and most have
accumulated substantial assets.[4]

And there's probably an Andre Blackburn for every Chris McAlister. Blackburn played in the same era as McAlister. A third round draft

choice and solid starter for over a decade, he never matched McAlister's star status or huge contracts. Nor did he subscribe to McAlister's spending habits: "My 12 years in the NFL, I didn't spend any of the money that I made through my regular season contracts."[5] Blackburn lived off his signing bonuses, postseason game checks, and side income. He's hosted radio and TV shows, done promotional appearances and autograph signings. Since retiring, he's run a modest chain of franchise ice cream shops. He lives a comfortable life, nothing extravagant, but the public never hears his story.

It's important to be realistic about both earning and spending in the NFL. First, players since the free agency era have earned a lot of money—often millions—*if they actually held roster spots for a few years.* Second, players prior to free agency made far less. Third, and perhaps most significantly, due to the vagaries of NFL contracts and salary structures, as well as the low pay scales for older retirees, the money made in the NFL is often overestimated.[6] When figuring a player's cumulative assets, we must also remember that a player may pay his agent around three percent of what he earns. Taxes take another substantial chunk of his salary, perhaps 35 to 47 percent for top-earning players, and around 25 percent for younger players on the bottom salary rungs. Subtract union dues, retirement savings, the cost of game tickets for family and friends, and other miscellaneous "payroll deductions," and some players actually take home as little as 40 percent of their gross pay.[7] No doubt most former players pocketed a healthy sum, but for many, it doesn't amount to millions.

We should also recognize that life in and after the NFL is legitimately expensive in ways that most people don't recognize. There are myriad hidden costs—expenditures that players themselves fail to properly take into account. Even the most frugal players can be surprised by the cost of NFL living. George Koonce never really lived in the "fast lane," but his life proved pricier than he anticipated:

Probably the biggest expense is your residence—your house. Actually, it's usually two houses, multiple residences. You go to Green Bay and you need a place to stay during the season. So you maybe take a hotel until you're sure you make the squad, then you lease an apartment or condo. That's not too bad in Green Bay, but it's a lot in New York or San Francisco. And it's probably for the full year. Most of the guys split right away [after the season] because they have families back home. So you leave town and you get a place there too. Everyone advises you to invest in property, so you buy a house. Lots of guys, for example, played at the "U" [University of Miami] so they buy nice places in Florida. But you still have the place in Green Bay to pay for too. So, even if you aren't trying to be extravagant, you're paying off two big houses. . . . You got property taxes, and upkeep. You got two sets of everything, one for each house. You might be paying somebody half the time just to look after each place, two yard maintenance guys. Then you have two telephone bills, two cable bills, two electric bills, and two homes to furnish.[8]

Players and their families also spend a lot on travel—moving back and forth between residences. Running a player's household has hidden expenses too. While wives and girlfriends typically manage all household details, unattached players often hire domestic surrogates—professionals to cook, or entourage members to manage mundane household details while the players are "at work." This isn't a personal extravagance. It's a household management strategy.

Then there's "personal maintenance" as well. Many players invest heavily in staying healthy, recovering from injury, working out, and staying in shape. Recently, standout linebacker James Harrison recounted just how much he spends on his body, admitting to keeping six different masseuses, a homeopathic doctor, chiropractor, and acupuncturist on his payroll:

My body is what helps me to make money. Whatever there is that I need to do to try and make myself better or get myself healthy, I'm going to do it. It wouldn't be unreasonable to say that I spend anywhere between $400,000 and $600,000 on body work, as far as taking care of my body, year-in and year-out. . . . I rent a hyperbaric chamber [a sealed, pressurized compartment used to deliver 100 percent oxygen] when I'm in Arizona [in the off season]. I have massages, and I bring people in from New York, Arizona to where I'm at.[9]

Harrison's former Steelers teammates used to call him a "massage whore," in honor of the several hours of massages he received each day. Excessive spending? Perhaps. But, for some, it's a reasonable career investment.

When all is said and done, most NFL players earn substantial money, yet their everyday lives are justifiably expensive. The complexities of their financial lives—both during and after football—certainly bear scrutiny, if only to understand how some do so well after they leave the game, while others' finances plummet.

Profligate Spending

"Man, you crazy!" exclaimed Terrell Owens when he heard about Adam "Pacman" Jones's spending spree. Evidently without hyperbole, Jones told a 2012 NFL Rookie Symposium that he once spent over a million dollars in one Las Vegas weekend.[10] Others drop $100,000 on birthday presents for themselves, burn hundred-dollar bills for fun, and run up $100,000 bar tabs.[11] Beyond such shocking anecdotes, however, a more substantial basis for the myth that most former NFL players are broke traces back to a 2009 *Sports Illustrated* article, "How (and Why) Athletes Go Broke," by Pablo S. Torre. Literally scores of journalists, authors, financial analysts, and internet sites repeat, if not quote, the following maxim:

> Athletes from the nation's biggest and most profitable leagues—the NBA, NFL, and Major League Baseball—are suffering from a financial pandemic. Although salaries have risen steadily during the last three decades, reports from a host of sources (athletes, players' associations, agents and financial advisers) indicate that . . . [b]y the time they have been retired for two years, 78% of former NFL players have gone bankrupt or are under financial stress because of joblessness or divorce.[12]

Torre is a highly reputable journalist and *SI* is a trusted source, yet a thorough internet search fails to reveal any further details about how this figure was derived. *SI* and myriad other sources provide copious anecdotal evidence that NFL players and former players are extravagant spenders, but the claim that four out of five former players "have gone bankrupt or are under financial stress" is vague and problematic.

Sociologist Joel Best cautions us about media aphorisms that use terms like "epidemic" or "pandemic" because such claims are often more sensationalized and rhetorical than factual. With the proliferation of internet journalists, pundits, and bloggers, word travels far and fast, even if it's not verifiable, so contemporary axioms are even more suspect.[13] While not questioning *SI*'s basic premise that many NFL players squander fortunes, we're skeptical about the "78 percent" figure.[14] The NFL Player Care study systematically assessed a large random sample of former NFL players and found little to support the claim that a vast majority "go broke"—"losing most or all of their money"—as *SI* trumpets and myriad others echo. The study did find that about ten percent of the former players surveyed had incomes below *twice* the poverty level, but also established the annual median income of the sample at around $88,000.[15] Retired players sometimes spoke to us about financial difficulties, but only one of several dozen that we interviewed indicated that he might be under *severe* financial duress. Many said that things were not as "flush" as during their playing days, but they didn't say they were broke. The upshot of our skepticism is not to deny that many former NFL players suffer financial woes, but to caution readers about accepting undocumented, sensationalized claims, and to temper the image of *all* former players as wanton spendthrifts.

That said, far too many former NFL players have little to show for their years of financial bonanza. Warren Sapp, former All-Pro defensive lineman and media star since his retirement, may be the most egregious recent example. According to media reports, Sapp made

$82,185,056 during his NFL career. He ended up with $826.04 in his bank account. In 2012, he filed for bankruptcy, declaring that he had $6.45 million in assets but owed more than $6.7 million. Among his assets: a 15,000-square-foot house, purchased for $4.1 million, complete with swimming pool, water slide, two-story wine cellar, five full bathrooms, a movie theater, and a lake of its own; 240 pairs of Air Jordan sneakers; and a $1,200 lion skin rug. Sapp had two children with his ex-wife. He fathered four other children with four different women. He owes them a total of $75,495 a month in alimony and child support. Since he quit playing, Sapp has worked on Showtime's *Inside the NFL* and the NFL Network's *NFL Total Access* as well as finishing second on season seven of *Dancing with the Stars*. He's probably made over $100,000 per month since he retired, but he can't seem to make ends meet.[16]

Andre Rison, an All-Pro veteran of seven NFL teams, used money to "make it rain"—tossing currency in the air and watching it float to the ground. Rison and Leon Searcy, who played 11 years with four teams, were fond of "bling"—expensive jewelry. "Custom diamond pieces, chains, crosses, you name it. I guarantee I spent $1 million on jewelry," admits Rison. Searcy indulged in clothes: "You got to dress up. Everybody has their suit guy. Tailor made. The Rolex and bracelet on your wrist. And then you had to throw in a mink."[17] Hall of Famer Deion Sanders reportedly owned nearly 2,000 suits.[18] Adds JaMarcus Russell, the first overall pick of the 2007 NFL draft, "Probably the dumbest thing I ever bought was a fox coat, with a big hood on it and a gray stripe running down it. Made me almost look like a silver back [gorilla]. I wore it maybe three times." But these are petty cash items compared to the extravagance of Keith McCants, the number four pick in the 1990 draft: "$7.6 million, 2.5 million a year. No. 1 all time—that's the biggest contract in the NFL for a defensive player. . . . I bought myself a yacht, a mansion, and a couple of cars. That ain't a million dollars. That's several million. I pretty much gave it away."[19]

Impulse Economics

Many players feel they've struck it rich when they reach the NFL. Top draft choices receive million-dollar signing bonuses, but even an undrafted rookie receives a $925 weekly stipend during training camp. If he makes the practice squad, he'll earn $5,700 a week. If he makes the roster, he jumps to over $400,000 for the season. It's new financial territory for most players.

Some say that an NFL player signing his first contract is like a lottery winner—a kid who's suddenly rich, with absolutely no financial responsibilities, acumen, or expertise. Virtually overnight, some players have more money than they know what to do with; even the lowest paid have more cash on hand than they've ever seen. But, like other lottery winners, NFL players discover pitfalls that they can't handle. Tales abound of lottery winners losing their winnings almost as fast as they get them via spending sprees, shaky investments, conniving wives or boyfriends, or shady money mangers.[20] Too often, newly minted NFL players take the same paths. Research on the happiness of lottery winners says there is no guarantee of contentment.[21] There seems to be a ceiling on just how happy new-found wealth can make a person. They call it "happiness adaptation." But with plenty of cash on hand, what's to stop a player from escalating his spending in search of greater heights, upping the ante on exhilaration.[22] Not all players take the financial plunge, but they're all tempted.

"With athletes, there's an extraordinary metamorphosis of financial challenge," says sports agent Leigh Steinberg, who has represented eight number-one NFL draft choices (and who, ironically, filed for bankruptcy himself in 2012). Some NFL observers say newly rich rookies often can't write a check and have never opened a bank account. They don't know a thing about taxes and payroll deductions. Steinberg adds, "Coming off college scholarships, they probably haven't even learned the basics of budgeting or keeping receipts."[23] The NFL and NFLPA are combating this through aggressive programming at the league-wide and team levels.

They hold orientation symposia and classes directed specifically at teaching younger players how to manage their finances.[24] Nevertheless, many players simply aren't ready to take advantage of the advice. Former NFL defensive back and current investment analyst Eugene Profit elaborates, "[Players] don't have the experience to handle the amount of money they are suddenly endowed with. Naturally, they want to go out and do the one thing they always dreamed about. 'I need to buy that house on the hill or that Mercedes.'"[25] It's not that football players or lottery winners are incapable of handling their good financial fortunes. It's just that they may be completely unprepared for the sudden opportunity and responsibility. They simply aren't ready for "prime time."

"It wasn't money. 'Loot!' That's what we called it back in the day. . . . My first check was for $500,000. Then I went on a splurge." That was Andre Rison's approach to money management. A cornerback for five different teams, Dante Wesley's first contract was relatively modest, but, as he recalls, "The first thing I bought for myself was a Cadillac Escalade." Bart Scott, a linebacker for the Ravens and Jets, was so far out of his element that he didn't know what to do with his bonus check: "I cashed my first NFL check at a check cashing joint, and they just laughed at me." But as Leon Searcy reminds us, "I am here to tell you. It doesn't last forever. Before you know it, I looked up and I was broke."[26] Take it from Raghib "Rocket" Ismail, former NFL and CFL wide receiver: "I was so busy focusing on football that the first year was suddenly over. I'd started with this $4 million base salary, but then I looked at my bank statement, and I just went, 'What the . . .?'"[27] Incredulous at today's relative wealth, Will Siegel, a 1950s veteran, agrees that contemporary players aren't prepared to manage their money:

How can you take a young man right out of college [and give him big money]. All the way from high school, he gets all this praise, praise, praise. Then they give him $20 million dollars, and you question that he has trouble. . . . I'm surprised there is not more trouble than there is. . . . You give them that kind of money, and you wonder why they go out and drink and party? Why would you not?[28]

Roman Oben sums it up in street terms: "It's 'ghetto economics.' Guys have been poor for so long that they have to show people how much money they make."[29] While the term "ghetto economics" is generally used derisively to characterize supposed patterns of economic behavior that trap ghetto residents in poverty, it does resonate with some players' experience. Tommy Jones, for example, traces his free spending after being drafted in 1993 to his "street" background, growing up poor, and wanting something better.

> It has to do with the habit that I brought to the league. . . . In Compton, where I grew up, gang banging was at the all-time high, but my mom was working two jobs as a nurse to barely support her family. . . . When I went to [the NFL], there was no supervision. I was on my own. I was an eighth round draft pick, so I made $118,000 my first year. I got $25,000 to sign, but now you are talking about a youngster in Virginia making $7,000, $8,000 every few weeks, and I had never seen that much money before, and to me that was a lot. . . . Now I had my own cash. That was my name on the check. I know guys that were making millions more than that, but when I cashed that $8,000 check, I was walking around with five of it in my pocket. We went to the mall. I went to the Ford dealer and put $5,000 down and got me a truck. . . . I wasn't thinking about any mutual funds.[30]

Kids like Jones from the impoverished inner city—often black kids— are probably less prepared to deal with sudden wealth than others. For example, sociologist Elijah Anderson suggests that urban street values discount prioritized spending and future-oriented saving. Ostentatious displays command respect, whereas "reserve" or "prudence" may be taken as weakness.[31] When he entered the NFL, Jones was no longer living in "the hood," but it still had its sway. At age 22, his prior experience didn't encourage a long-term, big picture approach to financial management, and vestiges of street values fueled his spending spree. He began literally establishing his worth by flaunting his cash.

While Anderson was writing about African American urban street culture, economically disadvantaged backgrounds of all sorts can leave players ill prepared to handle financial windfalls. In general, individuals from economically impoverished circumstances—black or white—are not inclined to save any surplus income, if indeed any surplus exists. There's some evidence that at low income levels, African Americans tend to save less than whites. In addition, due to their impoverished circumstances, the disadvantaged of all races tend to commit larger shares of their accumulated wealth to functional assets—such as houses and cars— and consumables. Again, blacks are more so inclined than whites.[32] This might suggest that black players are less prepared to deal with sudden wealth than their white counterparts, but the more compelling factor seems to be economic disadvantage.

While the NFL is predominantly African American—and has been for quite some time—there's little reason to believe that black players come into the league disproportionately prone to undisciplined spending, if we take socioeconomic background into account. The former players we studied come from a wide spectrum of racial and economic backgrounds, and among them, there's only a slight correlation between their socioeconomic circumstances and a proclivity for impulsive, extravagant spending. Race doesn't seem to be a deciding factor, either. Leaguewide, there's no systematic data regarding the socioeconomic backgrounds of NFL players, so we're reluctant to generalize from our sample. While players' socioeconomic backgrounds may influence players' readiness to deal with "financial challenge," other factors definitely come into play.

Obligated to Live Large

Credit the NFL player ethos for promoting a live-for-today, "spend it while you got it" mentality that drains some players' bank accounts. Listen carefully as even thoughtful players recount the circumstances surrounding the compulsion to spend. Player after player repeats this refrain: "I've made it to the NFL. I'm going to live the life." "I deserve to spend the money I've made." "If I want it, I can have it." They're axioms of the NFL ethos, embodiments of "livin' large." Raised in a frugal house-hold, George Koonce found it hard to resist:

I watched a lot of guys around me fall prey to the rampant spending that char-acterizes the professional football culture, regardless of their upbringing. I was no different. There is so much excitement; you have basically just hit the lottery. Once I made the roster, my first big purchase was a 1992 white Corvette with red interior for $38,000. . . . [Later] I bought a Mercedes and a Hummer. . . . Players really go overboard on automobiles.[33]

The ethos is ubiquitous and stealthy. It tempted the fiscally conserva-tive Koonce with cars, houses, and jewelry. When Tommy Jones flaunted his early earnings, his agent tried to intervene. He cautioned Jones to consider the future and curtail the spending. Jones would have none of it: "My mind was not focused on reality. It was focused on the whole persona of the NFL."[34] That persona, of course, was larger than life, and relentlessly trampled the more mundane aspects of Jones's reality. Jones ended up with very little to show for his five years in the NFL. Brandon Gold came from a white, middle-class background, much different from Tommy Jones's. But he, too, spent his money on cars, drugs, women, and "body maintenance." Livin' large clouded his long-term vision.

I had absolutely no knowledge whatsoever of money. . . . It takes a lot of money to sustain that [NFL] lifestyle. And when I talk about sustaining it, I don't mean [just paying for] your Benz. I mean upkeeping "the machine." That machine was me. . . . I felt like, "I'm in the pros. I'm living the fast life, and this money will continue to roll in for the rest of my life."[35]

At the start of careers, the compulsion for livin' large is hard to resist. As careers proceed, it becomes a habit that's hard to break. Former player and current coach Darryl Gatlin reflects on how extravagant spending isn't as much a character flaw as it is a cultural way of life.

> Most people think if you have $3 million in the bank, you set for the rest of your life. . . . That is really not true. . . . If you're obligated to living a certain lifestyle, human nature is going to say you have $3 million, you are supposed to live like you have $3 million. So you can spend $3 million. If you get a $15 million contract and you are making $4 million a year, it is hard not to go buy a million-dollar house or hard not to go buy a new Mercedes-Benz. I think players get caught up in a lifestyle that is hard to get out of when they get done playing. The more money you make, the higher your expenses are, and when you get done playing and you are not making that money anymore, it is easy to keep spending that money. You try to live that lifestyle after you finish playing, and I think that makes it hard.[36]

The key to Gatlin's analysis is the phrase "obligated to living a certain lifestyle." "Obligation" connotes a constellation of expectations that command a player to live large, to spend ostentatiously. According to Gatlin, it becomes a *habitual* way of living that doesn't go away when the NFL paychecks stop. That obligation is a form of peer pressure that seems irresistible. The player ethos becomes a lifetime social contract—a commitment to the NFL lifestyle—of which players are only vaguely aware, but that encourages them to live large, even when it's fiscally impossible.

Gatlin suggests that the mandate to live large gradually insinuates itself into players lives, but the player ethos is often boisterous and demanding. Around the locker room, players' cars, clothes, houses, and "bling" are constantly scrutinized. If they're not up to par, they're ridiculed. During his playing days, Roman Oben eschewed a new Cadillac for a Toyota Land Cruiser with 68,000 miles on it. His teammates taunted him mercilessly.[37] Back in the 1990s, former Pro Bowl linebacker Winfred Tubbs wasn't up to date with his electronic technology: "I got on a plane with a cassette player, and [a teammate] would tell me, 'They make CD players. You're in the NFL now.'"[38]

Livin' large is a competitive sport in the NFL. When winning is the only thing, players are easily trapped in a race to outspend one another. Herm Edwards calls it "keeping up with the Joneses."[39] Yet there's another colloquial use of the term "jones," suggesting that "keeping up with the joneses" might also mean fulfilling an intense desire for things seemingly irresistible. A "jones" is a sort of addiction. Both meanings come into play as NFL players measure themselves against their peers, practicing fiscal one-upmanship. "Stunting" to show one's financial wherewithal can involve pricey entertainment, "bling," cars, houses, entourages. Any form of conspicuous consumption can demonstrate livin' large. Leon Searcy liked to flaunt his largess: "I wanted people to know that, 'Hey, this is Leon Searcy at the big table, spending the money, popping the champagne.' . . . That was the coolest thing, to walk into a club and say I am here. I got me a bottle. Louis the 13th, $5,000 a bottle." Some of the off-field competitive drive comes from what some players call "helmet syndrome." When they're on the field, players' faces are hidden from view by their helmets. They are even penalized if they take their helmets off while they're in the game. Consequently, NFL players often compete for the sorts of attention that highlight their off-field personas and provide actual "face time" with the world.[40]

The competitive ethos and livin' large infiltrate even the most basic principles of money management. "Man, I'm growing my $10 million into $11.2 million. That's not sexy," facetiously notes Darren Rovell, ESPN business reporter. "It's not sexy to invest in a mutual fund. It is not very exciting," chimes in Wharton Sports Institute's Mori Taheripour. "Owning a bar, owning a club, that's far more exciting.[41] Ivan Thornton, a senior partner with the Fiduciary Management Group, notes that players often make bad investments because "the average adviser won't give pushback because he'll get fired. You'll have some players earning seven percent on their investments, but then they'll be listening to their teammate telling them there's a guy who can get them 18 percent."[42] Everything's a competition.

Bad Benchmarking

There's another subtle form of competition at work as players judge and juggle their finances. Everyone engages in self-evaluation. We compare ourselves to others, especially those who we figure are similar to us, in order to gauge just where we stand.[43] One way to conceptualize this process is "benchmarking." We envision standards for comparison, then see if we measure up. The trap for many NFL players comes when they set unrealistic benchmarks. This becomes obvious in spending competitions, but it also affects the more basic ways players think about life and money. Recall, for example, how Darryl Gatlin almost reflexively said that if "you have $3 million, you are supposed to live like you have $3 million." This axiom reflects the NFL ethos and embeds standards for comparison that few outside the league would share. Gatlin continues: "If a player is living off of $20,000 a month, in 12 months, he is going to spend $240,000, so he has to be making almost $450,000 to live that lifestyle after he finishes playing."[44] These are compelling observations to be sure, but they also reflect a highly skewed vision of the "real" financial world for most people.

The notion of spending $3 million sounds reasonable only in relation to circumstances where $3 million is commonplace. While that may be the case in the 21st-century NFL, it's a far cry from "normal" standards. Not everyone *needs* to spend $2 million dollars for the "nice house," as Gatlin says today's NFL life requires. Nor would most people agree that it's "human nature" to spend so freely, as he implies. Gatlin's benchmarks are products of his life in the bubble. They are understandable, given what he's seen and experienced *in the NFL*. When it comes time to inhabit a more mundane financial world outside the bubble, more modest benchmarks might be in order.

We see this in Andre Blackburn's post-career success story. His benchmarks stand in vivid contrast to those Gatlin mentions:

I could have come out of [my home town] probably making $65,000 a year working for Philip Morris or Allied Chemical, probably $45,000 escalating to $65,000 within five to seven years. So I figured, I'm seeing people with that type of lifestyle, . . . they had pretty good situations, pretty stable lifestyles, families were in good communities, kids were in good schools. I knew that would be enough money that I could actually maintain a very stable happiness. So that is pretty much where I put my monetary need for off the field. I didn't buy a car every year. I didn't buy a lot of expensive jewelry. I have a lot of patience. . . . I was able to do something that most players don't get a chance to do: be in the black when you leave the game.[45]

The key to this scenario is how Blackburn used modest yet realistic standards—lives and careers forged by college graduates entering near the bottom of a prominent local industry—as targets for his post-NFL life. Setting his NFL ego aside, he aspired to the lifestyle of others in his community who had done well for themselves by more "conventional" means. In doing so, as he modestly neglects to mention, he's probably achieved far more economic success and security than the guys he knows who went to work for Phillip Morris.

Bad Advice and Bad Investments

Profligate spending may be the reason some NFL players lose their money, but bad financial advice combined with injudicious investing comes in a close second. *Sports Illustrated*'s Pablo Torre argues that "hiring the wrong people as advisors and trusting them far too much" are often to blame. The "wrong people" range from scam artists, to inept or unscrupulous advisors, to well intentioned friends and family members without a hint of financial expertise. Magic Johnson, one of the most successful businessmen among former professional athletes, couldn't put it much plainer. He gets literally dozens of calls from star players asking for financial counsel, but ends discussions immediately if they mention friends and family managing their money: "It won't even be a conversation," says Johnson. "They hire these people not because of expertise but because they're friends. Well, they'll fail."[46] A bit less wealthy, but every bit as wise, Hakeem Chapman underscores Johnson's point: "These guys are hurting, and you know why? Bad decision making. Working with their brothers, aunts, and uncles, and everybody who is going to show them how to invest their money."[47] Nearly half of NFL alumni report some form of business or investment losses at one time or another, and about 42 percent say they have received bad financial advice.[48]

One source of trouble is too much money invested in real estate and private equity investments,[49] according to Ed Butowsky, managing partner of Chapwood Capital Investment Management. They typically involve personal connections and high risk, a recipe for far too many investment fiascos. Says Butowsky, "Coming out of college, you don't want to hear about the different and safe ways you can invest your money. You're more concerned about . . . the women, clubs and who knows who. You are concerned about the wrong things. . . . Young guys don't want to take the time to learn about how they should be investing their money."[50] Bart Scott elaborates: "Guys open up restaurants, and that is one of the most volatile industries that you can get into. . . . Restaurants in the hood. You know, [friends] ask you to do it, and then you ask for their business plan, and they say what is that? Exactly." Car washes are also popular investments, according to Andre Rison: "For some reason, professional athletes got this fad with buying car washes." One of these car wash deals went bad for Leon Searcy: "It wasn't no car wash. It was a fake deal. A friend of mine that I trusted. I gave him a lot of money to take care of it, and I haven't seen him or the money since." Rison also liked to dabble in the music industry: "I spent a lot of money in music. . . . If you bumped into me back in the '90s, and you were an aspiring guitar player or keyboard player, I gave you money to go buy equipment."[51]

Bad Agents

How do players get into so much financial trouble with the throng of prospective advisors trailing them around? Perhaps that's the problem. Many players fall under the sway of seemingly well-intentioned adults when they're mere teens. Remember, De'Anthony Thomas has been Snoop Dog's protégé since he was 12. Agents court players from the earliest opportunity, often skirting college rules and NFL standards. Unofficial advisors—often known as "street agents"—crawl out from under just about every rock. Even if players enlist legitimate professional help, there's no guarantee that an agent or legal representative will provide solid investment advice, or that financial advisors will handle players' money with players' long-range prospects in mind.

The NFLPA requires player agents and financial advisors to be registered and certified. An agent must pass a background check, have undergraduate and postgraduate degrees, attend two NFLPA-sponsored seminars, and pass a written examination covering the CBA, the salary cap, player benefits, NFLPA regulations governing contract advisors, substance abuse and performance-enhancing-drug policies, and other relevant topics. Ongoing compliance with the NFLPA regulations is required to maintain good standing. This includes paying an annual fee, having professional liability insurance, attending an annual NFLPA seminar for certified contract advisors, updating application information annually, and negotiating at least one player contract within a three-year period.[52] Registered NFLPA financial advisors must hold a bachelor's degree, have eight years of licensed experience (FINRA, CPA, insurance license, or license to practice law), have professional liability insurance, no civil, criminal, or regulatory history related to fraud, and have no pending client complaints.[53]

Regulated or not, shady advisors have made quite a mark on the NFL financial scene. According to the NFLPA, before closer scrutiny was instituted, at least 78 players lost more than $42 million between 1999 and 2002 because they trusted money to agents and financial advisors with questionable backgrounds. Included in these cases are Luigi DiFonzo, a former felon who claimed he was an Italian count and defrauded players such as Hall of Fame running back Eric Dickerson, and William "Tank" Black, who built a pyramid scheme that took about $12 million from at least a dozen players. In 2008, Atlanta hedge fund manager Kirk

Wright was convicted on 47 counts of fraud and money laundering in a scheme involving more than $150 million. His client list included at least eight NFL players and former players, several of whom lost millions. In 2008, Jeff Blake, who played for seven NFL teams from 1992 to 2005, sent a shady e-mail message to 102 other retired players on behalf of Triton Financial, an investment firm in Austin, Texas, whose "athlete services" department Blake directs along with several other former players, including Chris Weinke and brothers Ty and Koy Detmer. The e-mail unabashedly claimed that "Triton is averaging 32% annualized return on its investments within the past five years." A close examination of Triton revealed no such success. The firm wasn't even registered with the U.S. Securities and Exchange Commission. There are dozens of other documented accounts of scams and schemes, shady investments, and tax fraud that have cost players nearly everything they ever earned in the NFL.[54]

Not only are some agents frauds, but they overcharge their clients as well. "It's basically large-scale shoplifting," says Ed Butowsky. "Athletes don't know industry standards, so virtually every one of them is being robbed." Stock brokers, for example, may tout bonds with longer maturities because the commissions on them are bigger. Other advisors may overcharge for portfolio management, getting two or three percent instead of the customary one percent. Butowsky recalls meeting a former NFL player whose financial advisor—a former player himself—said that he couldn't reveal how much he was charging to manage the player's tax-exempt municipal bonds "because of the Patriot Act." Butowsky said the advisor was taking $146,000 every year.[55] ESPN business analyst Darren Rovell calls the NFLPA's efforts to regulate agents and advisors "a joke," claiming it's something of a scam itself, a revenue stream for the union. Says Rovell, "I don't think that they can look you in the eye and tell you that they are doing a better job at controlling who should be an official advisor and who shouldn't."[56]

Grave danger also lies in players' willingness to let agents take over other aspects of their lives. Butowsky says agents are more than ready:

"'I am going to take care of your insurance. I am going to take care of helping you find a house. I am going to take care of getting you endorsements,' which very rarely happens by the way. 'And I am going to take care of your finances.'"[57] Players don't see their bills, or keep track of payments. They're in the dark about taxes. They lose touch with their own money, learn only what their advisors want them to know, and often end up with far less than they thought they had. "You think of sharks in the hood, you think of gang bangers and drug dealers. You haven't seen nothing 'til you step into some of these white collar criminals. . . . Look at all the players who got caught up in the pyramid schemes," laments Bart Scott. Butowsky concurs: "I know many people who have had money wired out of their accounts to private equity accounts or into other accounts without their knowledge. A lot of signature forgery, and that is criminal."[58] Unfortunately, the humiliation of being duped keeps players quiet about their losses, allowing the scamming to thrive. It's a sad story, told too late, according to Leon Searcy:

> NFL guys are very egotistic. They don't like anybody to get the best of them on the field or off of the field. So, when they do get [scammed] by an investor or schemer, most of the time they are not telling you, because they don't want you to know they done got got.[59]

Family Fortunes
Most NFL players insist that they're good family men, a noble sentiment that sometimes can be costly. George Koonce learned the hard way:

> *You sign that first contract and you're overwhelmed with excitement and expectation. You made it. You've been drafted. Then you try to concentrate on football, making the team. And you turn to your trusted friends or relatives to help you stay focused on the job at hand, to earn a spot on that opening day roster. But are your friends and family relatives really equipped to manage your*

finances? In most cases no. But they are going to try anyway, and you want to let them.[60]

Like so many others, Koonce found his family descending upon him from all angles. Former coach Brian Billick warns that relatives suddenly emerge that players have never before met. "However big you *think* your family is, it will grow in the weeks leading up to your appearance at the NFL draft. At the 2003 draft, Charles Rogers had 98 people in his entourage."[61] Pulling no punches, Bart Scott warns that "getting money sometimes is like turning the lights on in a dark house in the ghetto. It exposes a lot of roaches and rats."[62]

These "new" families often start treating players as breadwinners—or lottery winners—even though their connections are tenuous. Koonce remembers feeling anxious and confused. Adult family members were suddenly asking him for financial advice and help. *"They felt that because I was making a lot of money I had all of the answers."*[63] At least they were asking. Bernie Kosar signed a $6 million contract in the 1980s and saw his family immediately take over:

> I wanted to get an agent to separate the money, football, and the family, so that we all could kind of coexist. But my family wanted to represent me; they wanted to manage my money. My father, he didn't really have a job after the mills had closed, and there weren't a lot of opportunities. I knew with my signing bonus he was paying off his mortgage and paying off the house and cars, and things of that nature. But, as I came to find out later, the Cleveland Browns also cut a contract with my father who also got a million dollars.[64]

Not only did Kosar's family hijack his income, he reports willingly loaning millions more to family members, teammates, and friends—money never repaid. He says financial advisors he "loved and trusted" mismanaged his money, losing as much as $15 million in a rash of bad investments.[65]

While Kosar's situation isn't typical, it's hardly unique. Some family members become de facto money and investment managers, while others approach players with "surefire" investment opportunities, showing up needing a little cash to get a hot new business off the ground. Says a former player's wife about how friends and family tap into NFL salaries: "My husband will go places and meet friends, and everybody has this wonderful idea that just needs some investors. Basically, they want to play with your money. If the investment makes it, then everybody is happy, but if it doesn't, they haven't lost anything; only you have. I think that people play on that. 'Hey, we've been friends for years.'"[66]

More commonly, friends and family are just looking for a little help from someone they've known all their lives who's now stumbled onto some good financial fortune. Koonce remembers an onslaught of requests from his family shortly after his first payday. His parents had never discussed family finances with him, but suddenly they were lamenting their tight situation. Aunts, uncles, and distant cousins he barely knew were telling him about their financial woes: "If you don't come through for me, I am basically going to lose everything I got." "I've been out of work, you know the situation with my car, the bills." Koonce remembers asking himself, *When did I become the bank?* He typically responded with compassion and measured generosity, with only one big regret: *"I started a trucking company with my sister. I think I lost over half a million."*[67]

Family members' sense of entitlement is sometimes overwhelming. They fail to recognize the burden their requests actually amount to; tickets to games, airfare to game sites, hotel rooms, and restaurants become expensive. Players sometimes support family members and acquaintances who previously helped them pursue the NFL dream, and married players find their in-laws are suddenly much more "congenial." Most of the demands aren't outrageous, but they presuppose the player's ability and willingness to take care of everyday expenses without batting an eye.[68]

Family and friends are generally ignorant of the player's actual financial situation. They're unaware that his salary is non-guaranteed and he's at risk of being released at any time with no compensation. One player and his wife were incredulous when his parents asked him to pay off their home mortgage, even before he made an NFL roster. An undrafted free agent, he had signed a $230,000 contract and received a $15,000 signing bonus. When he was demoted to the practice squad, his salary dipped to $73,950.[69]

Clearly, one of the greatest challenges of managing new-found wealth is learning to say "No." George Koonce isn't the only player to hear the "tragic" stories of folks he's known for years. Leon Searcy recalls some of his own:

> People that you have known all of your life all of a sudden can't function without you. "I can't keep the lights on. I can't pay the mortgage, my car note is due." They knew when payday was. They knew it better than I did. They had it circled on the calendar. . . . They were sitting out in the parking lot, leaning up against my car, asking me to help pay for their car note. . . . You give two or three thousand to eight to ten guys. "I got to have $200 here, $3,000 there. I got this child support; I got to pay my baby mama." I couldn't say no.[70]

But he had to learn. So did Bart Scott, who recalls taking care of five different households. "I paid more rent than government assistance." Or Bernie Kosar, who, over the years, claims to have helped out "25 to 50" families. Ed Butowsky chimes in: "I have clients of mine who literally have six houses, for their parents and friends. And they bought them all, and they are making mortgage payments. When their career ends, what are they going to do? Call up and say it is time to move out." Winfred Tubbs adds an exclamation point. "Out of 100 percent of the money I loaned out I didn't get one cent paid back." "It's hard to tell people that you love, 'No!'" says Herman Edwards.[71] Braylon Edwards amplifies the sentiment:

> It's hard as hell. You know, your sister might come up to you. Your auntie . . . You might have to tell your mother no. And I know that sounds ridiculous . . . . You have to own your money. The checks that they sending you . . . it says "Braylon

Edwards."... These are your checks. The bank account is in your name. The money that they're trying to come after is yours.[72]

Divorce and Child Support

Former NFL players are more likely to be currently married than comparable men in the general population. They're divorced at rates approximately the same as their age peers.[73] While it's inaccurate to say their married lives are just like everyone else's, their marriages are not as unstable as popular opinion would have it—or that the NFL apparently thinks they might be. Jerry Richardson, former NFL player and current owner of the Carolina Panthers, once told his team that divorce was the biggest financial threat they might face. He was probably referring to some of the huge financial settlements that have resulted from divorces involving highly paid NFL stars.[74] While Richardson is undoubtedly exaggerating, he reflects a prevalent ambivalence around the league about marriage and women. On one hand they are viewed as steadying forces. On the other, they're seen as threats to the NFL's pervasive control of players' lives. From management's point of view, marriage is a variable to be managed carefully.

This is a very instrumental outlook on players' domestic arrangements. By and large, management thinks marriage is a sign of maturity. Married players are likely to give up the "fast" life and become more committed to settling down to business. The message comes across to players, as George Koonce recalls:

I got caught up in what do the coaches want to see. I think the coaches feel like if you're married, you got a family, you're more responsible. [One player], my idol, he was married. Reggie White, the leader of the team, he was married. So I'm looking like this is what you're supposed to do.[75]

Some younger players think that being married actually improves their chances of making a roster, so they make the commitment. Of course, that commitment is sometimes just for appearance's sake. *"These same guys never stopped seeing multiple girlfriends because they never developed an understanding of what it meant to love another individual as much as they loved themselves and football,"* recalls Koonce. *"To them, it was perfectly normal to give themselves physically but never emotionally to these women. These same players were shocked when their wives filed for divorce."*[76]

The NFL's instrumental perspective carries over to divorce. It's viewed as a distraction that needs to be "handled" if it can't be avoided. Indeed, it's sufficiently important to be a prime topic at the annual Rookie Symposium, an orientation program for new players. The advice dispensed there, of course, comes mainly in the form of graphic warnings about women who will try to entrap NFL players to tap into their big contracts—"gold diggers," as they are called—and admonitions to players to protect themselves with prenuptial agreements and other financial safeguards.[77]

Realistically, while divorce won't be a major financial problem for most players, it has deflated many post-career bank accounts. Bernie Kosar, for example, claims his divorce cost him between four and five million dollars.[78] Troy Aikman reportedly paid over $1.75 million to settle his divorce.[79] There are plenty of accounts of other expensive NFL divorce settlements, which tend to emphasize the cost to players and overlook the investments that wives may have put into the marriages.

While there's no systematic evidence confirming that NFL players father more out-of-wedlock children than others of their age and background, anecdotal evidence abounds suggesting that a substantial number of players and former players are paying child support. Indeed, a 1998 *Sports Illustrated* article titled "Paternity Ward" reported that the number of out-of-wedlock children fathered by professional athletes is "staggering." One sports agent says he spends more time dealing with paternity claims than he does negotiating contracts. Court records document myriad cases where former players are being held responsible for up to a dozen children fathered out of wedlock.[80]

Paternity at this volume can be an expensive proposition. In some states, a man proven to have fathered a child may be ordered to pay roughly 20 percent of his income as child support until the child turns 18. While the average annual child support payment in the U.S. (2010) is about $5,200, 20 percent of an average NFL salary comes to quite a bit more than that (approximately $154,000). Sometimes judges will cap support payments—for example, at $10,000 per month per child—regardless of the father's income.[81] Recently, we've seen a number of highly publicized figures for NFL fathers: As already noted, Warren Sapp owes a total of $75,495 a month in alimony and child support.[82] Antonio Cromartie reportedly owes $294,000 a year in child support payments and recently took a $500,000 advance on his $1.7 million salary to cover child support.[83] Former NFL wide receiver Terrell Owens says he owes child support of $240,000 annually for each of his four children by four different women. Travis Henry claimed to have a child support bill of $17,000 a month in 2009.[84]

Affording Life after Football

Despite the financial horror stories, most NFL players fare pretty well financially after retirement. Even if the financial stream slows to a trickle, a modest lifestyle seems well within reach of most players. (Of course, as we've seen, modest aspirations aren't the NFL norm.) In an effort to contextualize the "Greedy Players" myth, journalist Hank Koebler of the *Huffington Post* has constructed a scenario describing just how long an "average" player's earnings might support himself (and his family) in an "average" lifestyle. Assuming an average career of 3.5 years, paid at the median salary of $770,000 per year, a player could expect total football earnings of about $2.7 million. Conservatively assuming that the player actually takes home around 40 percent of his gross pay after taxes, agent's fees, and other payroll deductions, that leaves the player with a bit over a million dollars in hand. The United States Census Bureau listed the median U.S. household income for 2011 as around $50,000. Continuing to assume that a player would choose to live within the means of the average household, the accumulated NFL take-home pay for his average career could last him around 20 years, not counting any interest or investment income the savings might generate. That should carry the player to the time when he can tap into his NFL pension (at age 45). While this financial scenario might be quite a comedown from high times in the NFL, it demonstrates that being broke isn't the only alternative for former players who haven't struck it rich.[85] And it provides an interesting counterpoint to Darryl Gatlin's account of players' "obligation" to the NFL lifestyle, raising the question: Does *human nature* inevitably say, "You have $3 million, you are supposed to live like you have $3 million. So you can spend $3 million"? It's more likely that this is the NFL player ethos talking.

Many NFL alumni turn down the volume on the ethos and manage their financial circumstances responsibly, adroitly, and *conservatively*. Spending isn't a personal compulsion or an irresistible cultural imperative. It isn't necessarily contagious. Most players avoid the "broke" syndrome. Vestiges of the ethos may keep former players from bragging about their conservative lifestyles or their tax-free municipal bonds, but their success stories also need to be told.

It goes without saying that self-discipline is the foundation of these stories. They also include chapters about sensible, supportive wives and families, and concrete plans for life after football. Prudence and foresight are cross-cutting themes. Hakeem Chapman—who grew up in the same Compton neighborhood as Tommy Jones—offers compelling reflections.

Prepare for tomorrow. That means look at the things that you want to do with your life. Do you want to be in a position where you are comfortable? That worried me a lot. . . . The kids now, they [should be buying] the things that you need right now, not what you want. That is the key thing. Later on, you can buy what you want. . . . There are players, they sign a $10 million guaranteed thing [contract], OK. They don't realize that the government gets one third of it, 35 percent. Then they [players] are going to go for [big ticket items that lose their value]. . . . You should buy the things that you need, not the things that you want.[86]

While there's no strict formula, the trick is to resist the NFL imperative to live large. Rod Smith, formerly of the Denver Broncos, points the way. Smith graduated from college with three business-related degrees but no ticket to the NFL. He wasn't drafted in 1994, went to training camp and was cut by the Patriots, made the Broncos practice squad, and eventually became a stalwart wide receiver. His humble beginnings taught him some important lessons:

I had a chance to be in the NFL, but not a chance to be in the NFL lifestyle, because I didn't have the income for it. I didn't come into the NFL with money. I started on the practice squad making $60,000 my first year. It was a whole lot of money to me, but nothing in comparison to the lifestyle of the guys I was around in the locker room. I was making $3,000 a week and people around me were making $100,000 per week. You could get caught up in that.[87]

Smith's first lesson was clear: Beware of "livin' large" beyond one's means. It stuck with him, and he remained frugal, even as his contracts grew:

The most luxurious thing I bought was my house. I wasn't a big jewelry or car guy. I don't have Ferraris and Bentleys. I had a motto that I lived by, "There are two places I want to look good at: home and practice." Most guys get caught up in looking good on the streets. If you have to show people you have money, you're not rich.[88]

Smith's caution was reinforced by fear—fear that it could suddenly end and he would be out in the financial cold, even if he was, by the latter part of his career, making good money:

I snuck up on my locker for 14 years. I saw them fire people, and when they did, the first thing they did was take their name off of the locker and put their stuff in a trash bag. That was my fear. For 14 years, I walked up to my locker, saw my name and thought, "I have one more day." I was always in fear that one day they were going to decide I wasn't good enough. I took advantage of every day and went to work.[89]

It's especially significant that this is *Rod Smith* talking: a 12-year veteran; twice All-Pro; three time Pro-Bowler; two Super Bowl rings; holder of the NFL record for catches, yards, and touchdowns by an undrafted player. If his fear of failure was eventually unfounded, it was powerful motivation to keep his eye on the eventual financial prize and stay focused on the big picture. Smith worries that today's players lack the work ethic, the foresight, and the humility to maximize their prospects: "You have these guys who call themselves celebrities now. They are not professional football players. As soon as the reality show is over, real life hits, your career is over and you are broke. If you look down and there aren't cleats on your feet, that's a problem." Smith's apprehension about his career ending made him "more conservative" and ultimately more financially successful. "That fear has me here [after retirement], living the way I want to live.[90]

When all is said and done, we're left with opposing images of financial lives after football. One has players literally spending themselves into oblivion during and after their careers, supporting family and friends, livin' large, taking bad advice, and making bad investments. A competing vision shows young men conscientiously building financial security, spending conservatively, investing wisely, partnering with sound advisors and, above all, planning for life after football. Why, then, do so many players choose the extravagant path?

There's no simple answer. Players and circumstances differ. There's one thing former players have in common, however. They've been in the bubble for years. Consequently many have had little responsibility for managing the mundane details their lives. As William Rhoden suggests, the "football machine" creates dependency. Players show up to play, Andrew Brandt reminds us, and colleges and the NFL take care of the rest. But who takes over when the end arrives? No matter how many times they're warned to plan for the long term, many players fail to see the big picture. What captures their attention? It's the locker room culture, the NFL player ethos, and the hypercompetitive, hypermasculine atmosphere in which they're totally immersed. It's the allure of livin' large. These influences are fundamentally incompatible with financial life *outside* the bubble.

6

WHAT'S NEXT?

"What do you want to do after football?" "After football? There's nothing after football!"
—NFL quarterback Tom Brady[1]

NFL players hold their dream jobs, but former players are "out of work" with time on their hands. They are "exes"—out of the bubble, no longer gridiron gods. "What's next?" is a complicated question with significant financial and identity implications most men their age don't have to face. Understandably, most former players want continuity in their work lives, but there's no NFL seniors league. They're not expressly looking to duplicate the NFL experience, but they do search for elements that made life in the bubble so satisfying. This process sometimes leads them to unrealistically narrow their options.

More Myths

Like the "broke and bankrupt" myth, there are several problematic narratives about NFL players' work lives after football. The first is that most players are financially "set for life" and never need to work again. A second holds that former players are broke and can't seem to find and hold respectable jobs. They wander aimlessly, living in the past, complaining about the present, and fading quietly and desolately into oblivion. While elements of these narratives are often true, they're also crude caricatures.

Given the shortness of the average career, most former players are in their twenties when their playing days are over. Only a very few are older than 35. And like others of their age cohorts, they typically settle into jobs to support themselves. The NFL Player Care study found that around 70 percent of former players say they are "working now" in some capacity. It's hard to know exactly what this means, especially since the study doesn't specify precisely what "working" means. Nearly 30 percent of those surveyed are over age 65—typically considered the retirement threshold. We wouldn't be surprised if they didn't have jobs. Over half the players surveyed have reached 55, the age when full NFL pensions kick in—another good reason not to hold a job. Nevertheless, most NFL alumni are working at *something*. Younger alumni (30–49), however, are about 12 percent less likely to be working than men of the same age in the general population (78 percent versus 90 percent), but older alumni (50-plus) are about eight percent *more* likely to be currently working (66 percent versus 58 percent). Overall, former NFL players appear to be better off financially than their age peers, as a group. These statistical trends correspond to several noteworthy challenges in former players' lives.[2] (See Appendix 2 for a brief summary of retired players' income. There's no good estimate of their current total worth.)

Recently, the *Wall Street Journal* noted that "just 49.2 percent of NFL retirees between 30 and 49 years old had jobs within a year of leaving the league."[3] Highlighting these "poor employment figures," the article implies that former players have trouble finding work, largely because they lack the background and training necessary to hold 21st-century jobs. The NFL and the NFLPA have been sensitive to this narrative for years. Embedded in this perspective, however, is a fundamental misunderstanding about the end of NFL careers. As we've seen, most players don't consider their football careers to be over for a year or two after they've played their final games. The fact that only 50 percent of former players have jumped into new jobs during that year in limbo isn't surprising. Most don't consider themselves to be finished with football. Their failure to find new jobs hardly indicates, by itself, that players are unemployable.

That's not to say, however, that finding jobs is easy. Accounts of post-career financial failures often implicate players' inability or unwillingness to find work after football. Not only do we hear of players going broke, but stories abound of players waiting idly for opportunity to come their way, bouncing from one venture to another, or mismanaging businesses.

We're told, for example, that less than one half of one percent of former players have historically been able to make successful transitions to business careers.[4] Nevertheless, this simply doesn't jibe with the Player Care study or other systematic research. Indeed, the percentage cited is so small that even anecdotal evidence challenges the assertion. As with similarly audacious statistical claims, it's hard to know where such figures come from and how they are derived. Regardless, the media have taken note and increasingly highlighted post-NFL problems.

Unfortunately, there's little systematic data on what sorts of jobs players pursue after they finish with football. There's no inventory of where they work or in what capacities. Given their proven willingness to work hard, their ability to learn complex plans and procedures, their capacity to analyze situations on the fly, and their discipline in pursuing success diligently, players have succeeded in just about every career imaginable: doctors, lawyers, business tycoons, investment managers, politicians, judges, coaches, teachers, preachers, movie stars, and owners of bars. But not everyone succeeds, and their challenges and failures aren't arbitrary or capricious. There are some notable patterns to former players' work lives—both successes and failures—that emerge in relation to the unique circumstances of living in the bubble for years, then confronting an involuntary and uncertain ending.

Starting Up, Starting Over

Refusing to concede that their playing days are over, many players spend months, if not years, working out and trying to make a roster. This keeps them out of the job market for a year or two, with long-term implications. It took George Koonce a couple of years to go back to school and get a job in athletic administration. Others have similar stories. They are often "paralyzed," and sometimes the paralysis isn't temporary. Recall, for instance, how Brandon Gold ended his career. He stayed home, relaxed on the beach, worked out, read the Bible. But somewhere along the way he realized he had another life to lead. That involved a decade-long struggle.

> [Finding] a job is extremely difficult. I have humbled myself so much
> now. I will do whatever. . . . I'm a great guy, but I don't know what I am
> supposed to be doing. . . . You have to reinvent yourself . . . and you are
> going to need to do something totally normal.[5]

Gold is ambivalent about assuming new professional statuses and
roles. He was "humbled" after all the excitement, glory, and money of
the NFL. He needed to become someone new, doing something "totally
normal." Money and identity were both at stake. These dilemmas resonate throughout Tommy Jones's saga:

> [Entering a new profession] wasn't going to pay me the type of money that
> I want right now. I wasn't thinking about [the job] being beneath me. Yeah,
> that was part of it. . . . I was used to having checks for thousands, and to
> just be on a salary for $15 an hour, I just couldn't do that.[6]

Entangled in family finances and poor decisions, Jones had fiscal qualms,
but also had ego problems. He put off getting his college degree or getting
onto an alternate employment path. Suddenly, he was 15 years down the
road, having made little progress. "I kind of put everything on the back
burner. I wasn't even thinking about going to school at that time. . . .
To be honest, the years just went by. . . . It was tough to swallow at first,
and for four years after retirement, I didn't want to get a job."[7] A decade
later, Jones had no steady job or source of income. He'd dabbled in some
investment schemes in the clothing and recording industries, but those
failed. While he still had plans, he remained captive to his initial post-
football inertia and lofty expectations.

Aversion to the Ordinary

Gold and Jones both allude to the ego sacrifices entailed in taking ordinary jobs, doing something "totally normal." One of the most frequent
observations former players make about their football careers is how
exciting they were, how much players craved the intensity and attention

that were part of the bubble. Hakeem Chapman, a veteran of five Super Bowls, sums it up:

> There is nowhere in the world you can go and get that same feeling you got when you were out there on that football field playing ball. You didn't have that type of excitement when you got married or with the birth of your child. You can't find it anywhere. You played in the Super Bowl. You tell me [where] to find that kind of excitement that you had in the Super Bowl. I'm still searching for it—that high.[8]

Having been special for years, players love the adulation. They're virtually addicted to the excitement and attention. Doing something else for a living pales in comparison. So, when Tommy Jones balks at taking a mundane job—"Not necessarily that that was beneath me to do, but I just didn't want to do that right now"—he's looking down from a lofty professional pinnacle. It's hard for another line of work to measure up. Recall George Koonce's reaction to the initial job offer he received to work in the ECU Athletic Department for $36,000 a year.[9] He was insulted. His agent was appalled, and egged him on: *"He said, 'George, you got to be kidding me.' He said, 'You need to go up there and tell them to kiss your ass.'"*[10] The mundane job and the ordinary salary had Koonce on the verge of declining the job offer, until reason, in the name of Tunisia Koonce, took over. Koonce was disheartened by the same realization many former players have—that few jobs will actually pay them the amounts to which they had become accustomed—but his wife helped him adjust to that reality.

Some players are humiliated when they're confronted with being normal—taking ordinary jobs. That doesn't prevent then from going to work, but it may steer them into particular kinds of occupations. Throughout our research, we've come across relatively few former players who hold conventional, salaried, nine-to-five jobs. To be sure, many are self-employed and set their own hours. Others are professionals, who by definition, work until the job is done. Whereas there was a time when former NFL players would turn to teaching, or sell cars or insurance, younger alumni are more likely to be entrepreneurs or cobble together combinations of money making activities that generate income, but that don't constitute a conventional professional résumé. It's not necessarily due to an aversion to work. Rather it's a desire to maintain a high public profile, combined with a penchant for control over personal time and effort—a desire to be their own men, not someone else's employees. Players want to continue being distinctive in some capacity, not just one of the crowd. And they hope for jobs that provide a modicum of the excitement they used to feel in going to work: jobs in entertainment or the mass media; professions with tangible, immediate payoffs; high-risk, high-reward occupations and business enterprises. They're looking for jobs that embody the NFL ethos and resemble aspects of the bubble. They're not exactly spoiled by success, but their past success shapes how they evaluate prospects for the future.

Bad Benchmarking Revisited

Looking for vestiges of their former careers, former players often set high standards. We've seen how using questionable standards for comparison leads players to extravagant spending and fiscal shortsightedness. This practice infects post-football career planning as well. As Hakeem Chapman suggests, if you're looking for a comparable career, "You can't find it anywhere." It's hard to get seriously interested in a mundane job like teaching or coaching high school football, where the take-home check might amount to less than $3,000 a month—less than a rookie free agent training camp stipend. When even a former journeyman player can walk away from a weekend of autograph signing with thousands in tax-free cash, nine-to-five office work has muted appeal. Most former players immediately make more in severance pay and their annual cut of the NFLPA's group licensing agreement than they might earn at entry-level administrative or service positions.[11] With NFL salaries as a benchmark, almost any other occupation falls short.

A second type of problematic benchmarking creates a more subtle challenge. Former players often claim they've spent their "best years" in the NFL, but those days are over and they are back at square one when seeking new jobs and careers. They frame time spent in the NFL as time lost on the job track. George Koonce elaborates:

When we was off playing football, our classmates on campus, they were doing internships, they was working their way up the ladder. While we were on the practice field learning how to tackle, they were learning the game of life. Now, all of a sudden I am 32 years old, I'm out of the league, and my classmate that was in my industrial technology classes, he is 32, but he has had ten years on me, going through the interview process, closing deals, so now, I am at 32, trying to compete with him. That's tough.[12]

Anderson Smith concurs: "I was frustrated because I wasn't as far along as [his contemporaries]. These guys have been doing it for 15 to 20 years while I was playing football. They're the lucky ones."[13]

Some former players who see themselves lagging behind use this as a reason for not getting into the race. They feel they'll never catch up. Such accounts, however, are often grounded in faulty assumptions about the careers being compared and how occupational advancement proceeds. First, the careers they envision for comparison apparently begin even before college graduation and proceed with steady direction and purpose. That's far from the reality of today's job market, where even college graduates take time to settle into career paths. Many take time off after they graduate, move back in with their parents, travel in Europe, do volunteer or mission work, join the Peace Corps or Teach for America, or take temporary jobs just to make some money and enjoy their youth. Others bounce from job to job, trying to "find themselves," looking for career traction before they actually settle on an enduring line of work. In short, they don't get the running "head start" that former players imagine.[14]

In addition, if the average NFL career is 3.5 years, many former players haven't necessarily fallen that far behind. Most former NFL players don't start the occupational race that long after their contemporaries, certainly not so far behind as to prevent catching up. They are, after all, still in their mid-twenties. Anderson Smith, for example, was 24 when he played his last NFL game. He distorts the time frame when he implies that his contemporaries have a 20-year head start on him.

The competitive disadvantage some former players describe is often more imagined than real, and is likely to be erased by the many benefits and career enhancements that the NFL provides. Players don't stagnate while in the NFL. They learn discipline. They meet potential employers and investors. They learn communication skills—to be media savvy, to speak in public, to deal with advisors, lawyers, administrators, and bosses. There's a long list of "self-improvement" programs provided by teams, the NFL, and the NFLPA, all aimed at honing job skills and improving career opportunities. Even if time in the NFL is time out of the job market, those years provide players with sufficient advantages to offset the hardships they claim to face. To say that those who didn't have NFL careers are "the lucky ones" is stretching the point.

Generational Differences

Many players also claim that players who played in the days before big money are the "lucky ones" because economic hardship forced them to develop job skills and income sources outside of football. While it's mainly younger alumni who subscribe to this theory, many old-timers agree that they were better prepared to face life after football, even if they weren't as financially blessed.

While players from the 1950s through the 1970s generally made decent money by everyday standards, most of them routinely worked in the off season. Today's players—young and old alike—eagerly valorize the old-timers for their resourcefulness and industry, such as James Sutton, the All-Pro cornerback from the 1970s who spent several years as a substitute teacher in the off season. "I went into real estate," recalls Sutton, "but all the time I was playing I had to be thinking about what was next. It was good money for the times, but I knew it would end when I quit and I always kept an eye out for how I would make a living when I was done [playing].[15]

Sutton wasn't alone. The Player Care study found that 75 percent of older alumni worked during the off season, compared to 23 percent of younger retirees. It's likely that even fewer contemporary players hold jobs in today's off season. Hakeem Chapman elaborates his story:

Every year, I did something different because, back then, we worked [in the off season]. One year, I got my real estate license. Another year, I got my stockbroker's license. Another year, I worked for Zales Corporation. I learned about jewelry. I did a lot of things. . . . You never know how long [football] is going to last, and when I quit, I had made enough relationships networking with people. I wanted to turn it into something. . . . I put myself in a position where if I got hurt or when it was all over, I would have a place to fall back on. [Working] those six months [each off season], I had about six occupations to fall back on.[16]

There are literally dozens of accounts of players like Sutton teaching in the off season, or getting into sales, like Chapman. All-Pro players from the 1950s such as Leo Nomellini and Eugene "Big Daddy" Lipscomb took up professional wrestling. Others started their own businesses, sold insurance, or took low-level management positions with established firms. Doing so made it possible for players to support themselves relatively comfortably despite low football salaries, while simultaneously preparing for future careers. Perhaps old-timers weren't exactly "lucky" to be paid so little, but it accustomed them to normal jobs and prompted them to explore diverse possibilities.

By comparison, contemporary players end up with relatively little job preparation or experience. This isn't an insurmountable obstacle for these otherwise talented and ambitious young men, but it leaves them in uncharted territory when they're done playing. Rather than weaving football into the broader fabric of their lives, football has become their lives. They have gone "all in." That said, even though past generations of players were forced to work during their playing careers, this was no guarantee of post-career success. There are plenty of stories of old-timers who never found stable employment and ended up struggling financially, even if they didn't wantonly squander their money.[17] Indeed, former players and NFL alumni organizations have complained vigorously for years that the NFL and the NFLPA have turned their backs on the financial difficulties faced by older players who retired before the era of free agency. Looking at the bigger picture, it's hard to say these guys are the "lucky ones." (See Appendix 2 for an overview of the finances of NFL alumni.)

Paths to Success

Former players who have done well after football often mention planning, preparation, and hard work, but they also highlight fortuitous opportunities and good fortune. There are common threads, but no surefire recipes. Hakeem Chapman's eclectic skills—the six occupations he explored— certainly came in handy as he became successful in real estate development, sales, equities investment, and motivational speaking. He was true to his own motto: "Prepare for tomorrow, meaning look at the things that you want to do with your life." Although his path is exemplary—replete with valuable lessons—Chapman's success story is far from typical. Many routes to post-NFL careers are more straightforward, more conventional. Prepare by getting a college education in an appropriate field. Develop job skills. Explore alternatives. Seize opportunities. Former cornerback Eugene Profit, for example, set himself up for success in textbook fashion. Raised in South Central Los Angeles—just blocks from where Tommy Jones and Chapman grew up—Profit hit the books as well as the gridiron, set his sights on an Ivy League education, then the NFL. During his five-year NFL career, fellow players and coaches thought he was sure to go into coaching, given his keen intelligence and dedication to the game. But he also had a Yale degree in economics and a fascination with "the study of money and capital flows." Profit decided on Wall Street.

Forced out of football by injury in 1991, he became a financial consultant at Legg Mason, a global asset management firm, then founded his own financial management company in 1996. Profit Investment Management's assets have grown from $300,000 to over $2 billion, making it one of the largest and most successful African American–owned businesses in the United States. Profit had an average NFL career for his time. His income was modest, never more than $200,000 in a season. But he parlayed his skills, preparation, and opportunities—many of them afforded by his NFL career—into a success story that rivals, if not parallels, Hakeem Chapman's.[18]

But there are myriad unconventional success stories, too. Jesse Dampeer, a contemporary of Chapman's, wasn't a planner, and his journey was strikingly serendipitous. He never thought his football career would last, nor did he intentionally prepare to start over when his unanticipated football career was done.

> I grew up in the woods, logging between semesters and had some interest in that but really had no idea about what direction I would go and just thought it was a wonderful experience to play in the NFL. Things weren't quite as large as they are today, and so I just assumed a couple of years after I left [his team], that would be the end of it.[19]

Like many of his contemporaries, Dampeer worked in the off season, mainly jobs in construction and small businesses. He never thought he was holding down a "real job." "I've had projects," he says. "I've had a business that I was trying to put together or something I was trying to create, something I was trying to do to generate income." His insights reveal an important aspect of many former players' attitudes about work, money, and identity. He had *projects*, not jobs. It's an important distinction.

Dampeer's projects included cattle ranching, television work, publishing, motivational speaking and filmmaking, real estate development, coal mining, oil, gas, geothermal energy, and telecommunications. There's little to tie these ventures together, except that they all required skills and qualities that Dampeer honed in the NFL: "I had confidence, and I knew about preparation, and consistency, and commitment, and discipline, and how to treat people, and all those things." These traits worked for Dampeer, no matter where he turned.

Combining his "tools of the trade" with his distinction between projects and jobs, we see some important parallels between Dampeer's football and business successes. His diverse ventures seemingly have little in common, but fundamentally they were independent, individualistic enterprises. Dampeer had no bosses. He had financially successful enterprises, but no jobs. He was an innovator, an entrepreneur, an impresario. It was part of a larger career pattern that mirrored significant aspects of his football experience:

> I want to have something interesting. I want to enjoy it. I want to have fun. I want to be excited about what I do. . . . I know I started thinking about what was pushing me, and I believe it was my Super Bowl experiences, my championship experiences. I was chasing an emotional high that I had experienced in football. I was chasing that feeling of victory . . . of that incredibly emotional moment when you win the Super Bowl, and you are on top of the world. . . . I think I'm trying to recapture that.

In many ways, Dampeer is the antithesis of both Hakeem Chapman and Eugene Profit. He didn't plan ahead and he didn't stay a true course. But there are common themes. Each was dedicated to success. Each pursued high-risk, high-reward ventures. They sought situations where the spotlight might find them. They were their own bosses. While most former players don't succeed at their levels, many speak of their post-NFL accomplishments and aspirations in similar terms. Perhaps it's an extension of their individualistic, personally motivated selves that excelled at football. Or perhaps it's a reaction against the strict regimentation, oversight, and coaching they've received since they were kids. In either case, post-NFL success stories often evince football-related themes.

Most strikingly, nearly every time former players talk about post-football jobs, they drift back to Jesse Dampeer's concluding sentiments. They want something flashy, exiting, fun. They want the exhilaration. You can hear the NFL player ethos seep into their aspirations as well as their descriptions of normal jobs and lives. It plays out in their occupational choices. It's present in their wildly speculative business decisions, in their impulsive spending, in their investment strategies. Where's the excitement in mutual funds? Who wants to run a dry-cleaning franchise when you can open a recording studio with your own record label? Who wants to sit behind a desk? Stanley Davis sums it up: "My career after football? Oh my God: pro wrestling, I won an Emmy on a TV show in Chicago. I wrote a book, I am a head coach and part owner of an indoor football team. I have done a myriad of stuff, and still nothing compares to walking out that tunnel with the boys."[20]

Coaching

Craving vestiges of the bubble, most players would like to remain close to the game, near the limelight. One obvious way is by coaching. Coaches roam the locker room and share in the culture. They bask in the thrill of victory and suffer the anguish of defeat. While it's seemingly the closest thing to being a player, it's an option relatively few players choose. The overwhelming reason: it's too much work![21] George Koonce is adamant:

I put so much time in as a player, now I'm thinking, "I wouldn't want to work those type of hours as a coach." I'm not that type. You know how much damn film they have to watch to get ready for the Cowboys or Southern Miss? I really enjoyed that aspect of the game as a player, but I wouldn't want to do it as a coach.[22]

Coaches at the pro and big-time college levels easily put in 100-hour work weeks. Former Super Bowl winner Jon Gruden was legendary for his 20-hour work days, reportedly arriving at the office at 4:00 a.m., if he hadn't spent the night there. Coaches generally figure the key to success is outworking the other guys, so they see an intrinsic value in working long hours.[23] There are no days off, no off season. And, by and large, the work isn't glamorous: countless hours of film study and planning, endless repetitive meetings. Only a small fraction of a coach's time is actually spent on the field, working with players or coaching games.

Coaching does pay well at the elite levels. Head coaches in the NFL and NCAA can make millions. Even assistant coaches make six-figure salaries, with some coordinators topping $1 million.[24] But compared to what players make, that's peanuts. Most NFL assistant coaches earn far less than the players they coach, even their rookies. For ex-players, coaching is a big step down the salary ladder. If a former player takes an NFL coaching position, he could be the lowest paid guy in the locker room.

The descent is even more precipitous at other levels of coaching. It's not uncommon to hear players and retirees say they'd like to work with kids, keep their hand in the game, coach high school. Their visions, of course, are often romanticized. High school coaching requires more than showing up at the end of summer and throwing the ball around with a bunch of eager teenagers. It's not as demanding as the NFL, but it's hard work. Most high school football head coaches have teaching or administrative responsibilities, which stretch their days from dawn to well past dusk. And their compensation pales in relation to what NFL and college coaches make.

Generally, high school coaches receive stipends for their coaching, over and above their teaching salaries. According to the U.S. Bureau of Labor Statistics (2011), high school teachers average around $55,000 annually. Special coaching contracts or coaching stipends can raise a football coach's income substantially, but exceeding $100,000 is rare. In Texas, the hotbed of prep football, coaches on average make around $30,000 more than their non-coaching teaching counterparts. The head coaches at two of the nations most storied high school programs Odessa Permian and Odessa High each make around $100,000, plus several thousand dollars worth of extra perks. After winning ten consecutive district titles and three state championships, the head coach at Euless Trinity High School was awarded a contract in excess of $114,000. In 2012, the ten highest-paid head coaches in South Carolina averaged around $100,000. Salaries for top flight head coaches in other football strongholds are comparable. At the same time, coaching stipends for head coaches can be as little as $4,000, with assistants making $3,000 or less.[25]

When former players do get into NFL coaching, it's usually at the bottom rung, and most NFL coaches are not former professional players. In 2013, only eight of the league's 32 teams had head coaches with NFL playing experience[26] and only 26 percent of all NFL coaches have played in the league.[27] Nevertheless, the NFL and individual teams sponsor coaching workshops, internships, and boot camps, as well as minority coaching fellowships, that give former players the opportunity to experience the game from a coaching standpoint, but these are not salaried positions and don't guarantee coaching jobs. While many players try their hand at high school coaching as volunteer assistants, they discover that it's no way to make a living. The NFL alumni landscape is littered with former players who have given it a try and quickly gotten out.[28] On the other hand, many players who don't really need the money have gotten heavily involved as volunteer assistants in high schools, and have found the experience fulfilling—a good way to stay close to the game without the commitments of full-time coaching.

Media Careers

If coaching is the most logical extension of playing, then becoming a media sports commentator is a close second. Take it from Mark Schlereth, former NFL lineman and current ESPN broadcaster: "My father told me, 'Do something you like to do and you'll never have to get up in the morning and go to work.' That's what I did. I got to live out my childhood dream, played 12 years in the NFL and I've been talking about it ever since.[29] Radio, TV, internet outlets, and programming of all sorts make it possible to make an impression, if not a living, commenting on sports. The demand for commentators, pundits, and critics seems insatiable. NFL player credentials lend authenticity as well as expertise to a media presence.

By and large, players and former players view jobs in the media as viable and attractive ways of making money, if not a living, after football. They've been on camera and the other side of the microphone throughout their careers. With the advent of social media such as Facebook and Twitter, they're becoming skilled in textual communication—in 140 characters or less. Hakeem Chapman was ahead of the media game as far back as the 1960s, when he began taking acting classes in anticipation of moving behind a microphone or in front of a camera. Today, players routinely appear on TV and radio year-round, and post blogs and maintain web sites devoted to football and related issues. They've already got a foot in the door.

The demands of actually *working* full time in the media, however, often surprise former players. As in football, excellence requires preparation and practice, and media work involves many of the aspects of coaching that turn players off. Some former players would like media jobs, but only want to work a few hours a week—mainly on the air. Former linebacker Derrick Brooks, who worked as an ESPN analyst before becoming president of the Arena Football League's Tampa Bay Storm, decries this attitude: "When guys tell me they want to be on television, I'll ask if they're willing to broadcast a high school game for nothing to gain experience. And their response is, 'No. I'm such-and-such.' I tell them, 'Well, you're nobody in this game.' You need to put as much effort into this as you put into being a player."[30]

Players are sometimes caught off guard by the pay scale. Celebrity broadcasters with national network jobs make good money, maybe millions, and that's presumed to be the norm. But apart from the relatively small handful of jobs with major networks and in large local media markets (e.g., New York, Chicago, Dallas, and L.A.), TV and radio jobs aren't necessarily lucrative, especially if one only works a few hours a week. A big-market sports talk radio host might make close to a million annually if ratings are good, but the norm falls well below six figures. According to the Bureau of Labor Statistics, the median salary for radio "announcers" and "talk show hosts" was around $27,000 in 2010, ranging from as little as $17,000 up to nearly six figures for the top ten percent. Television pays a bit better than radio. Former pro stars can expect to make more initially than "sports geeks" who are starting out in the business, but some "on-air personalities" make as little as $20 an hour on a part-time basis.[31]

To establish a serious media career, former players need to learn the ropes. There are a wide variety of roles to learn: play-by-play announcer, color analyst, pundit, talk show host, comic sidekick, and others. Each demands its own skill set. Some players believe that doing a talk show simply involves showing up and talking, but according to professionals in the industry, that's far from the case.[32] One needs to learn the "off-air" technical workings of broadcasting as well as develop the requisite on-air talents. Analytic acuity, expert knowledge, a quick wit, an engaging sense of humor, and the ability to engage or infuriate others are important assets to cultivate. For radio work, a voice must be clear and distinctive, while TV makes its own visual demands. And being well organized and committed to planning are crucial in broadcasting. This sounds a lot like coaching, if not playing, football.

Many players get their first taste of professional media exposure by appearing on weekly local TV or radio shows centered around their teams, while others pick up a few hundred dollars by calling in to radio stations once a week during the season for brief conversations. The professional possibilities are tantalizing, but deceptive. Transforming brief engagements into media careers is challenging. Recently, the NFL has been helping players make that leap, offering formal training in media work, including "boot camps" in "Broadcasting" and "Sports Journalism and Communications."[33]

Beyond the money, and perhaps most importantly, jobs in the sports media supply many components of life in the bubble that players treasure. First, there's public attention, if not adulation. Second, there's excitement of performing before a crowd. It may not be the adrenaline rush of running out of the tunnel at the Super Bowl, but there is something exhilarating about going on the air for a vast audience. Former Green Bay Packer LeRoy Butler provides a glimpse of what motivated his budding media career: "When the crowd noise stops, you got to turn it back on . . . and that is why I like being on [the radio] everyday. . . . Score a touchdown, do a Lambeau Leap. . . . This [being on radio and TV] is Lambeau Field to me."[34]

Third, sports broadcast settings often involve the sort of camaraderie that players experienced in the NFL. The importance of this can't be overstated. Former players miss their teammates. They miss the locker room. They miss the teamwork and striving for a common goal. Some media jobs provide all of these. According to longtime broadcaster Rich Eisen, working for the NFL Network is as close to recreating NFL camaraderie as one can get. It's a "frat boy" version of an NFL locker room, with all the hijinks, bawdy humor, misogyny, and comradeship that can be packed into a workplace.[35] Taken together, these aspects of media work make it especially inviting to former players if they're willing to pay the price.

Cashing In on Celebrity

Many former players would like to be paid simply for being popular icons or celebrities. Lending out their name or their presence can be both lucrative and ego boosting. Product endorsement, for example, cashes in on gridiron fame without requiring extensive new or specialized skills. Few players, however, have the cachet or star power to garner lucrative nationwide endorsements. Once you get past the elite quarterbacks, few players hit the motherlode. The Manning brothers, Aaron Rodgers, Tom Brady, and Drew Brees have multimillion-dollar advertising deals, but even other stars have trouble attracting six-figure endorsement money. For most, it's far less and the well runs dry rather quickly. Only the occasional icon—such as Joe Montana—or other players who have maintained high entertainment-media profiles—such as Terry Bradshaw—continue to cash in on their names and personas years after they've left the game.[36] Occasionally, former players like Jim Brown and

WHAT'S NEXT? * 187

Carl Weathers parlay their NFL notoriety into substantial Hollywood careers. Many others dabble at the periphery of the film industry before fading away. As with most professions, becoming a serious actor requires talent, commitment, training, and work.

Numerous former players, however, are able to trade on their NFL celebrity on a smaller scale. Autograph signings, often combined with memorabilia sales, are ubiquitous. Depending upon the locale and market, they can be quite lucrative, even for players with minimal name recognition. The venues run the gamut from convention halls to sports bars and strip mall openings. Fees run from a few dollars per signature charged directly to autograph seekers to several thousand dollars for extended sessions with autograph and memorabilia dealers, who pay for hundreds of signatures at a time. Internet booking agencies hook up players with events, offering either a set fee or a percentage of the revenue generated.[37]

Some former players remain in demand as entertainment "personalities" or motivational speakers. Even 40 years after his final game, Hakeem Chapman still capitalizes on his modest fame:

[After I retired] I did films and a lot of stuff. I was on the first *Mod Squad* series. I wasn't one of the lead principals, but I was on the show every week. I did a lot of acting, and I started [motivational speaking]. I took those acting qualities and put them in front of the audience. Now, when I talk, I entertain the people, and I keep them awake. I have about three gigs a month. . . . I'm at a church tailgate party, and I am at a casino and they pay very handsomely. You make yourself $4,500 or $5,000.[38]

We need to keep this success in perspective. Chapman is an extraordinary character, with keen foresight and adaptability. He planned and prepared to make the most of his celebrity, and it's paid off. A journeyman, he played on several championship teams, but was never a star. But he recognized the opportunities that came with an NFL career and industriously and intelligently pursued them. Recall that he laid the groundwork for jobs in business, real estate, and stock sales. He anticipated a possible entertainment career and trained for it, too. As he observes about his current success as a celebrity, "So, how did I do this? I prepared for it. I knew how I would be on stage. I can address people. I can talk. Studying acting, I can relate to the people and give the people what they want to hear and see."[39] Many former NFL players like to be paid for who they *were*, not what they do now. Chapman maximized both through planning, preparation, and the willingness to provide something people would pay for. He realized he had to deliver a viable product, not simply show up at a gig.

Being paid for who one is—or who one *was*—can be easy money, but it's an occupation with limited horizons. The perilous side of selling yourself as a commodity is your value is completely market dependent and you've got only one aging commodity to sell. You're not producing anything, or providing a value-added service. When a player is valuable in name only, he may be employed by a business, but he might not actually be part of the business operation. His place in the hierarchy is peripheral, and he's gaining no professional capital. His name and his past are all he's got. That's fine for selling autographs, but it holds less currency in more substantial professional ventures.

Philanthropy

Ask former NFL players what they've been doing with their time since retiring and many of them mention their "charity work." They acknowledge their good fortune and genuinely want to "give something back" to the community. By and large, they are genuinely altruistic, although many aren't averse to mixing business with philanthropy. Done right, everybody wins. David Jordan's story, for example, puts charity work squarely in the middle of his post-football career and introduces some ways in which philanthropy, earning a living, and the player ethos intertwine.

> The whole first year [after being cut] I just worked out. I did a lot of charity work. I got involved in the March of Dimes. Then I started traveling

the country doing a lot of different things, getting a lot of golf events for charity. As the years progressed, I wanted to do more charity work but also have a job. So I cut back a little bit on the charity work. Then, finally, two years ago, I took it upon myself that I wanted to become a world long drive competitor in golf. I made it to the world championships. So now what I do is I travel the country doing charity and corporate celebrity events, doing all different types of golf, trick shots, long-drive exhibitions. I will do charity events. I will do corporate events. Number one is making an income for me and my family, and also making money for some of these charities.[40]

Clearly, Jordan is playing off his NFL celebrity for both personal and charitable gain. Much of his time, and often his signature, is given for free, but he also shares in the revenue, receiving an appearance fee to assist in fundraisers. It's not uncommon, for example, for a charity autograph and memorabilia signing session or a golf outing to generate thousands of dollars worth of donations, as much as $10,000 of which may go to the former player as an appearance fee or honorarium, plus expenses.[41]

When they initially come into big money for the first time, NFL players' gratitude often leads them to establish charitable foundations, which the players continue to run after they have retired. Some of these become major philanthropic forces, especially if the player is a star and his commitment is abiding.[42] Other foundations are well intentioned, but less than efficient in funneling money to worthy causes. Their activities tend to wane, especially when players' salaries run out after retirement. Still other foundations are thinly veiled money-making schemes, if not outright scams. Sometimes it's hard to tell the difference. Individually, or through their foundations, players may provide fund raising services (e.g., motivational speeches, appearances at golf tournaments or other outings) for which they (or their foundations) are paid. The same services might also be sold to corporate entities or philanthropic organizations, with fees varying widely. Foundations may hold fund-raisers of their own, often passing along the money raised directly to established community agencies or indirectly through other charitable organizations (e.g., the American Cancer Society).

Too often, however, little of the money donated finds its way to the causes for which it was ostensibly intended. An ESPN *Outside the Lines* investigation of 115 charities run by high-profile athletes (including NFL stars) found that most of these charities "don't measure up to what charity experts would say is an efficient, effective use of money." Seventy-four percent of the charities fell short of one or more acceptable nonprofit operating standards, including how much money an organization actually spends on charitable work as opposed to administrative expenses and whether there is sufficient oversight of its operations. Unfortunately, too many former NFL players have been involved in questionable practices. It's not uncommon, for example, for players to use their charities to provide jobs for friends and relatives. Sometimes they use them to support indulgent lifestyles.[43]

To be sure, former players aren't getting rich running charitable foundations. But operating a foundation supplies former players with a bit of the "action" they lost when they retired. They deal with large sums of money. They rub elbows with the rich and famous. They place themselves in a flattering public spotlight. They get together with their buddies— often former players—to live large for a little while and experience the camaraderie of the good old days, restoring vestiges of their former lives.

Challenges and Solutions

Former players consistently mention a set of common job-related challenges they encounter in moving beyond the NFL. Some are largely generational, but persist in present-day laments. Others seem timeless, testing young and old alike. The most vociferous complaints come from players who retired prior to the free agency era, who never made big money. Old-timers bemoan their meager pension checks, blaming both the NFL and the NFLPA for leaving them high and dry. Some of the inequities have been addressed by recent revisions of the pension program, putting more money in the pockets of NFL alumni across the board. Still, old-timers are never going to catch up with their younger peers. Some have already endured decades of hardship. While younger retirees have less to lament, they also know that their retirement plans aren't as good as those in other sports, MLB, for example.

Younger alumni have somewhat different concerns. Across the board, they wish they had more guidance regarding life after football. Having spent most of their lives in the bubble—being treated as special and having things done for them prior to, and during college, and certainly in the pros—they feel they were walking into the wilderness when they walked out of the NFL. Suddenly, they were responsible for taking care of personal matters that others tended to before. Jamaal McDaniels, a veteran from the late 1980s, for example, observes that "A lot of these kids [current players] don't have a clue. . . . You have to start early. You have to start getting into these kids' minds a lot earlier, so they can get a jump on things."[44] He thinks aspiring players as well as those who make it to the NFL need to be forewarned about challenges along the way, and better prepared for the issues that emerge at the end.

McDaniels felt abandoned: "I didn't have anybody to hold my hand and help me get a job, a good and decent job." For some, mentoring or formal programming seem to be viable solutions. They regret not having more systematic opportunities to learn about financial, professional, occupational, and social challenges. George Koonce is one of them:

I didn't really have the mentors. I didn't really have the life coaches. I had [football] coaches in my life from nine years old until I turned 32, but they were coaching me to play a position. They were coaching me to strive to get better out there on the practice field and in the off season, but I didn't have anyone really coaching me per se, giving a road map or playbook to be an athletic director or a VP of administration for an NFL team. I kind of had to learn all that by chance, or on the fly. I wanted to do it. I wanted to reach my potential, but I didn't have anybody that took the time to show me.[45]

Times have changed since Koonce's playing days. Players today receive a full menu of formal guidance through NFL and NFLPA programming. NFL Player Engagement and NFLPA programs address nearly every aspect of life in and after the NFL including transition advice, career building, financial training, coaching academies, and "boot camps" for broadcasting, entertainment industries, retail franchising, real estate, and capital investment.[46] There's even a budding service industry cropping up around the NFL aimed at helping players deal with life away from the field. Increasingly, we're seeing the emergence of professional guides to escort players into the real world: "life coaches" or "transition coaches." Ken Ruettgers, for example, played in the NFL in the 1980s and 1990s and prepared well for his days after football. In 2001 he started GamesOver. org as a resource to help athletes transition into retirement.[47] In 2013, 11 former NFL players—including Troy Vincent—were trained and certified as transition coaches by the league.[48] Several of the former players we interviewed expressed an interest in getting into this line of work, and a couple have already established web sites advertising their services.

Of course these are recent developments, resources not available to older alumni. But many younger alumni seem uninformed about their availability. Despite vigorous efforts by the NFL and NFLPA to develop and publicize these resources, most players and former players fail to take advantage of the opportunities. According to Troy Vincent, NFL vice president of player engagement, his office is aggressively promoting its programs and if players aren't taking advantage of the league's workshops, boot camps, internships, career counseling services, and other programs, it's their own fault. "The player today," says Vincent, "has to make a conscious effort not to engage, because the service and program offerings are robust. There is no excuse."[49]

Despite the proliferation of development programming, some players and alumni mention internships as a possible missing solution. As we've heard, younger alumni feel that their older counterparts had a post-career advantage because they held jobs in the off season. Internships are touted as the contemporary equivalent. The NFL has recently developed a wide-ranging internship program and the NFLPA is in step with its own programming.[50] Occasionally, internships lead directly to jobs, but that's the exception, not the rule. Recently, for example, David Howard, who has signed with four teams since 2010, but has not played in a regular-season NFL game, turned an internship at Merrill Lynch Wealth Management into a full time position as a financial planner. His managing director at Merrill Lynch says Howard brought a skill set that's impossible to teach: "Work ethic and discipline. I attribute a lot of that to a tough Ivy League academic regimen and from the requirements of pro sports. David is hungry and has great determination."[51]

This underscores an aspect of internships that players and alumni sometimes fail to grasp. An internship isn't a job offer or a promise. It's a glimpse into how an organization operates, how it looks from the inside. It provides limited on-the-job training, but interns usually aren't given serious management-level responsibilities. They are more likely to be "gofers" or perhaps allowed to shadow organization members without substantial responsibilities. Internships aren't entry-level positions or even management traineeships. This means, of course, that it's unrealistic to expect an internship to turn directly into a job.

Internships, however, are an excellent way for players to get a feeling for post-NFL career tracks, and to find out whether they might be interested in, and suited for, particular careers. But players must pursue those career tracks at their own initiative. They need to bring something to the table, so to speak. Like David Howard, they have to demonstrate a skill set that makes an employer want to hire them and a work ethic that will impress prospective employers. Today's players have a prominent role model to follow: NFL commissioner Roger Goodell began his NFL career as an intern in the league office, clipping newspaper stories and performing other menial media-related tasks.[52]

Last, but certainly not least, many NFL players contend that education is a prevalent barrier to career development, but also a surefire remedy to the problem. Brandon Gold, as we've seen, has had a rough time gaining post-NFL traction, and he views education as part of the problem:

I'm a former NFL player. I have a lot of confidence. I'm good looking. I'm a white guy. I have a lot of going for me. . . . But I realized once I was in the real world, to be a high school coach, you need a degree. If you want to be a college coach, you need a degree. . . . It is important, I realize now.[53]

While myriad others echo the sentiment, less than half of NFL alumni have degrees when they leave college. Today, the NFL provides special resources to assist payers in finishing their degree requirements (see Appendix 2), and eventually around 80 percent of alumni get their degrees. But it still remains a challenge, as Daryl Gatlin notes: "They encourage players to get their education and go back to school, but it is really hard to get away and go back if your school is not in the city that you are playing in, because the obligation in the off season is a lot greater now."[54] George Koonce summarizes much of what he's seen, both during and after his NFL career:

Education is the key building block to success. It does not matter what arena you go into. You can be a teacher, an accountant or an attorney, but education has to be at the forefront. On the job, you have to be able to process information and think strategically, that's where education comes in. In many cases, NFL rookies are handling significant amounts of money for the first time in their lives. If they had an educational base in finance, they would be better prepared to make that money work for them. Having an educational base helps immensely.[55]

These observations reveal a subtle distinction regarding education that eludes many players. There's a difference between getting a degree and getting an education. Otis Tyler puts it this way: "Many players go to college and even get a degree, but they don't have a clue about how they are going to use it, how they are going to make something out of the rest of their lives."[56] In college, while majoring in "eligibility," many players earn degrees that might have little to do with their occupational designs after football. This is not to say that education for education's sake isn't valuable, but degrees in "recreation and leisure" or "hospitality business" may be of little use if a former player wants to go into teaching, real estate, or investment banking. Similarly, if players don't take the college experience to heart, they may not develop those analytic and critical thinking skills to which Koonce alludes, which could be assets in a wide variety of post-football ventures. Having a college degree probably isn't the panacea that some players imagine, but it's an available resource that opens otherwise blocked career paths.

Success Is in the Details

While there's no recipe for success in life after football, success stories are instructive. There's one legendary tale circulating among former NFL players that we've heard several times. Willie Davis played for the Green Bay Packers in the 1960s and is often lauded for making the perfect transition from the NFL to a productive life after football. Players repeat Davis's story in glowing, broadly romanticized terms. As their story goes, Davis came out of a small college to become a Hall of Fame defensive end and team captain for Vince Lombardi's Packers dynasty of the 1960s. When he retired, Davis parlayed his football connections into a lucrative career as a beer distributor, then as owner of a fleet of radio stations. As his empire grew, Davis eventually sat on the boards of over a dozen major corporations and several universities.[57]

For many players, Davis embodies the ideal approach to life after football. They view his success as the optimal confluence of personal achievements on the field and ripe business opportunities off it. To be sure, these are two significant factors, but to modify the timeless cliché, success is in the details. There are significant aspects of Davis's remarkable success that most of his NFL admirers overlook.[58] For example, during his playing days, Davis actually *worked* in the brewing industry—even during the season—assuming positions of managerial responsibility, not just doing public relations appearances. He also worked tirelessly to earn an MBA from the University of Chicago, one of the world's most prestigious and demanding graduate programs. He made the dean's list, and got an education, not just a degree. Along the way, he conscientiously cultivated both skills and relationships in the business world.

After retiring from football, Davis took *two* jobs. He began a seven-year run as a major network broadcaster, and he used money he saved from his playing days to buy a beer distributorship in South Central Los Angeles. He was no absentee owner. He built a floundering distributorship into a thriving success by literally loading his trucks and delivering his product in order to make sure his customers were satisfied. Within a few years, Davis parlayed his business and media acumen into the purchase of several radio stations, which then became the cornerstone of his multimillion-dollar financial empire.

Davis's story offers several lessons in how to move from one successful career to another. First, financial success didn't necessarily follow from football fame. Indeed, for Davis, they grew simultaneously, side by side. Like so many other successful retirees, Davis lived his life on parallel tracks, and put supreme effort into both. Typically, players who achieve post-career professional success have actually been living "dual lives" or riding multiple tracks while they were in the NFL. Players who didn't put all their eggs in the NFL basket—who moved beyond the indulgences of the bubble—were generally ready to step into other lines of work when their NFL careers ended. They were willing to invest more into their second jobs than just their names.

Davis got a formal education, not just a degree. But he also got a priceless *practical* education by learning his businesses from the bottom, up. He wasn't averse to starting on the ground floor—even at the "advanced" age of 35—and didn't expect to be handed anything simply because he was a football star. Like other ex-players who have been successful after the NFL, Davis lived by the adage, "You need to work as hard at your second career as you did at football." He was also fond of saying, "Luck is when preparation meets opportunity," to explain his career success.[59] The details of his life make it clear that Willie Davis worked at being prepared, never waiting for opportunity to capriciously bless him with success.

Hakeem Chapman, quite a success in his own right, underscores many of the lessons we learn from Willie Davis. His counsel is straightforward and unpretentious, yet eloquent:

> Educate . . . and prepare. . . . [Get to the players] before they get intoxi-cated, before they get addicted, before they get the lights, and the camera, and the action. You talk to them before that, and say, "Hey, this is going to have an impact on you. . . . You are going to be a little crazy for a while, but remember, the game is only a short period of time." I would tell them to think back to how hard they worked to become a professional athlete. Think of the hours and hours of weight room and sweat and effort and blood and sweat and tears, and then find you a profession. . . . Find you something you like. Get involved somehow. Any kind of job. It doesn't matter where you start. Don't expect to be the CEO. Expect to be the low guy on the totem pole. And that is an advantage, because you can understand the business as you work your way up. And work as hard at that business as you did at becoming an athlete. Take it with the same degree of seriousness. Put the same passion into it, the same heart into it, the same need, the want, the fire, the hunger. Then if you work anywhere close to how you worked as an athlete at your business, you will succeed. It is so simple. Just to change the focus a little bit. Change the focus from your game to your job. But it takes the qualities. It takes the preparation. It takes commitment. It takes discipline. It takes all the things that you have, or you would have never played the game at a high level. So you have everything you need, just refocus it.[60]

7

PLAYING WITHOUT A PLAYBOOK

One thing about athletes, they are guys of structure and guys of habit. . . . When you don't have that in life, it is kind of like you are out there on an island.
—Anderson Smith, former Cincinnati Bengals tight end[1]

Speaking about post-career challenges, former players sometimes mention money or thwarted career aspirations. Surprisingly, however, they're much more likely to lament the loss of everyday routines, the camaraderie, and the sense of common purpose.

Facing a life without structure is no picnic. "The hardest part is your daily routine," says former quarterback Trent Green. "For 15 years, I knew exactly what I was doing in March, June, and September because there was a schedule. When you take that away, you suddenly have a lot more time on your hands. I've been out of the game since 2008, and I still have a tough time with it."[2] Former Vikings linebacker Ben Leber agrees: "I'm such a creature of habit, the void of not having a daily schedule, it was tough. Tougher than I expected."[3] Another retiree elaborates: "It was just very difficult for me to make my own schedule because I always had my life scheduled for me. . . . So keeping the focus and maintaining the focus throughout the day was very, very tough."[4]

Many players feel this way immediately after they're out of the league, but, for some, the feeling lasts for years—if it ever disappears. Without the NFL script and the reassurance of custom and ritual, everyday tasks and relationships are problematic. It's unsettling for many, excruciating for some. Out on a social island, former players are metaphorically lost, socially isolated, and psychically demoralized. They find themselves morally adrift, no longer captivated by the sacred ethos and brotherhood of the locker room. Football has been the players' refuge, their sanctuary from both large personal problems and the bothersome minutiae of daily life. Now outside the bubble, those annoying details begin to gnaw. As Derrick Brooks puts it, "Players always say the football field is a safe haven, that you can go there and block everything else out. But what do you do when that's gone and you have to deal with life?"[5]

Languished Life Skills

Dealing with the routine matters of everyday life can be troublesome, from issues of money and jobs to the details of how to allocate free time. The loss of structure forces former players to fend for themselves in ways they've never experienced, and they often lack the fundamental life skills to get by. As an NFL alum from the late 1990s points out:

> From the time you wake up [when you are playing], you have an agenda on what to do, where you need to be, where you need to go, what time you need to get back. All these things are done for you so it's almost like you're a baby or a child while you're playing and when you get out of there, it's like you have to grow up. It's time to grow up."[6]

This epitomizes the infantilization William Rhoden highlights as part of the "conveyor belt" that ushers players through big-time football. Colleges and NFL teams act like surrogate parents, sheltering, nurturing, and controlling players as fully as they can. When players are let go, they're often little better prepared to take care of themselves than teenagers leaving home for the first time. Shielded from the outside world, with others handling all mundane responsibilities, many players have been denied the opportunity to "grow up." Consequently, managing one's time and daily affairs is sometimes easier said than done. Troy Vincent recalls killing time in his unscheduled life by washing clothes every day until his wife told him that normal people don't do laundry that often. So he started cutting the lawn three times a week. He literally didn't know what else to do.[7]

Some ex-players seemed trapped by their freedom. They know they need to develop new social routines, but they aren't prepared. They've been consummate professionals in the NFL, but haven't ventured far afield. The mundane transactions of everyday life confound or bore them. They lack basic social skills that others outside the bubble take for granted. Anderson Smith poses the dilemma in gridiron terms:

> When I was in a situation in a football game, I knew that third and eight, I need to get to that pylon down there or we ain't gonna convert this first down. So, I got to extend my route more steps and make this head fake and a break, and make this catch. Whereas now [after retirement], you don't know where the pylon is, you don't know where the first down is. You don't know which play is going to be the big play. You are playing the game without a playbook. So it is a whole different ball game. . . . When you get out here in the real world, you got to figure out what you need to work on today, what I need to do over here. How do I develop more relationships with people? How do I become a people person? How do I become able to communicate with diverse people of each age? That is really different from "This is what you need to do, Smith."[8]

Without a playbook, social dexterity is at a premium, but it's in short supply with many former players. In the bubble, they just didn't need the full arsenal of social skills and graces most people rely on to navigate their everyday lives. Jillian Beale, the wife of a former player from the 1990s—speaking realistically, but compassionately—puts it bluntly:

> You know what? They have a complete lack of people skills—most of them. They don't know how to interact as anything but football players and team-mates. They have their own ways of behaving with one another that are pretty outrageous to people from the outside. But when they end up on the outside, that's all they know how to do. That's how they behave and they discover outsiders aren't really impressed now that they aren't playing for the [team].[9]

To paraphrase Anderson Smith, many former players aren't adept at social interaction, at making social connections. They don't know how to cultivate lasting social relationships. They're uncomfortable with people different from themselves. All these deficits may impede personal and professional growth. Even more importantly, they can stunt social lives, especially, but not exclusively, when women are involved, as Jillian Beale observes:

> Most of them have trouble relating to women. For their whole lives—at least since they became football stars—they've had access to women sexually. They haven't had to really relate to women as people. They just keep score. A lot of sex without relationships. Then, when they are out of the game, they can't relate normally to women—or anyone else for that matter. Too many of them can't change and the situation has changed for them. They've been special all this time and they don't know how to behave. They've acted one way and once they've retired they don't know how to get along in the real world. They've lived in a world of their own and when it ends, they don't function very well in normal society. They've lived a life where the team was always there to look out for them and clean up their messes when they screw up. Once they retire, there is no one left to look out for them.[10]

Scarce Social Support

When Anderson Smith left the game, he not only lost the structure of his life, he lost an important source of encouragement and sustenance that might have eased his transition out of football. As he puts it, "When you are out there on that [retirement] island, there is no support system for you."[11] George Koonce relates a similar experience:

> *I found myself alone for the first time in my life. I'd always had the support of my teammates, my friends, my family. But that just disappeared. Leaving football is like getting a divorce. You're separated from the life and the people you knew. It's*

all behind you now. Or maybe even like death, the loss is so complete. I tried to reach out to my former teammates, but it's just not the same.[12]

Not only does the end of NFL careers deprive players of the basic structures of their lives, it robs them of many of their closest relationships. Players lived life in the bubble to the fullest, but almost exclusively in the company of teammates and others connected to the NFL. Stripped of that life, former players sometimes have no one to fall back on. When the free tickets and the parties run out, so do the friends and hangers-on. When the paydays stop and the there's no money to loan, distant relatives keep their distance. When the investment capital is gone, so are the financial "partners." Koonce recalls how others abandoned ship when he lost his job:

Everybody seemed to disappear. Your agent's gone. I talked to that guy once, twice a day for years, and suddenly he can't return my calls. . . . My family didn't know what to do with me. My Mom was thinking, "What's going on here? Is he all done?" My sisters—a bad business deal went down and they are gone. They may be at Mom's house when I go there, but I don't have a relationship anymore. Your uncles, all that, that's gone.[13]

Even football friends and teammates slip away. Like Koonce, Anderson Smith found himself virtually on his own when he "retired."

I went through a very lonely time, without having anyone to talk with. Your friends are going on with their season, so a lot of guys don't really understand where you're coming from. . . . A lot of the friends that you had in college already have a career started and they are doing [their thing].[14]

It's nice to have the formal retirement resources of the NFL and the NFLA to help establish new directions in life after football. But programs and workshops can't replace the people who've disappeared from the scene.

Fellow players would seem to be the most obvious source of social support, but as Smith intimates, a significant gap emerges between men who may have been virtually inseparable for years. Koonce explains the distance.

Why wouldn't I just call some old playing buddies, or maybe somebody who's been out of the league for a few years? Well, a player just doesn't call another player when he's been cut. He's embarrassed and vulnerable. Up 'til then, the player had been the best . . . a warrior, a hero, a victor. Now what is he? He's a failure, a has-been. He doesn't want people to think he's weak. So, he keeps it all to himself.[15]

All players fear the end, but they also refuse to believe that it will happen to them—at least not until they're ready. The last thing they want is a reminder of their vulnerability staring them in the face. When the end comes for someone else, players feel sympathy and compassion for the other guy. They know that he's suffering. They care about their friend and compatriot. But they also know that, sooner or later, they will walk in those shoes and they steel themselves against the prospect. Denial overpowers empathy. So, when a player is cut, he knows what his former teammates are thinking and feeling. He feels as though he's lost nearly everything, and he doesn't want to lose what little remains of his self-respect and the regard of others. So he won't allow himself to suffer in public, or seek the solace of guys in the locker room. He knows that they have compassion, but he also knows their instinct for self-preservation is going to erect protective barriers. Having lived through both sides of the situation, George Koonce remembers: *"When you've been released, it's like you have a disease, some kind of infection. Everyone else is afraid it's contagious. They avoid you like the plague. Players worry that they might get cut just for hanging out with you."*[16]

Domestic Distress

In most respects, NFL marriages are as solid. According to the NFL Player Care study, in contrast to popular belief, retired NFL players are no more likely than the general population to be widowed or divorced. In fact, they are *more* likely to be currently married (over 75 percent) than comparable men in the general population. Less than 15 percent of NFL marriages end within five years of retirement.[17] Nevertheless, players encounter a unique set of domestic challenges that may be especially onerous because family is expected to be a solution, not the problem. It's supposed to be a refuge from the trials and tribulations of everyday life—a "haven in a heartless world."[18] But often it's a mixed blessing, and sometimes players end up "twice divorced"—from both the NFL and their wives and families.

One source of difficulty is the fundamental structure of many NFL marriages. Out of practical necessity, many players' marriages are "one-sided." Indeed, they may be one of the last bastions of the traditional gendered division of household labor.[19] Due to their round-the-clock, full-time commitment to football, players aren't around the house very much; they're drive-by husbands and fathers. Their primary contribution to the household is financial. In return, they ask their wives to manage the household and hold down the fort socially and emotionally. Wives put their own lives on hold to help players devote their full attention to the game. Taking care of the player—managing nearly every detail of his life—often becomes an NFL wife's full-time job. Few wives maintain their own careers outside the home.[20]

As a result, wives identify so thoroughly with their NFL husbands that their own lives are completely entwined with their husbands' NFL role, status, and fate. When he's out of the league, they, too, are cut off from a life to which they have become deeply accustomed and attached. *Their* routines and rituals—the structures of *their* days and years—are disrupted just like his. So are their identities and emotions. Player wives live in a bubble of their own, and it bursts for them, just as it does for ex-players. That makes being supportive a difficult task.[21]

NFL wives have their own aspirations for life after football, expectations that sometimes conflict with players' needs. While most players' wives don't eagerly anticipate retirement, they typically think it will bring a much-needed equilibrium to their marriages. Many are glad to be done with the stress of game day and have had their fill of being the weekend activity director for out-of-town friends who've come for the game. They look forward to not worrying about football groupies hounding their husbands. Wives may even plan new post-career possibilities for themselves and their marriages, expecting husbands to be more attentive to family matters and help out more around the house. Most hope their husbands' health will improve without the weekly injuries.[22] One player's wife explains: "He's worked so hard for so long. Let him have his time [when he retires] to rest and golf. Then it will be my turn to be out there, and he will be the one taking the kids to practice, volunteering, and doing homework."[23] But when that moment finally arrives, players and wives may be on decidedly different pages of the new script.

Retirement typically introduces new household dynamics to players' lives, with realigned family organization replacing the everyday structure of life in the bubble. Recalls Kim Singletary, wife of former All-Pro Mike Singletary, "[After retirement] I started saying, look, I have needs. I have interests. I have desires. I am not saying it's all about me, but I am saying it's going to be like 50/50 here, you know. Not all you."[24] Players typically haven't spent much time around the house during their playing days, and, according to their wives, they may not be fully "there" when they are home. They haven't been responsible for many household chores, and were minimally involved with childcare. After retirement, wives often demand that players do their fair share around the house—something a temporarily shamed and emotionally vulnerable player may resent. Players find out that being a good father requires more than simply hugging the kids on the field after a winning game. Being a good husband means more than bringing home a paycheck. *Providing* support, rather than receiving it, is a new and difficult role.

Kim Singletary says it took about five years to adjust her marriage: "We all had to retrain his energy. I really had to train him to see me, see a different side of me, see my gifts, see my talents. He had just been so used to looking at everything from his perspective."[25] And this all took place at a time when her husband was going through his football withdrawal. Everything he'd always done and been was now up in the air, at the same time that pressures mounted at home to get with a new program. If former players are being retrained, it's often reluctantly, if not against their will.

In some instances, however, players are eager to jump headlong into family life, even though they've merely been drive-by husbands and fathers for years. But that can cause trouble, too, because they may not be fully welcome in this new role. A wife of a former NFL player offers the following observations about her husband and other NFL players' reemergence as family men:

> This is my turf. Who are you? You have not been here for how many months, and you want to tell somebody WHAT? The guys came back and they really didn't know how to act. They didn't know the family's customs. They didn't know the language. They weren't familiar with the slang. They were total foreigners. My husband would come back into the home and think he had an established position, but he really didn't, because he was never really there to establish it all those other months.[26]

When players retire, it may be the first time in years the couple is actually spending time together. Some NFL wives describe that first year as "unbearable." "He would not get off the couch and he was always in a bad mood," recalls one ex-player's wife. "He didn't go to any of his former team's games—not that they ever invited him. To this day, he doesn't watch any football on TV. Maybe it's terrible to say, but I was done being supportive. I was sick of it."[27]

This may be the gist of the family's failure to provide a haven in a heartless world. Whereas ex-players may expect their wives to support and comfort them when they're dismissed from the game, that backing and encouragement is suddenly problematic. Perhaps for the first time in players' adult lives, others around them aren't knocking themselves out to make *former* players feel special, to keep *their* lives perfectly on track.

But post-football life has its emotional trials for players' wives, too. Many of them are as unprepared for the end as their husbands. They deny that their lifestyles might change. In the same boat as retiring players, some wives are shocked when the money stops flowing in and the spending needs to stop. Says the wife of a former player:

> I never knew that I liked the limelight, but whenever my husband and I went out, we never had to wait on a table, and we never had to wait in line for anything. Now, sometimes we have to wait. Well, if I have to stand in a line, I won't go. You get used to a certain way of living. When your husband retires, you are a commoner, and you miss the perks.[28]

Lost Camaraderie

I'd say the thing [retired players] miss the most is the camaraderie. That's the thing guys talk about most. Not being a part of the team. They miss the locker room. They were a part of an elite group of guys . . . and a lot of those guys miss the conversation, miss the time being among their fellow teammates.[29]

It's not the money or the glory; it's the loss of the team atmosphere that hurts the most. Not being able to "hang with the boys" has profound consequences.

Part of what former players miss is the shared experience and the knowledge that everyone went through the same thing *together*, regardless of when or where they played. Will Siegel echoes Koonce's observations, stressing the complete acceptance by his teammates:

> It's not just me. All the guys feel this way. I was fortunate to play for ten years. It was unbelievable. . . . But [the best thing] is the relationships you

make. . . . It's like being in the Marines. You are immediately accepted when you come back. It's just like you have never gone. They are just acceptive, because all of us know what each individual had to do to be in that group in that period of time.[30]

Many players compare their relationships to the bonds that are literally forged in combat and are hard to duplicate when the battle's over. As one retiree puts it, players literally depend on their teammates for their livelihood—if not their lives—and that common purpose and connection is hard to relinquish:

> Your livelihood depends on them and you do everything with them. . . .
> You live with them for six weeks in the beginning, you go to work with them all during the year from 7 a.m. to 8 p.m. 9 p.m., and you fly with them, and you travel with them, and then all of a sudden, it's gone, that's tough. . . . You play dominoes and you play cards and video games and go out and drink beer and eat hot dogs, you know, and go for a steak. . . .
> When we were playing, we would be with our teammates more than our wives. . . . I've missed that more than playing.[31]

Often, in moments of high passion—especially after big wins—emotions flow. "When you see people win championships," said Ray Lewis after winning the Super Bowl, "they do it based off love." "We were ready to die for each other out there," added his teammate Brendon Ayanbadejo.[32] Players typically aren't this emotional. They're more likely to use the term "camaraderie" than "love," or even "friendship." There's a subtle, yet important distinction in their choice of words, because players' sentiments generally emanate from, and are directed toward, the football milieu and circumstances, not necessarily the people involved. That's not to say that players don't appreciate their comrades in arms, that they don't feel a strong sense of masculine love. But they are much more apt to say they miss "the locker room" or "hanging out with the guys" than to refer to lost friendships or deep affective ties. Listen closely as Michael Arrington speaks of what he misses most about his NFL days:

> I think [it's] the relationships that you have with the people in the locker room. You can work in a lot of different places, you can go in a lot of different environments, but there is no environment quite like the locker room and the camaraderie you have with those guys you bleed, sweat, cry, and celebrate with. A lot of those relationships you have for the rest of your life. So I think that is the biggest thing you walk away with. . . . Being around that environment . . . that is one of the biggest things I miss.[33]

To be sure, Arrington thinks the relationships are important, and many last for years. But it's the *environment* that promotes and sustains them. This doesn't diminish the friendship that is certainly a vital component of camaraderie, but it underscores the situational nature of those friendships. They're based on the locker room and its special culture.[34] According to Tommy Jones, it's a unique environment former players aren't likely to duplicate because of its special demands:

> Being in the locker room, I know everybody misses that. . . . That camaraderie, you can't replace that with nothing else, not even money, really. . . . We were in the trenches fighting. . . . That is all we did. We didn't work a regular job. That is all we did all of our lives, and us, the select few to get to that level, that right there is a special thing that can't be replaced.[35]

Stanley Davis has similar recollections, especially of the spirit of "one for all, and all for one." There's a special bond that comes from feeling like you and your teammates are taking on the entire world, with everyone rooting against you.

> It's the camaraderie, the brotherhood that you're in, that gang mentality really. Us against the world. You know, you got my back and I got your back. . . . People ask me that all of the time: "Well, have you seen the guys?

Are you still hanging out with the guys?" You never get to [hang out] like you used to do it. So it never lives up to it anymore. You see them every now and then, but it's not the whole gang in the locker room, where it's all for one and one for all, like the fucking Musketeers.[36]

But it's more than just a siege mentality or bonding against a common threat. Hanging out with the guys was *fun*, in a way that's off-limits to most grown men. Charles Nobles is up-front in his assessment: "Honestly, it was the camaraderie, playing with guys and just having that group of guys come together and just fun. It was *fun*."[37] For Walter Canady, a running back from the 1970s, the camaraderie meant he was able to be himself, exactly the man he wanted to be.

That is what you miss the most. The big thing is you are around guys, and you know guys get criticized about this and that, and so people like to take shots at guys. In the locker room, you can be exactly who you want to be. You can be as ridiculous as you want to be, and nobody judges you on that. Guys tell their stories, or they do silly things, but nobody is judging them. So you miss your boys . . . when it is gone all of a sudden, it is a big hole in your life.[38]

Canady is hinting at a bigger picture of the locker room culture. Accounts of NFL life—fiction, nonfiction, biography, exposé, or technical descriptions—are full of tales of locker room hijinks, trash talking, practical jokes, card games, dominoes, sexual escapades, and wild adventures. Nothing is too outrageous in this bastion of masculine solidarity. As Canady says, no one judges, and everybody's got your back. It's the player ethos.[39]

Kevin Best puts everything in perspective. While he's more analytic than many of his colleagues, the bottom line is basically the same:

Camaraderie is something where you are in an intimate setting with someone, and you are able to enjoy that experience together. . . . Billy Herbert and I would play hooky while the rest of the players were out practicing special teams. They were running special teams, so we would come out here and play golf, sometimes two or three balls a hole. That is the kind of thing that you miss. . . . The flights going to an away game or coming home from a game or heading to practice. The days off. All of that kind of stuff. . . . You had guys in the locker room from all over the country. All walks of life. And that [the locker room environment] is the common denominator.[40]

Best eloquently captures the essence of NFL camaraderie: a sense of familiarity and trust, fellowship, team spirit, common bonding, shared goals—solidarity built on the NFL ethos. But there's an almost imperceptible restraint in the way former players describe the missing camaraderie. As much as they enjoy each others' company, players know that teammates are transient. They can be traded or cut at any time. Free agents move from team to team, especially later in their careers. When speaking of trades and other roster moves, players uniformly observe that "it's a business" and relationships are bound to be transitory. Mike Golic, a former defensive lineman, chooses his words carefully: "Most of the guys you play with, most of the guys in the locker room, you consider them 'acquaintances.' I guess I wouldn't call them friends. They were guys I worked with, guys I hung out with. But when the season ended we'd sort of go our separate ways."[41] Golic is a gregarious man, and was certainly an integral and well-liked member of any locker room he inhabited. But he draws an important distinction. Locker room camaraderie is an intense and highly valued *workplace* relationship, but it may not reach the depths of enduring friendship.

Nearly everyone working outside the NFL has had workplace friends who are stalwart companions eight hours a day, five days a week, on the job. The work week would be intolerable without them. When one retires or moves to a new position, everyone extends heartfelt best wishes, promises to "get together," and vows that "nothing's going to change." But everything does change. At first, the e-mail keeps flowing. But lunch once a week becomes an occasional get-together on Friday after work. Maybe a phone call every now and then to "catch up." Eventually it's a Christmas card or e-mailed announcement of a child's graduation. It's no different for NFL players. When their careers end, they're embarrassed and they steer clear of their teammates, and their teammates avoid them "like the plague." A few of the guys stay in touch, and some make a point of getting together. But mostly it's running into one another at alumni reunions, autograph signings, or charity golf outings. The joy on these occasions is heartfelt, but it serves mainly to remind former players of the camaraderie they once had and the locker rooms that they can never share again. They miss the guys, but they miss life in the NFL bubble even more.

Cut from the Congregation

Many players take their eviction from the bubble in stride. They revel in their newfound family lives, and many build new social circles and meaningful careers and pastimes. But for some, it exacts dramatic changes that players can't anticipate. Losing the locker room is obvious. Shifts in marital dynamics probably shouldn't come as a surprise. But other collateral consequences of leaving the NFL are hard to foresee.

In other walks of life, for example, when dramatic challenges and changes lead to personal turmoil, some individuals may turn to what's typically considered an ultimately stabilizing source: religion and the church. Many players, George Koonce included, seek spiritual support in dealing with their departure from the NFL:

I went to church. I tried to keep myself as busy as possible with bible study on Wednesday and going to church on Sunday. I did that for the second year out of the game. The first year I drank. Then I cleansed my system and did not drink anything for six months. I fasted and prayed for three months.[42]

For Koonce and many others, religion is a major source of solace. Without diminishing the importance of spiritual commitment, however, in one very important way, former players' religious lives may let them down. The NFL Player Care study found that former players and alumni claim to be more religious and attend church services more than their counterparts in the general population.[43] Religion seemingly plays an important role in the lives of NFL players and teams—for better or worse. It can bond a team, or at least groups of players, or it can be divisive, providing the basis for judgment, factions, and cliques.[44] In many respects, however, this is no different from the world outside. In the NFL, however, there's one important difference. Teams organize their players' spiritual lives just like they organize everything else. That is, the team has a hand in most of the *practical* details of players' religious lives. When Andrew Brandt listed the ways in which the league regiments players' lives, he mentioned meetings, practices, workouts, meal, transportation, recreation, and team prayers. He left out bible study, fellowship groups, and chapel services. NFL teams often have team chaplains, usually selected by, and certainly approved by, the organization itself. Occasionally, religious leaders, such as Reggie White, emerge from the ranks of the players. Religious services are scheduled on Sundays, and sometimes during the week. Weekly bible study groups are common, typically held in team facilities and attended exclusively by team and organization personnel. In effect, players in the bubble are served up "room service religion."

For many active players, this is a convenient and highly valued source of fellowship and spiritual support. For some, it's a launching pad for bigger and better ministries and "good works" after their playing days. Players such as Reggie White, Tony Dungy, and Bart Starr have gone on to become influential spiritual and community leaders, especially reaching out to former players. But room service religion lacks the broader sense of community—literally widespread congregation—that typifies most organized religion. Getting their religion along with their training table meals and their physical therapy, NFL players aren't fully integrated into a broader religious community in the same fashion as their outside counterparts. They have *team* prayers, *team* chaplains, *team* prayer meetings, and *team* bible study groups. The team chaplain accompanies the team on the road. Services are held right in the team hotel. Religion is delivered directly to the player's door, just like room service burgers and fries.

This is not to imply that it's spiritually deficient or superficial. To the contrary, most religious players in the NFL take their spirituality quite seriously, even if the NFL ethos demands an occasional compromise. But the fact that players engage in the formal and social aspects of religion and worship within the guarded confines of the bubble makes the experience one more source of insulation from the real world.

Players get a homogenized version of religious practice and a homogeneous blend of fellow worshipers. They don't contact the broad range of congregants one often finds in a thriving community church—people of different ages, backgrounds, and genders. They don't form *social* relationships with fellow spiritual travelers from outside their inner circle. While this may or may not be spiritually limiting, it deprives players of a *social* support network to which they might turn when their playing days are over. When NFL careers end, and players are cut from the team, they may also be cut from their church. Whereas a congregant who loses his job, goes through a divorce, or is otherwise displaced can turn to members of his church community for support, the former player is "deselected" from his spiritual home at the same time that he's cut from his team. He's left on his own—perhaps not spiritually, but definitely socially. There's one more page missing from his playbook.

8

TRIALS OF TRANSITION

After everything I went through, I still felt like something was missing. It was like things were upside down and I wasn't sure which way to turn. It just felt strange and I didn't know what to do about it. I've been very fortunate to get my life together but something still doesn't feel quite right.[1]

Why doesn't retirement feel right for so many NFL players? They undergo many of the same processes of role exit that confront other retirees, but something's qualitatively different. The sports retirement literature suggests that most elite athletes are likely to move successfully out of their sports and into other satisfying life endeavors.[2] While this is largely true for NFL players, too many of them never seem to "get over it." Otis Tyler, for example, has done very well for himself. He has a rich family life and a healthy local media career. But ask him about his 25-year transition into life after football: "Oh, God, I think we are all still transitioning. I feel like I'm doing OK, but I'm not there yet. . . . We're out there on an island, just drifting. And that can last for a long time."[3] Why? Drew Raymond, a wide receiver from the 1990s, has an answer: "Man, when that bubble breaks, you just don't know what to do. It's all you know. You never get used to that new life."[4]

Culture Shock

The key here is the "new life." When they speak of transition, former players seldom focus on new jobs or different roles. Instead, they lament the passing of a way of life that they've experienced since they were boys. An anthropologist overhearing their conversations might say former players were experiencing something akin to "culture shock." Culture shock is the process of disruption and adjustment to an unfamiliar environment that sets off emotional, behavioral, psychological, and cognitive crises for those involved. It can arise in any new situation—moving to a foreign country, going away to college, taking a new job, even entering a new relationship—that has consequences for patterns of behavior or identity. Under these circumstances, we lose our cultural cues and bearings, the familiar signs and guidelines that keep us "on course" in dealing with our daily lives and interactions. When this happens, a person can feel like a "fish out of water." With familiar cultural props removed, anxiety and frustration set in.[5]

It's easy to see NFL players experiencing culture shock at the end of their playing days. They're not just out of the game; they're out of the bubble. But culture shock is generally short-lived, a passing phase. Why might it persist for NFL players where others seem to adapt more quickly? Again, we've heard the answer before: "When that bubble breaks, you just don't know what to do. It's all you know." Is this overly dramatic? People from other walks of life manage major life transitions without as much lingering trauma. But very few individuals exist in an environment so completely captivating as the NFL bubble. The bubble establishes patterns of acting and interacting that are deeply engrained. Its way of life is all encompassing. It provides players with a cultural toolkit that they *habitually* use to craft the everyday features of their lives. At the same time, however, the bubble also insulates players from other ways of seeing and doing everyday life. Players are short-handed when it comes to adapting to other circumstances. We've seen how undisciplined spending, "livin' large," uncertain job prospects, flagging social support, and injury pose serious challenges as players move out of the NFL. These can certainly be daunting problems. But not all players succumb to them. Nor are these challenges the source of many former players' disenchantment with life without football. And it's not just losing jobs or changing roles. These can be radical changes, to be sure, but viewed simply, they are parts—not the totality—of players' lives. Something more radical is going on. Perhaps the scenario resembles the circumstances where military personnel are discharged from active duty, or even when prisoners are freed from incarceration. When they leave the bubble, NFL players change worlds. They literally swap realities, often against their will and frequently not to their liking. The cultural imperatives inside the bubble are so pervasive and enduring that, as a practical matter, they've become the very structures of a player's consciousness.[6] Some players are lost without them.

This may seem exaggerated. Is the bubble, with its player ethos and locker room culture, so unique and powerful that players can't adjust to other circumstances? A recent locker room controversy offers a unique window into the cultural milieu that dominates NFL players' lives. In November 2013, offensive tackle Jonathan Martin—an African American—walked away from the Miami Dolphins' training complex to seek treatment for emotional distress. Through his agent, he said that he could no longer tolerate the emotional abuse he was taking from Dolphins teammates. Debate immediately erupted on several fronts, often centering on whether Martin was simply unwilling or unable to put up with the typical "hazing" to which younger NFL players have traditionally been subjected. Some argued that he was being maliciously "bullied" by veteran teammates. The conversation took a serious turn when Martin released an incendiary transcript of a voicemail message left on his phone a few months earlier by teammate and fellow offensive lineman Ritchie Incognito, who is white.

> Hey, wassup, you half-nigger piece of shit. I saw you on Twitter, you been training 10 weeks. I'll shit in your fuckin' mouth. I'm gonna slap your fuckin' mouth. I'm gonna slap your real mother across the face [laughter]. Fuck you, you're still a rookie. I'll kill you.[7]

Incognito has a longstanding reputation as an NFL "badass." A key member of the Dolphins offensive line, he was voted into the 2012 Pro Bowl. But he is also known as one of the NFL's dirtiest players and most outrageous characters. Throughout the controversy, no one challenged this depiction, nor did Incognito deny his actions or words. For his part,

Martin was known as a "soft" player who seemed strangely out of place in the tough-man's world of the NFL, even though he had been a two-time college All-American and second round draft choice. Initially, the bullying accusations seemed entirely plausible, given Incognito's background and the damning voicemail, and he was quickly suspended by the Dolphins.[8]

As time passed, however, new pieces of the puzzling story began to emerge. Fellow Dolphins reported that Martin and Incognito had been close friends. Black and white players alike denied that Incognito was a racist. Alternate explanations recast acts of intimidation in terms of practical joking and solidarity-building rites of initiation. Moreover, Martin himself was portrayed as willingly going along with the jokes. Indeed, teammates said Martin had played the incriminating voicemail for them, and they laughed along with him. To them it was one more instance of Incognito's outrageous "macho man" persona. Evidently, no one at the time—including Martin—took Incognito's rant seriously. Indeed, text messages were ultimately released in which Martin exchanged seemingly light-hearted, vulgar insults with Incognito that approximated the tone and content of those sent by Incognito.[9] Eventually, teammates began to explain the entire mess within the context of everyday locker room banter and a request by the Dolphins organization for Incognito to bring Martin out of his shell and toughen him up.[10]

Regardless of what develops out of this scenario, the terms of the discussion provide telling insights into the culture of the NFL and its inner sanctums. This cultural environment—the NFL bubble—provides players with a field of consciousness that is so different from other everyday social worlds that former players are lost and disoriented when they have to fend for themselves. If the worst impressions prevail, they would underscore a racist strain that runs through the league. But that's certainly not a version to which most players subscribe. Indeed, players, black and white, commonly say that there's less racism in the NFL than in any other setting they've experienced.[11] Fellow players dismissed Incognito's racial slurs as familiar, good-humored banter—almost terms of endearment—between teammates that demonstrated a genuine lack of racial animus rather than racially motivated contempt. Nevertheless, Incognito's words still stand, "nigger" prominently among them. Racist or not, they inscribe a crude vulgarity upon the NFL scene.

Amidst all the protestations, players tacitly acknowledge that the NFL locker room tolerates virtually any form of aggression as long as it contributes to a winning edge. There's a "take no prisoners" attitude that's demanded in the NFL. As players interpretively packaged the Incognito–Martin rift as an instance of normal locker room behavior being misunderstood or gone awry, the powerful contours of the NFL player ethos became obvious. Toughness is the foundation of the ethos, so, from players' perspectives, Incognito wasn't culturally out of line. As the discussion evolved, it quickly became apparent that no one thought it was OK for one player to bully or seriously harm a teammate. But it was just as clear that crude language and rough treatment—especially cloaked in humor—aggression, and intimidation are bywords of the NFL locker room. It's a world where it's *normal* for veterans to use intimidation to toughen up the new guys. While many players initially thought that Incognito may have gone too far—perhaps lost perspective on how much "razzing" Martin could take—the practice of "toughening up" itself was never fundamentally questioned. It's OK to use threats and humiliation to further team ends. "Winning's the only thing."[12]

There were several other culturally revealing twists to this scenario as well. Many players and observers asked why Martin didn't fight back. Why didn't he just punch Incognito in the face? Said teammate Tyson Clabo: "If Martin had a problem, he didn't show it. . . . I think that if you have a problem with somebody . . . [you should] stand up and be a man."[13] Others point out that the NFL is full of bullies. That's how they got there and that's how they keep their jobs, through aggression and intimidation. Those are supreme virtues when directed on the field, and if they spill off the field, well that's part of the package. Every player in the NFL is a little crazy, they all admit, and sociopaths are often vital to winning. Backing down, on the other hand, is a sign of fatal weakness. "You can't let [a bully] see that it [hazing and intimidation] got to you," comments Mike Golic. "If you let this be known [that there was hazing or bullying going on], if you go public, you won't be able to go back into the locker room."[14]

In the NFL scheme of things, being soft is a greater sin than being crazy, crude, or barbaric. From this perspective, it's Martin who is culturally out of step. Former Dolphins teammate Lydon Murtha virtually damned Martin when he characterized him as shy and standoffish, with "a tendency to tank when things would get difficult in practice."[15] Martin came off as the antithesis of Incognito's "badass." After all he'd majored in classical studies at Stanford and came from a long line of Harvard graduates. Coy Wire, a former Stanford and NFL player, knows what that might mean: "If you don't fit into the mold, and the culture in the locker room, you won't last. Sometimes, in a gladiator sport like football, intelligence can be perceived as being soft."[16]

And perception matters. As Mike Greenberg, Golic's media sidekick, notes, "The NFL is probably the only place where having parents who went to Harvard, and you went to Stanford, is something you have to 'overcome.'"[17] In the warrior culture of the NFL, one can't even *appear* to be soft. "This is a game of high testosterone, with men hammering their bodies on a daily basis," says Lydon Murtha. "You are taught to be an aggressive person, and you typically do not make it to the NFL if you are a passive person. There are a few, but it's very hard. Playing football is a man's job, and if there's any weak link, it gets weeded out."[18]

If toughness is the coin of the NFL realm, loyalty also carries considerable currency. Not surprisingly, after initial outrage from a few players not associated with the Dolphins, Incognito's teammates—black and white—rallied to his support.[19] To a man, they said that Martin should never have taken his complaints outside the locker room. Players stick together like a "band of brothers, like a fraternity" says former coach Brian Billick.[20] "It's a brotherhood, a pure brotherhood," adds Ray Lewis.[21] Airing dirty laundry in public is a cardinal sin. "Keep it in the house," says Martin's teammate Bryant McKinney.[22] Remember, the code of the NFL is "What happens in the locker room stays in the locker room."

When Martin sought outside help, he was not only admitting to weakness, he became a traitor to the cause.

Some compare the NFL code of loyalty to the code of silence and allegiance of gangs, prisoners, the military, or the police. [23] By exposing the situation to the media, says Murtha, Martin broke that code. "It shows that he's not there for his teammates and he's not standing up for himself. There might be a team that gives him a chance [to play again in the NFL] because he's a good person, but the players will reject him. They'll think, *if I say one thing he's going to the press.* He'll never earn the respect of teammates and personnel in the NFL because he didn't take care of business the right way."[24] According to Murtha and others, the Dolphins aren't unique. Conflict breaks out routinely, but there are routine ways to handle it. "This racial slur would be a blip on the radar if everything that happens in the locker room went public," claims Murtha. "All over the league, problems are hashed out in-house. Either you talk about it or you get physical. But at the end of the day, you handle it indoors."[25]

This is the culture of the NFL: the world of the tough guy, the loyal teammate, the gladiator. Commentators often dismiss locker room culture as an immature, ephemeral anomaly into which otherwise respectable men sometimes slip for good fellowship and light-hearted respite from adult responsibilities. But in the case of the NFL, it's much more. It's the quintessence of "team," and its ethos is the heart and soul of its inhabitants. The local culture is fully embodied in players' attitudes and lifestyle, which they carry with them wherever they go. It's not that they are compelled to act this way. Rather, they opt to hold themselves accountable to the ethos, using it to justify a very distinctive set of behavioral habits.

Of course, all this might easily be dismissed as the outlandish behavior of a rogue ball player—an aberration. Richie Incognito could be the exception to the NFL rule. Indeed, it's this sort of extreme case—the deviant or outlier—that actually helps society identify the boundaries of what's normal and acceptable.[26] It would be easy to characterize Incognito as such a boundary setting renegade, an anomaly. Tellingly, however, his behavior is *not* beyond the pale—at least not in the NFL. Incognito has been voted the league's dirtiest player. He was dismissed from two college teams for inappropriately aggressive behavior. He's appeared on national TV ranting vile obscenities and racial slurs in a bar.[27] He was investigated in 2012 for sexually harassing a woman at a Dolphins golf tournament. According to police reports, a 34-year-old female volunteer told police that Incognito had been intoxicated and molested her with a golf club.[28] Incognito routinely uses the term "nigger." Despite all this, he was still a teammate in good standing. He wasn't considered a deplorable anomaly, one who stood beyond the boundary. In fact, teammates considered Incognito *more* than acceptable as a member of the locker room brigade. He was a leader, an exemplar of the player ethos. In 2013, before the controversy broke, he was a member of the Dolphins' leadership council.

All of this speaks volumes about life in the NFL. If Incognito is "within bounds," what might be "out of bounds"? Where are the limits of normal or acceptable in the league? Where are the lines drawn separating the upstanding from the intolerable? The NFL culture and player ethos not only abide Incognito's demeanor and behavior, they honor them. At the same time they question Jonathan Martin's character because he's mild mannered and not loyal to the core. To listen to players comment on the controversy, it's Martin who sets the standard for unacceptability. He's too soft and disloyal.

In February 2014, NFL-appointed investigator Ted Wells issued a report on the Dolphins' situation that concluded that the team's locker room supported a "culture of intolerance" and a "pattern of harassment" directed at Martin as well as another young Dolphins offensive lineman and a member of the team's training staff. The Wells Report verified most of Martin's claims, but stopped short of castigating the locker room culture that fomented the situation. It implied that the locker room ethos sometimes got out of hand, but the report never condemned the culture as pathological. At least for the moment, the discussion adopted the terms of inappropriate workplace "bullying."[29]

Reaction among NFL players was decidedly mixed, echoing arguments made earlier. The league itself offered pubic displays of grave concern, and even raised the possibility of penalizing players during games for any use of the "N-word" (although never publicly voicing the actual term "nigger" that was ostensibly to be penalized). Ultimately the discussion was tabled on the grounds that the use of racial slurs was already covered by unsportsmanlike conduct rules. The issues of locker room culture, threatening conduct, and racial animus were set aside in order to debate changes in the "extra point" rules.[30]

The Wells Report is conspicuously noncommittal in assessing underlying factors precipitating this particular incident. "Our mandate did not include setting standards for what types of behavior should be permitted or prohibited within the Miami Dolphins organization," says the report.[31] For their part, the Dolphins vowed to continue reviewing relevant team policies and procedures to seek "areas of improvement."[32] Ultimately, we're left with the report's summation:

> The behavior that occurred here was harmful to the players, the team and the league. It was inconsistent with a civilized workplace—even in a professional football league and even among tough football players whose very profession is defined by physical and mental domination of players across the line of scrimmage. There are lines—even in a football locker room— that should not be crossed, as they were here. *We leave the determination of precisely where to draw those lines to those who spend their lives playing, coaching and managing the game of professional football.*[33]

Such a conclusion essentially downplays the larger cultural issues underpinning this situation. If NFL standards for what's "normal" allow for Richie Incognito's extremes—or anything in the vicinity—how do they guide players operating *outside* the locker room? Of course most NFL players don't act like Incognito. Many of them think he's a jerk, even if they do respect what he brings to the game. But with standards established so far out on the periphery, nearly any excess seems tolerable. It's no wonder players feel disoriented when they're evicted from the locker room. The rules of the game radically change. Excess is called into question. It's no surprise when things seem upside down, that former players don't know exactly what to do. That's culture shock: the disruption of the familiar, the loss of cultural cues and bearings. If Richie Incognito signals what's "normal" inside the NFL, there may be problems when players step outside.

Richie Incognito also helps set the parameters for what it means to be a real man in a tough guy's game. The term "macho" was coined with him in mind. Masculinity is the bedrock of the NFL player ethos and in an environment where one's manhood is challenged on a daily basis, Incognito pushed the limits. It was certainly the subtext of the controversy involving Jonathan Martin. To call Martin "soft" was essentially saying he wasn't man enough for the NFL. As Lydon Murtha reminded us, it's a "high testosterone" game.

Just as the NFL ethos thoroughly conflates toughness and masculinity, it uses homophobia and misogyny to further highlight the contours of being a man. Homophobic slurs—such as "fag" or "faggot"—are so commonplace as terms of generalized derision that they lose their ostensible pejorative connection to sexuality. If players are suspected of malingering or refusing to play though pain, for example, they're labeled "faggots." Players don't really believe that the targets of such remarks are actually gay. They simply use the slur as a way of condemning behavior or character that's perceived as insufficiently masculine.[34]

This practice was underscored throughout the Incognito–Martin controversy. The Wells Report documents multiple instances where Dolphins players (including Martin) "teased" a fellow teammate about being gay (although there's no evidence confirming the teammate's sexuality), calling him, among other things, "fag" or "faggot." Other taunts were far more vulgar and sexually suggestive. Even members of the coaching staff participated. The report also revealed that the Dolphins kept an unofficial "fine book" that recorded players' finable offenses, including being a "pussy"—which apparently referred to being "soft" more than sexuality.[35]

It remains to be seen if such manifestations of locker room masculinity will thrive in the future. In February 2014, Michael Sam, All-American defensive end and Southeastern Conference defensive player of the year, publicly announced that he was gay. Initially considered a near certainty be taken in the NFL draft, Sam would become the first openly gay player in the league. While many players were immediately supportive, there were plenty of skeptics as well. *Forbes* contributor David Lariviere wrote that "With the recent announcement by Michael Sam . . . that he is gay, it is even more urgent that a tolerant atmosphere exist throughout the league. The frequent use of homophobic insults undermines this goal."[36] Some NFL executives were more explicit: "Outness" they suggest, is "an employment hazard" in a "man's man's game." Drafting Sam will be a risk, one said, because "there's nothing more sensitive than the heartbeat of the locker room." A more general sentiment among NFL general managers was that Sam would probably still be drafted, but, that all things being equal, they preferred not to draft players who brought with them unnecessary "distractions." This is the same caveat often used when discussing players with criminal records or histories of substance abuse, suggesting that being gay carries a stigma comparable to breaking the law or using illicit drugs.

Eventually, Sam was drafted at the end of the seventh round by the St. Louis Rams., the 249th out of 256 players drafted. For an SEC defensive player of the year to slide this far down the draft board is nearly unprecedented. At the same time, however, the consensus among NFL personnel evaluators was that Sam's "tweener" size, mediocre "measurables," and lack of fit with conventional NFL defensive schemes diminished his value. Regardless, official reaction to Sam's drafting from the league, the Rams, and the national news and sports media was extremely positive, embracing the occasion as a groundbreaking, historic moment. Still, a few players and former players offered strong negative comments implicating Sam's sexuality. Sam was cut at the end of training camp but performed well enough that he may still catch on with an NFL squad. The extent of the league's acceptance of an openly gay player remains to be seen.[37]

The objectification and vilification of women plays a similar role in fortifying the NFL's culture of toughness and masculinity. Locker room banter and sexual braggadocio is legendary. Players use outlandish and derisive comments about mothers, sisters, and girlfriends both to humorously denigrate one another and to distance themselves from all things feminine. Indeed, to be a man often seems to require demeaning women. During the Incognito–Martin controversy, for example, Martin's attorney, David Cornwell, alleged that an unnamed Dolphins teammate reportedly directed the following remarks toward Martin and his sister: "We are going to run a train on your sister. . . . She loves me. I am going to f*** her without a condom and c** in her c***."[38] The Wells Report offered additional graphically demeaning examples. These remarks almost assuredly had nothing to do with Martin's sister personally. They are simply depersonalizing and degrading slurs aimed at challenging *Martin's* masculinity by debasing his sister. Once again, we see just how far behavioral boundaries are stretched in the name of "normal." As former NFL quarterback Danny Kannell observes, players simply treat race, gender, sexuality, and toughness in ways totally different from how they are handled in other work places or social settings.[39]

Sociologist Michael Kimmel would certainly recognize the rites of masculinity in an NFL locker room. Indeed, he might suggest that we see their roots in the everyday pursuit of manhood across the landscape of 21st-century American society. Based on years of field research, Kimmel argues that contemporary young men occupy a social world he calls "Guyland."[40] It's a phase of life and social arena dominated by "buddy culture," with minimal demands from parents, partners, and casual outsiders. Its occupants skirt the responsibilities of mature adulthood and the nuisances of everyday life as they try to develop mature masculine identities. Largely in the company of other young men, they test and prove themselves as men and develop the defining attitudes and self-images they will carry into mature adulthood. In Guyland, peer approval and tacit adherence to the "guy code" are the prime forces in shaping young men's behavior and identities.

The guy code exhorts a commitment to relentlessly masculine attitudes and camaraderie. Kimmel describes it using a widely known indigenous shorthand: "Bros before hos." The code is simple: Be a man among men (no sissies allowed). Be important, successful, and powerful. Be reliable and loyal. Be daring and aggressive. The camaraderie of Guyland is key. Male bonding and a commitment to a "band of brothers" are scaled-down versions of the masculine fellowship that emerges in wartime combat, or among the ranks of the police and firefighters. The social world of Guyland revolves almost exclusively around other guys. In Kimmel's terms, it's a "pure, homosocial Eden, uncorrupted by sober responsibilities of adulthood."[41]

Does this sound familiar? The NFL locker room is Guyland on steroids, where players aggressively exaggerate the "guy code." Masculinity lives large, with the volume turned way up. It's hypermasculinity. Just as individual men aren't the virtual embodiments of Guyland, not all NFL players are fully committed to locker room masculinity. In the bubble, they strike their own deals with the pervasive normative order. But the NFL culture definitely leaves its masculine imprint, even when players leave the game. The bubble packs a more powerful cultural punch than the more amorphous Guyland, leaving lasting habits that shape not only what former players do, but how they see their worlds, even when they are out of the league. Out of the game, it's difficult for players to find their hypermasculine-identity bearings, to know *society's* limits.

At the same time that the NFL culture offers an exaggerated version of masculinity, it also provides unique cultural cues about race and race relations. The manner in which players rallied to deny Incognito's racism elucidates a unique aspect of NFL culture that's sometimes an additional source of culture shock. In fact, the entire controversy offered a rare glimpse into racialized interactions between NFL players, as well as into some of the ways that race is insinuated into NFL culture.

The topic of race was almost never volunteered by anyone associated with the NFL in all the narrative materials we've collected about life in and after football. Periodically, league and union officials and self-appointed watchdogs assess the state of racial parity in the NFL, offering statistical analyses of percentages of white and non-white players, coaches, and administrators.[42] There's been a longstanding conversation about "stacking" black players at particular positions (i.e., assigning them to positions demanding extreme athleticism but excluding them from "thinking positions" and positions "close to the ball," quarterback in particular). Today, the general tenor of the discussions is that the NFL is far from perfect, but has made steady progress over the decades, and is presently at the forefront of institutional race relations in the United States. With the exception of outright ownership, African Americans have been prominently and successfully represented throughout the NFL, including upper management (there have been a small handful of black minority owners/partners). The fact that most current players (and a growing proportion of alums) are non-white, however, receives relatively little critical inquiry.

This can't be ignored when we ask how race affects players' transition out of the NFL. The answer, however, is somewhat oblique. Players and former players virtually never explicitly mentioned race as a factor in their discussions with us. We've found nothing substantial in media accounts. Players frequently refer to the problems that emerge when families descend upon players who've signed big contracts, and they implicitly suggest that this is more a problem for black players than whites due to the relative economic needs of the two groups and the perceived differences in kinship structure.[43] When Bart Scott, an African American, says, "Getting money sometimes is like turning the lights on in a dark house in the ghetto. It exposes a lot of roaches and rats," it's hard not to infer racial connotations.[44] But that's as close as most former players come to invoking race as a post-career factor. Still, we're reluctant to conclude that race simply doesn't matter. As the Incognito controversy shows, race is important, but perhaps not in conventional ways.

For example, at first, Incognito drew the ire and indignation of nearly everyone who heard his racially charged voicemail message to his black teammate: "Hey, wassup, you half nigger piece of shit." While the media is loathe to even print the term, the focus was squarely on Incognito's use of the typically redacted word "nigger."[45] As vile as the term may be, we explicitly use it here to make a set of important analytic points relating to race, culture, and meaning.

Incognito was initially castigated throughout the sports media—indeed throughout the sports world—by both blacks and whites. For two days he was vilified as a racist. The overwhelming consensus was there was no place in football for language and attitudes like his. Indeed, there were indignant calls to uproot a locker room culture of racial animus and bigotry that was clearly infecting the NFL. But in an unanticipated turn of events, rejoinders from NFL locker rooms—again from both black and white players—turned the discussion upside down. Player after player—mainly Dolphins, but also from other teams around the league—rose to object. Ritchie Incognito was not a racist, teammates (black and white) proclaimed. He was a good teammate, one who embraced all his "buddies" in the locker room with the sort of camaraderie and fellowship that built team cohesion. Like his black "brothers," Incognito used the word "nigger" as a way of signifying solidarity that crossed—even dissolved—racial lines.[46]

Why, when the Anti-Defamation League was calling for investigations into NFL locker rooms, were Incognito's black teammates dismissing the racist allegations? One of his black former teammates sums it up:

> Richie is honorary. I don't expect you [reporter] to understand because you're not black. But being a black guy, being a brother [in the NFL] is more than just about skin color. It's about how you carry yourself. How you play. Where you come from. What you've experienced. A lot of things.[47]

The importance of this and related exchanges isn't about Richie Incognito, per se. Rather it's about cultural understandings of race in the locker room more generally. Player after player insists that the NFL is "the least racist environment I've ever been in."[48] But significantly, players don't say that locker rooms are color blind, that race doesn't matter, that the environment isn't racialized. The NFL is among a very few formal organizational environments that's dominated by black men—rich, powerful black men. A large majority of the players are black. Team leaders are black. Most of the star players are black. Even the new generation of star quarterbacks is predominantly black. There are black coaches and general managers. NFLPA leaders are black. The locker room culture can't help but reflect this fact. Certainly there are racial animosities. Race is sometimes invoked to explain perceived inequities. But NFL players also believe deeply that the league is a pure meritocracy. It's part of the ethos. Talent wins out over everything else. For players, it's an arena and an opportunity where anyone can achieve the American Dream on a level, multiracial playing field.

Players leaving the league are probably never going to encounter such an environment again. They'll return to the small towns of white west Texas or the black neighborhoods of Miami. For those who jump into the corporate world, they'll find nearly all white colleagues, as well as increasingly more women. How does this affect former players' retirement transitions? Black players, especially, but whites as well, will be venturing into new social territory. It's not necessarily hostile or threatening, but it's different. Players are imbued with the NFL culture and ethos as it pertains to masculinity, gender, and race. They are fluent in the language—both literally and figuratively. But locker room culture, demeanor, and behavior are out of place in the corporate world where "loose talk" about race, gender, sex, and sexuality are decidedly out of place. While many organizational environments leave much to be desired in this regard, they hardly compare to the NFL locker room, even at its worst.

After inhabiting a culture where masculinity and race distinctively define social relationships in somewhat unconventional ways, former players may simply find the world *outside* the NFL to be "out of the ordinary." Perhaps encounters with broader cultural standards regarding race and masculinity don't constitute full blown "culture shock," but, for former players, there's a fundamental cultural "strangeness" with respect to these pillars of American social life that may be disorienting. Considering the extreme limits of cultural acceptability within the bubble—what's "normal" in the NFL locker room—former players may understandably feel like "fish out of water."

Dealing with Disjuncture

While the notion of culture shock helps explain the initial displacement and disorientation experienced by former players, another factor contributes to prolonged transition troubles. Culture shock usually dissipates, sooner or later. A different sort of disjuncture, however, may compound the lingering malaise that plagues some former players. It's a form of social disconnection or misalignment that's known in classic sociological terms as "anomie."

Emile Durkheim famously invoked the term to refer to social circumstances where standards or expectations for behavior are confused, ambiguous, or missing. It's often called a state of "normlessness." Anomie emerges when community standards no longer regulate member's activities. Under such circumstances, rules on how people ought to behave don't seem to apply and people don't know what to expect from one another. Without normative guidelines, individuals can't find their place in society.[49]

Robert Merton modified Durkheim's term to refer to social conditions whereby adherence to cultural imperatives is thwarted by social structural circumstances. In Merton's terms, anomie is a disjuncture between culturally prescribed means and socially valued goals. Culture instructs individuals in the acceptable ways of pursuing societal objectives: acceptable means to valued ends, so to speak. Those ends are legitimate aims for the group's members, the things worth striving for. Anomie exists when means and goals fail to align, producing a cultural-structural disjuncture resulting in *social strain* that provokes individual adaptive responses.[50]

When players leave the NFL, they carry the insider's *ethos* and the bubble's norms with them. Outside the bubble, however, the norms no longer apply. Former players find it difficult to act "instinctively" or naturally because the larger social world doesn't honor the code to which they've become habituated. They experience their own version of normlessness. At the same time, former players' value structures are also in flux. The goals of dominance and winning don't necessarily disappear, but they're transformed, and become less clearly defined. The outside world has no direct counterpart to winning a game, a championship, a Super Bowl. While there are analogous socially valued goals such as financial success, personal accomplishment, or celebrity, they aren't as clear-cut as those that NFL players pursue each Sunday.

In this state of anomie, social accountability falters, feelings of belonging weaken, and the sense of a coherent social world evaporates.[51] The structures of former players' experience are suddenly in flux. Being in a state of relative normlessness doesn't mean that former players now inhabit a world without norms, however. To the contrary, they're well aware of the normative expectations and constraints that characterize the NFL bubble; they're deeply internalized. But former players realize that the standards of the bubble don't necessarily apply in the world outside. So they're carrying the ethos of the bubble around with them, with no way to live up to it. They don't have the same opportunities to "live large," compete in the extreme, or be a tough guy anymore. It's ingrained in them—the essence of who they once were—but now they have no legitimate means to pursue those goals or live by their former code of ethics.

The *psychological* consequences of anomie are sometimes called "anomia." This is a mental and emotional state whereby a person's sense of social belonging is broken or disrupted. Anomia is the *feeling* of disorientation, accompanied by a sense of emptiness or apathy—a sensation of meaningless, accompanied by anxiety and confusion.[52] It was part of George Koonce's state of mind as he worked out for months on end, keeping himself in shape for the opportunity to get back in the NFL—an opportunity that never came. It's the emotional place in which he found himself as he drove aimlessly to the beach, not knowing what he was looking for, and when he took that turn too fast in his Chevy Suburban, just to see what would happen. It's the psychological space where Otis Tyler and Drew Raymond occasionally still find themselves.

Former players' responses generally aren't as dramatic as Koonce's. Merton, however, would not have been surprised. In circumstances where original goals or aspirations are out of reach or have been abandoned, some individuals persist in their futile pursuit. They adhere to culturally prescribed conduct, even though it's pointless. Continuing the old ways approaches a compulsion, especially when there is no payoff in sight. Merton calls this adaptation "ritualism."[53] We've heard myriad accounts of former players ritualistically rehabbing serious injuries, working out hours each day, "running laps" from training camp to training camp, all in the futile pursuit of a withered dream. Merton tells us to expect something like this when the individual's social status and worth is largely dependent on a particular kind of achievement, as is the case in the NFL. Most players move beyond this in a year or two. The unrealistic goals succumb to the reality that no NFL team is going to call and the comeback attempts and the ritualistic workouts cease. The cost to former players, however, is considerable delay in getting on with their lives. In some instances, the inertia established in the first year or two out of the league keeps some players from moving on to something new with any enthusiasm or momentum.

Merton also wouldn't be surprised by former players who seem to give up altogether. When a loss of goals combines with a perceived lack of avenues to success, individuals turn away from social engagement. Merton calls this "retreatism"—the abandonment of both cultural goals and institutionalized practices.[54] It's an extreme response to acute anomie, where there's been an abrupt breakdown in the familiar and accepted normative framework and where goals are suddenly out of reach. This is often the case when individuals unexpectedly become exempt from role obligations, such as with military discharges, leaving the priesthood, or being deselected from the NFL.

The most common symptom of retreatism, according to Merton, is a generalized apathy. Retreatists simply don't connect with society.

The most extreme manifestation is suicide. Although infrequent, we've seen it far too often among former NFL players, and we've noted many examples of despondency and several suicide attempts. Sometimes we hear accounts of players breaking ties completely with the league, selling their memorabilia, and avoiding all contact with former teammates. Some simply languish, without serious attempts to establish new careers or pastimes. Such adaptations certainly resonate with Merton's model.

As with culture shock, we need to consider why responses to anomie can be so extreme among former NFL players. Again, the answer lies in the degree to which football has dominated players' lives. The culturally exalted goals have been with most players since childhood. The socially structured means to these ends have been in place for nearly as long. And they're all encompassing. Players' entire lives have been structured around their NFL dream. When that structure disappears, there's little to which former players can cling, nothing left to shoot for. The social disjunctures at the end of NFL careers are serious fractures, not minor fault lines.

Identity under Siege

Former NFL players confront myriad challenges on the social psychological front, too. Retirement places their identities at stake. Viewed abstractly, the ways in which players experience, apprehend, and appreciate their lives after football are filtered through the ways that they conceive of and evaluate their selves. The social objects that individuals understand themselves to be provide the experiential anchors for making sense of their lives. We live by and through those selves. Associated identities claim our places in the world around us.[55] But when these selves are in flux—when identities are challenged—the ways we navigate everyday life, and the way we feel about our experience, are put to the test.

If feelings of disorientation and distress derive from the cultural shock of leaving the NFL, there's even greater cognitive and emotional turmoil when players' fundamental sense of who they are is cut adrift. This isn't just a sense of cultural confusion or normlessness. It's a loss of *personal* bearings. Certainly losing the central role in players' lives is unsettling, but the persistent feeling that something's wrong or something's missing signals greater social psychological upheaval than simply role exit or job loss.

The concept of "role" is useful in thinking about the various enterprises and activities in which individuals engage, but it's too limiting and static to capture what it actually means to *be* an NFL player. There is no script or set of normative role requirements that captures everything that's involved. By the same token, "role exit" simply doesn't convey the radical change that sweeps over former players' lives. They aren't losing roles; they're losing *selves* they've known for a lifetime. "I am 48 years old and I still have dreams about it," says Jamaal McDaniels, speaking about being an NFL player. "You never get that out of your system, man."[56]

What they never get out of their systems are the selves and identities that were firmly established during the years in the NFL bubble. As Mike Flynn, a veteran of five NFL teams, recalls, "You come out of that tunnel [onto the playing field], you feel like you're a god."[57] That's a powerful self-image, but it's only one of many that players have come to know. There's the "football" self—the person identified with being an elite athlete on the field.[58] This self encompasses the football player role, to be sure, but goes far beyond into the realm of the self-defining player ethos. Being a player involves far more than suiting up on Sundays. There's also the "celebrated" self that basks in the limelight of being an elite, highly paid, widely recognized athlete. We've also heard of the "gladiator" self—the warrior who fearlessly and violently sacrifices everything, body and soul, for his team and teammates. The gladiator marches into battle with his brothers, the "masculine" or "macho" self, who is all man, all the time. Then, of course, there's the "large self," the one that thrives on excess, on "livin' large" at every opportunity. These are all selves that NFL players live by—socially structured and socially structuring sets of identities, personas, and related practices that serve to ground players' everyday activities and their notions of who they are.[59]

These selves are related—siblings of a sort—and the end of NFL careers places them in jeopardy. A seven-year veteran linebacker speaks of what he's lost to retirement: "It [being a football player] is always what I've been and what I've done. So there's a little bit of identity change. . . . You know what I miss is . . . being an NFL football player. That status, that prestige, the respect."[60] Aspects of each identity fall away when players leave the NFL. Former players may grieve for some of them, but never miss others. Some may never go away. But former players' accounts of their transition troubles repeatedly come back to an ubiquitous loss:

> I miss lining up on the opening snap and 65,000 people screaming, and making a big tackle. High-fiving my buddies, getting high-fived and knowing that 'Man, I played good!' or I made a good play. . . . I miss men saying, 'Hey, there goes [player]! He plays linebacker for the [name of team]. . . . I miss the Super Bowl, 850 million people watching you and you only. I mean, nobody else is watching anything else. It's awesome![61]

Patricia and Peter Adler's revealing sociological study of a Division I NCAA basketball team offers keen insight into the identity implications of playing big-time sports. The "gloried self" is the centerpiece of their story. College basketball players are similar to NFL players in many respects; most importantly, they're elite athletes who garner considerable attention for excelling at their sport. The basketball players the Adlers studied were campus, if not national, celebrities, perpetually occupying the spotlight. As a consequence, write the Adlers, "The experience of glory was so existentially gratifying that these athletes became emotionally riveted on it, turning away from other aspects of their lives and selves that did not offer such fulfillment. . . . They thus developed 'gloried' selves."[62]

Like other versions of the self, the gloried self is the product of social feedback. Constantly told that they are great, athletes come to see themselves that way.[63] Even the most modest, self-effacing NFL players sport gloried selves. They've been celebrated and idolized since they were kids. Consider the impact of seeing yourself—actually *being* yourself—in an EA Sports *Madden NFL* video game. In a sense, players can literally become "Prime Time" (Deion Sanders) or "Megatron" (Calvin Johnson). Internalizing all of this, being cheered by millions, and feeling like a god or a video icon, who could resist the gloried self?

The gloried self is also greedy. It elbows aside other identities. The Adlers say it's intoxicating and addictive. It becomes the primary self through which players process their experience. Once players embrace the gloried self, they're "all in." According to the Adlers, they may abandon all other aspirations and identities. They are virtually engulfed in the athletic role, which leads them to center their attention on the present while abandoning any future orientation. Their self-esteem and self-worth come solely from one source of gratification: athletic fame. As this happens, the field of identity options progressively narrows, so that the gloried self is both dominant and one-dimensional. College athletes, for example, ignore their student and social roles, while immersing themselves completely in the athletic role. NFL players are similarly consumed. The gloried self is so closely tied to the NFL life that it can't survive without it. And therein lies the problem when careers inevitably end.

While most elite athletes struggle with identity loss when their playing days are over, NFL players are especially vulnerable. Their careers stretch back to childhood. They've pursued no other options. They've made myriad "side bets" on their athletic success, attaching not only their identities, but their financial well-being, their work lives, their social lives, and even their health to their success as football players.[64] When careers end, the rest can crumble, and the existential damage can be overwhelming. Their gloried selves dissolve. The Adlers note that the loss is especially sudden and devastating for college athletes, for whom "it's all over" once their eligibility runs out.[65] It's not quite as sudden for NFL players. They stretch out their departure and milk their celebrity until it runs dry. Nevertheless, while they've banked more notoriety than their college counterparts, most former players eventually exhaust their NFL capital and the glory days come to an end, along with their gloried selves.

Totalizing Tendencies

The NFL is a realm of excess: exorbitant salaries and extravagant spending; unbridled aspirations; hypermasculinity; near-lethal aggression and violence; extreme tolerance for pain; fanatical work ethic; total commitment. The league demands these qualities, and, for the most part, players eagerly comply. Earlier, we called the NFL a "greedy institution." Perhaps it's even more demanding.

Another classic sociological concept aptly applies to players' seemingly total immersion into, and infatuation with, the NFL bubble. Erving Goffman popularized the term "total institution" to refer to institutions that have exceedingly high "encompassing tendencies."[66] These places typically segregate themselves and their inhabitants from the outside world with formal and informal barriers to physical and social interaction. Goffman had institutions such as prisons, mental asylums, and concentration camps in mind, noting that they typically surrounded themselves with high walls, locked doors, and other physical barricades. But he also included nursing homes, orphanages, rehabilitation clinics, monasteries, convents, and the military. The common linkage is their near-complete and intentional isolation from the rest of the world.

The goals of total institutions vary widely, from caring for the infirm or helpless, to protecting society from the dangerous, to providing contemplative sanctuaries or spiritual retreats. Again, what they all have in common is the aim of reforming. In Goffman's words, total institutions are "part residential community, part formal organization . . . they are the forcing houses for changing persons; each is a natural experiment on what can be done to the self." Total institutions, he notes, are established to produce particular types of individuals.[67]

The resemblance to the NFL here is largely suggestive. We're not saying that the NFL meets all of the requirements for being a bona fide total institution, but there are sufficient parallels to adopt it as a useful analytic guide. For example, Goffman suggests that total institutions aim to break down the separation of typically independent spheres of everyday life by consolidating all activities in one place, under a single authority. All members' needs are explicitly anticipated and provided for on site. All phases of the day's activities are highly planned and tightly scheduled, and are concertedly aimed at the institution's goals and guided by formal rules and strictures. Intense surveillance accompanies the high degree of regimentation. Each phase of a member's daily activity is conducted in the immediate company of fellow members, who are similarly guided and motivated.[68]

The NFL isn't literally a total institution because players aren't confined to NFL facilities—at least not 24/7. They are, of course, mandated to be at team facilities for early morning treatment, meals, and meetings. And they stay until the full workday is done. They're fined if they miss meetings or appointments, or even if they are late. And they are "locked up" for training camps, as well as the nights before games. While the accommodations are far better than those of most other total institutions, players are still confined to their quarters, required to observe curfews, and subjected to bed checks. Minor details aside, the NFL has much in common with other total institutions—at least metaphorically.

Like other total institutions, the NFL aims to mold men into institutionally desired forms. It replaces competing agendas with its own. It disrupts players' alternate behavioral habits, totally and radically reshaping the structural and moral contours of daily living. The resulting "disculturation" renders players manageable, hopefully maximizing their productivity. As Goffman warns, however, disculturation is likely to leave members with a sort of childlike dependency, "incapable of managing certain features of daily life on the outside."[69]

What's more, Goffman claims that a central aim of total institutions is the "mortification" of self, whereby members surrender outside identities to those preferred and cultivated by institutional authorities. Insulated from outside interaction, immersed in institutional culture and regimens, and surrounded by others undergoing the same process, outside identities are systematically and ceremonially stripped away, to be replaced by selves constructed to institutional order.[70] This is more than institutional socialization. It's fundamental identity transformation, which Goffman says leaves members with severe deficits in "adult self-determination, autonomy, and freedom of action."[71]

Effectively "colonized" by the institutional experience, members of total institutions lose confidence in their ability to function outside institutional confines. Transition to the outside world triggers "release anxiety," in Goffman's terms.[72] Members simply aren't up to speed with the cultural guidelines and cues of the outside world. Perhaps retiring players wouldn't call it "release anxiety," but they know the trepidations that come with being released. Absent the literal walls of the classic total institution, the NFL erects metaphorical, cultural walls that may be just as confining.

We should be cautious, however, in drawing literal comparisons with other total institutions, because the NFL differs in some very significant respects. Prisons, for example, command *every* aspect of prisoners' lives, something the NFL can't and doesn't claim to do. Plus prisons are both involuntary and unabashedly coercive, again quite different in degree from the circumstances of the NFL, where there are tremendous incentives to seek membership. Prisoners neither enter nor leave at their own discretion. But they do leave on schedule, another difference from the NFL, where the end is poorly anticipated.

Despite these differences, however, the challenges of "reentry" for prisoners and former players bear significant similarities. Inside prisons, for example, there's tremendous pressure to assimilate prison norms, which often leads to a sort of "institutional dependency." Prison life teaches prisoners to rely on the prison structure for all aspects of their existence and the NFL bubble has its counterparts. Prisoners often lose the ability to make their own decisions and cease to realistically envision life after their sentences are up. They can't plan a new life and provide for themselves when they finally get out. They aren't prepared to face the social, economic, and emotional challenges on the outside. They even lose the social-relation skills necessary to reconnect with intimates and close associates in the outside world. Taken to the extreme, some prisoners become totally "institutionalized" or "prisonized," in Donald Clemmer's famous terms.[73] Having forgotten how to live in "free society" with its mundane complexities and demands, they're ill prepared for the transition they face. They're essentially incapable of surviving outside prison.[74]

While former players seldom encounter difficulties of this magnitude, we've heard player narratives that closely mimic these concerns. NFL players certainly aren't "prisonized," but they encounter many of the same institutional stumbling blocks and parallel transition troubles. The central lesson of the prison experience for NFL players is clear, however. The deeper and more complete the immersion in the institutional culture, the more difficult it is to make the transition to the outside.[75]

Comparisons between the military and the NFL as total institutions may also be instructive. Entry into both is voluntary and there are significant incentives to join both. Exit is "semi-voluntary" and, like most NFL players, some military personnel are not especially anxious to muster out. We need to be careful to distinguish the experiences of actual combat veterans. They face a constellation of traumas that we don't intend to compare to those in the NFL. Still, members of the military and NFL players share the experience of "totalization." And once again we find that discharged armed service members (not necessarily combat vets), like prisoners and NFL football players, have trouble readjusting to the "real world."[76] They must relearn the practical and social skills needed to survive in a less regimented environment. Today's military attempts to deal with these problems aggressively, conducting discharge preparation programs and manning a web site and online informational brochures in ways remarkably similar to the NFL's Player Care programs and web site.[77]

Dr. Ramon Hinojosa of the Veteran's Administration observes that military personnel also routinely receive preseparation debriefings as they leave active duty. Specially designed programs address the social, psychosocial, and economic challenges that return to civilian life may pose. But many discharged service men, according to Hinojosa, ignore the information or reject the advice, often out of masculine pride, denial, disregard, or ambivalence about life after the military. These responses are symptomatic of a military culture that, in many ways, resembles that of the NFL. In both cases, "exes" insist that they will be fine, although post-retirement evidence says this isn't always the case.[78]

While working on this book, George Koonce received a handwritten letter from an officer in a middle-size Wisconsin police force. He'd read a newspaper interview Koonce had recently done on the subject of his post-career transition. This note offers some additional insight into how still another totalizing institution creates challenges similar to those confronted by players leaving the NFL:

> I'm just a middle-aged cop in Wisconsin who enjoyed watching you play. . . . Cops are in a similar situation. We spend our career somewhat isolated. Our unique duties, life and death dependency on each other, the 24/7 schedule, shared experiences (tragic and funny) really create that camaraderie that must be similar to a football team. Being a cop sometimes creates an identity that becomes your whole life. So, when we retire, we lose something that can't be replaced. . . . It can send you adrift, trying to fill that void in many ways—some destructive (which partially accounts for our high rates of divorce, suicide, alcoholism, etc.).

The letter is a compassionate gesture grounded in common experience. It's also a warning about the challenges of stepping outside of totalized environments such as the police department or the NFL bubble.

Keys to Transition

Perhaps the essence of leaving the NFL with good prospects and positive momentum is to actively resist "totalization." Players who thrive after football often defy cultural and organizational pressures to become full-blown NFL "organization men."[79] This doesn't mean they've failed as players. Rather, it means they've poked their heads out of the bubble occasionally, sheltered aspects of their selves from the locker room culture, and developed talents that might serve interests other than football. In doing so, they've inoculated themselves against engulfment, rejecting total institutionalization in favor of personal diversification.

Does this limit their success in the NFL? Perhaps. If they don't pay the price, they don't make the roster. If they don't go "all in" all year round, there careers might be short. But one thing seems certain. If players put all their eggs in the NFL basket, they're inviting serious challenges when they leave the game because they haven't built a foundation of post-career options. In today's greedy NFL, the trick may be to hold football at bay— at least sometimes—in order to keep options open.

Players often claim that the contemporary game demands all their time, but that's an exaggeration. The NFL is not a voracious predator, gobbling up *every* second of every day. It's not irresistible. We've seen plenty of examples where planning and prudent time allocation allow players to get college degrees—and educations—while still in the league. And examples abound of players launching second careers while they're still playing.

Still, players are reluctant to branch out, and for good reason. They don't want to imperil the NFL dream. Michael Oriard, for one, occasionally wonders if he would have been more successful in the NFL if he'd put more of himself into the game. He speculates that he might have been more than a backup lineman if he'd made greater sacrifices, wanted it more. Ultimately, Oriard concluded that football success wasn't worth the price that might have been extracted from other dimensions of his life. "How ironic is it," he notes, "that the better players and the players for whom football has greater personal importance must pay the penalty in a more difficult adjustment to retirement." "Blessed are the mediocre," he concludes, "for they shall inherit the future."[80]

While Oriard is far too modest about his football career, he still conceives of himself as a football player and this deeply informs his identity. But he also sees himself in more enduring, far-reaching terms:

The long career [as an English professor at Oregon State] is clearly what's more important, because it was the longer career. . . . I've been more successful as an English professor than I ever was as a football player. . . . I've written seven books—I've been a very productive scholar. I was named a distinguished professor at my university. Of course, that old cliché, that "sports is life with the volume turned up . . ." Well, it's true that my successes as an academic have been more routine than my going from walk-on at Notre Dame to the NFL. . . . I paid my dues and it all worked out OK.[81]

Michael Oriard, George Koonce, and countless other players committed major portions of their lives and selves to NFL success, yet they still had enough left over to thrive after football. Indeed, Koonce and Oriard offer exemplary lessons in avoiding "institutionalization," even though they're studies in contrast. It's easy to peg Oriard as the white, cerebral offensive lineman, while Koonce is the black, athletic middle linebacker. It's tempting to conclude that Oriard's social background alone predicted life successes that Koonce likely wouldn't achieve. Probabilistically, that's the case. The range of choices available to them were definitely conditioned by their socioeconomic, racial, and educational foundations, but each made crucial choices within his range of possibilities—choices that either opened or closed options.

Oriard grew up in a middle-class family, was an honor student at private schools, and had the luxury of being socially positioned to choose from a full slate of possibilities. His football dream led him to Notre Dame, but not on a football scholarship. What if he'd chosen another university, say, Miami or Michigan? Would those schools have embraced a walk-on who wanted to study physics and English lit? Being middle class or white doesn't necessarily mean one takes education seriously, or makes the most of one's opportunities. Remember Jim Harbaugh's experience at the University of Michigan. Nor does it insure prudent planning. Former first round draft choice Todd Marinovich planned his pursuit of the NFL down to the smallest detail. The son of a football coach, Marinovich had seemingly every social advantage. He made every choice of his young life (or had them made for him) with NFL success in mind. His commitment was as "total" as one could imagine, but these choices left him floundering when football was done with him, with an unfortunate legacy of homelessness, drug abuse, and jail.[82]

Being poor or black, on the other hand, doesn't necessarily mean that one majors in "eligibility" or "sport and recreation." It doesn't prescribe "livin' large." Eugene Profit and Charles Nobles testify to this. George Koonce came from modest means, where school was an afterthought to many of his peers. But his parents wouldn't let him slack off, even when he sometimes lagged behind. When he couldn't qualify for a Division I football scholarship, Koonce did his time at a community college rather than quitting in despair, laying an academic as well as a football foundation. He got a degree in industrial technology and construction management—a field which dovetailed with past work experience, as well as with his future investment plans.

In a sense, Koonce and Oriard got onto paths running parallel alongside football. Perhaps it was a luxury for Oriard and more of a necessity for Koonce, but both actually had to work for their livings while trying to land positions in the NFL. Once there, Koonce had a far more productive and lucrative career, while Oriard just managed to get by. But Oriard also managed to complete most of his doctoral studies with his NFL income paying the bills. Koonce, on the other hand, had his bouts of minor excesses, but basically trod a conservative path through his playing years. He maintained ties with his alma mater. Keeping true to his roots, he bought rental properties and other real estate and preserved his financial solvency, even though he had some bad investments and terrible luck with injury and non-guaranteed NFL contracts. He didn't simply blow through his NFL money and end up broke at the end of the line.

Given the chance and the choice, both Koonce and Oriard cultivated varied opportunities rather than immersing themselves totally in football. To invoke a useful cliché, both chose to keep other irons in the fire while pursuing their NFL dreams. "Educate and prepare," said Hakeem Chapman. "Change the focus from your game to your job. . . . You have everything you need, just refocus it." Oriard and Koonce got the message.

Neither was totally "institutionalized" or completely swallowed up by the NFL and its culture. The NFL player ethos didn't rule their lives with an iron hand. It wasn't mediocrity that insured their futures. It was diversification: their defiance of totalization.

Forging the Future

Clearly, there's life after football, and for many former NFL players, it's full, rich, and rewarding. Unfortunately, that's not always the case. Some of the post-career pitfalls we've seen leave us with grave reservations. Our qualms stem from seeing players close down options and make short-sighted or poorly informed choices among limited alternatives. The pertinent question, from our vantage point, is what might be done to enhance players' lives when they finish playing? Can they have *better* lives after football, where players and their families won't be overwhelmed by physical injury, financial woes, bleak job prospects, and social voids?

Certainly post-career plans, programs, and opportunities play a role, and the NFL and NFLPA have finally stepped up to take responsibility for helping players transition to the future. They're encouraging education, work training and experience, internships, media training, investment advice, financial management, and even "life coaching." While there's still room for improvement, opportunities are there for the taking.

But there's even greater need for change within the NFL bubble and its prevailing culture. We've argued that one key to successfully transitioning out of the NFL is to resist the league's totalizing tendencies. That means being wary of going "all in," even when that's the optimal strategy for succeeding in the game itself. In nearly all walks of life, when a person is "all in," it's challenging to get out with any degree of success.

Prisons and the military are two well-know "totalizing" institutions. Even more than the NFL, they command all aspects of players' lives; their cultures are all encompassing. Reintegration problems for their "exes" are famously difficult, but they may be instructive. The prison literature, for example, stresses two major "reentry" challenges faced by those going back to the "real world." First, "prisonization" is a *functional* adaptation to the institutional and cultural demands of "the inside," but it inhibits success on the outside. Second, the more "prisonized" the individual, the more difficulty he or she has reentering normal society. Deeply socialized and enculturated, those who are "prisonized" have lost the tools to rejoin society. We aren't claiming that NFL players are fully "prisonized" and it would be unfair—and maladaptive—to ask them to reject unilaterally the demands of the NFL, its culture and ethos. But in light of recent developments, perhaps it's reasonable to suggest that the NFL culture better align itself with wider cultural values, mores, and practices.

We're not suggesting a wholesale abandonment of the NFL ethos, just a tempering of the violence, coarseness, hypermasculinity, and excess that dominates life in and around the NFL. A continued insistence, for example, on defying injury and emphasizing toughness borders on pathological. Bodies, if not lives, are severely endangered—as the recent concussion controversy demonstrates—in ways that are counterproductive for the game, its players, and its alumni. The crude vulgarity of locker room culture and its hypermasculine, homophobic atmosphere strikes most outsiders as outrageous. The compulsion to live large is hard for outsiders to comprehend. To the extent that the NFL can curb these excesses to bring locker room culture more in line with workplace cultures in the wider world, the better chance NFL players have to succeed in that wider world.

It may increase the NFL's chances of thriving as well. With today's concern about the league's antisocial images and culture of violence—where players themselves resist nearly all safety measures that might impugn their toughness or masculinity—there's a growing apprehension about football's future viability. While it appears to be a thriving financial enterprise, a recent NBC poll found that 40 percent of American parents would steer their kids away from playing football.[83] Whereas this would have minimal impact in the immediate future, without the conveyor belt from peewee football, to high school, to colleges, the player supply chain might eventually dry up.

In 2014, the NFL finds itself under scrutiny on myriad fronts. The concussion controversy, the Richie Incognito debacle, and the addition of its first openly gay player, however, present opportunities to reconfigure some cultural components in ways that might keep players from becoming so culturally isolated in the bubble that they can't function outside. It's a chance for the league itself to check its totalizing tendencies, allowing players to exercise discretion and responsibility in ways that will help them better prepare for life after football. Fifteen-yard penalties for on-field racial slurs aren't the answer.

For their part, players need aggressively to promote these changes themselves. They should recognize and revamp some of the more limiting and debilitating aspects of the NFL ethos as they expand their own personal horizons. To remain captivated by the "gloried self" is immensely and immediately gratifying, but ultimately, the NFL spotlight fades for most of them. Just as they should diversify their financial and career options, they need multidimensional selves that can serve them well once the cheering stops and they're confronted by an increasingly diverse social world. Their talent and potential are boundless, and their opportunities today are burgeoning. Former players simply need to move forward to claim new limelights in multifaceted lives after football.

APPENDIX 1

METHODOLOGY

This book offers a naturalistic examination of former NFL players' lives during and after their playing days. It aims to understand players' social realities on their own terms. Such an approach seeks rich descriptions of lives in relation to the actual circumstances in which they unfold. The focus is mainly on *what* those lives and realities are like from players' perspectives—that is, the phenomenological complexity of those worlds. To that end, the primary data for the study are former players' personal narratives about their experiences as they prepared for and played out their football careers, then moved into the uncertainty of life after football.[1]

From this perspective, we conducted approximately 50 life history interviews with NFL players and former players. As a former player, George Koonce had unprecedented access to research subjects and took the lead in forging research relationships. He also conducted most of the interviews—generally in one-on-one situations, but occasionally with one of the other researchers participating.

The interviews varied in their formality, structure, and timing. Approximately 30 were prearranged as more or less formal interviews. The others were more impromptu, being set up "on the spot" when players were available and willing to talk for more than just a few minutes. All of the interviews were semistructured, organized around a set of guiding topics but no strict interview schedule. Interviews lasted from about 45 minutes to several hours, sometimes across multiple occasions. Interview subjects were promised confidentiality to promote honest, forthcoming responses. Consequently, we use pseudonyms for interviewees throughout the book, and have disguised teams, places, and other persons mentioned in our research interviews.

The interviews were supplemented by direct observation on several occasions, where we were able to watch and listen to former players interact in casual settings like autograph signings, team reunions, charity events, and informal get-togethers. Talk of retirement issues inevitably and naturally developed at these events. On some occasions, our observations were purely "noninterventional" in that we merely watched and listened without interjecting our research agenda into the ongoing interactions. On other occasions, however, we joined the conversations, inquiring about issues that piqued our interest. On still other occasions, we parlayed an initial conversation into relatively formal interviews. Most of the interviews were audio recorded and subsequently transcribed, although several were recorded in field notes.

What distinguishes this study from others is its use of various techniques of "participant observation," "auto-observation," or "autoethnography."[2] George Koonce played football for most of his young adult life, including nine years in the NFL. After the end of his football career, Koonce earned his Ph.D. from Marquette University, where his doctoral dissertation examined role transitions of NFL players. Most of the life history interviews were conducted for this research. Perhaps more importantly, Koonce's three and a half decades of being an "insider" in the world of elite football afforded him unparalleled opportunity to experience firsthand the issues explored in this study. The research draws heavily upon his retrospective descriptions and analysis from this insider's perspective. Holstein and Jones also interviewed Koonce for several hours concerning his experiences as a player and, subsequently, as a retiree.

There are advantages and disadvantages to Koonce's unique researcher role. Any attributes of a participant observer's role affects data collection and analysis. A primary advantage of collecting data "from the inside" has been called "intimate familiarity."[3] In his "complete membership role,"[4] Koonce experienced firsthand many of the phenomena under study, so his knowledge was multidimensional: cognitive, emotional, and visceral. This, in turn, sensitized him to issues for exploration when he interviewed other players. His status as a former player—sometimes a former teammate—gave him access to interview subjects and promoted their willingness to talk openly with him. The sort of authenticity to which he had access due to his full participation in the players' social world is often credited with contributing observational and analytic depth and understanding not available to more detached outsiders.[5] At the same time, however, his insider status undoubtedly shaped interviewees' responses, since they knew they were talking to "one of their own," which placed their conversations *within* the same cultural context that they were ostensibly asked to describe.[6]

In addition to formal interviews, data were also collected from the myriad interviews conducted in the sports journalism media. It's unlikely to find lives more thoroughly questioned and examined than those of professional football players. Collectively, they are interviewed virtually every day of a seven-month-long season, and occasionally during the remaining months of the year. Between 2010 and 2013, while this study was conducted, we found hundreds of interviews with players and former players on the subject of life after football, plus even more on what it was like inside the actual players' worlds. Add to this the dozens of biographies and autobiographies of players and former players, and we had a nearly endless supply of narrative material at our disposal.

In all, we collected and analyzed approximately 2,500 single-spaced pages of interview data, not including narrative materials contained in the approximately 40 biographies, autobiographies, and journalistic books we consulted. We also drew upon two rigorous interview studies of former NFL players (S. Coakley 2006) and their wives (O'Toole 2006) that provided dozens of additional interviews that were pertinent to our study. All of our transcribed data were coded and analyzed using NVIVO qualitative data analysis software. Including multiple coding entries, our NVIVO data set amounted to nearly 1,000 single-spaced pages of coded data entries.

In addition, we consulted dozens of public and organizational documents produced by the NFL, the NFLPA, the NCAA, and other organizations dealing with player welfare issues. Finally, we relied upon systematically collected data sources whenever possible, although these are rare. The Player Care study is probably the best available, but has its limitations.[7]

We used an inductive "grounded theory" strategy for analyzing our data, employing a constant comparative method.[8] The grounded theory approach methodically organizes unique individual experiences collected in the field (interviews, observations, documents, etc.) into comparable categories so that commonalities as well as variations in personal experiences emerge. Analysis starts with open coding, a process of line-by-line analysis of data in order to identify significant experiences and/or phenomenological themes. As patterns emerge, a more focused coding process synthesizes these patterns into hierarchically organized themes that are then systematically coded around core categories, or central themes, thus tying the data together. Data properties and dimensions are then systematically compared within and across thematic categories. The systematic comparison of data involves comparing case to case (i.e., individual to individual), case to category (i.e., individuals' issues to emergent themes), and categories to categories (i.e., themes to themes) along their various dimensions and properties—hence the process is constantly comparative.[9]

Interviews and other material gathered from internet sources pose special challenges. As a rule of thumb, we used materials only from legitimate sports and news journalism sources and web sites, and eschewed the use of personal blogs and other unauthorized sources. In addition, we considered internet data to be "legitimate" only if we found multiple references to the same (or similar) facts and themes. We did occasionally explore "deviant cases" for their comparative value, but attempted, first of all, to assure that emergent issues were not so idiosyncratic as to be unreliable or inaccurate. We have used only direct, attributed, documented quotations in our analysis.

APPENDIX 2

RETIREMENT BENEFITS

Misapprehensions about player retirement benefits are rife—both among the general public and among players and former players themselves. This appendix briefly summarizes the benefits provided by the NFL, with special emphasis on limitations and qualifications for eligibility. We also note some controversial and contentious issues in this realm.

Financial Context

Some financial context is necessary to place retirement benefits into proper perspective. The following synopsis, taken from the NFL Player Care study, outlines the general financial picture for players who are "vested"—that is, who have spent a minimum of three to five years in the NFL, depending on the era in which they played, and are thus eligible for the benefits package.[1]

Vested retirees have substantially higher incomes than men of similar ages in the general population. Younger NFL alumni report median total incomes of $85,000 (2008) and older alumni report a median of $93,400 (2008). As points of reference, the median total income for all U.S. men aged 30–49 was $55,000 and for all men 50 or older was $48,169. When NFL alumni are compared with U.S. men with some college experience (not necessarily four-year degrees), the income gaps are cut nearly in half. Still another picture emerges when we look at those at the lower end of the income ladder. Younger alumni report incomes below the poverty level at the same rate as the general population. These numbers are even more noteworthy when NFL veterans are compared with men of comparable education. NFL alumni are twice as likely to report income that is below the poverty level—8.4 percent versus 4.1 percent in the general population.

Remember, these figures are based on alumni who had roughly average careers; they don't include players with careers of three years or less.

In terms of income sources, 49.2 percent of older alumni reported that they had annual incomes from earnings (median: $70,000), while 65.5 percent of younger players had earnings income (median: $65,000). Other sources of "labor" income include bonuses or commissions, professional practices, endorsements, and business. About a third of former players have some sort of business income. Surprisingly only around ten percent of NFL alumni make money from endorsements, and those amounts are relatively small (the median is less than $10,000). The study does not indicate how many players have no income at all, nor does it report data on players' current total wealth.

Benefits
While the current NFL benefits package is extensive, if not comprehensive, this hasn't always been the case. Alumni from earlier eras received only a small fraction of what's presently available. NFLCommunications.com and other NFL sources specify the following benefits.[2]

Severance Pay
Under the severance pay plan, a released player with two or more credited seasons in the NFL receives termination pay of $12,500 per credited season. A season is "credited" if the player is on (1) the active roster, (2) the inactive list, (3) injured reserve, or (4) the physically unable to perform list for at least three regular season or postseason games. A nine-year veteran such as George Koonce, for example, would be due $112,500 upon filing for retirement.

Bert Bell/Pete Rozelle Retirement Plan
The retirement plan provides both pension and disability benefits. Under the latest CBA, to be eligible (i.e., vested), a player must be credited with being an active player for (1) five credited seasons if he played before 1973, or (2) four credited seasons if any of his seasons were after 1973,

or (3) three credited seasons if any of them was after 1992. At the age of 55, vested players receive monthly pensions based on years in service, not based on earnings in the league. The amounts differ according to the credited seasons played. Alumni are given $250 per month for each year played before 1982, $255 per season for 1982–1992, $265 per season for 1993–1994, $315 per season for 1995–1996, $365 per season for 1997, and $470 per season for years since 1998. For example, George Koonce started his nine-year career in 1992. His monthly pension payment would be calculated as follows: (1992) $255 + (1993) $265 + (1994) $265 + (1995) $315 + (1996) $315 + (1997) $365 + (1998) ($470) + (1999) $470 + (2000) $470 = $3,190 monthly payment for life ($38,280 annually at age 55). In comparison, the occasional player such as Brett Favre, a recently retired veteran of 20 years, will pull down nearly $100,000 annually when he reaches age 55. Players may elect to receive pension checks as early as age 45, but the monthly payments are substantially reduced. If players elect to defer payments until age 65, the monthly checks are substantially larger.

Second Career Plan (401[k] Savings Plan)
Rookie players may contribute to the 401(k) plan, but only players with at least two credited seasons get matching contributions. A player with at least two credited seasons in the league can contribute up to a maximum of $10,000 in pretax dollars per year and receive a matching team contribution of $2 for each $1 the player contributes.

Player Annuity Program
This program provides tax-deferred earnings on contributions made by NFL teams. NFL contributions are $5,000 for each of a player's second and third credited seasons, $55,000 for his fourth credited season, and $65,000 for each credited season thereafter.

Health Insurance
The NFL provides continued health care coverage to vested players and their families *for five years* after leaving the league. Medical insurance covers

100 percent of all in-network medical costs for a player and his dependents. The annual deductible for medical insurance is $400 per player and $800 per family with a lifetime maximum benefit of up to $2.5 million. Dental insurance covers 100 percent of all preventive dental care along with 85 percent of general services and 50 percent of major services. The annual deductible for dental coverage is $50 and there is an annual maximum benefit of $2,000. *Players who never vested are without NFL health insurance.*

"88 Plan"
This plan provides retired players with as much as $88,000 per year for individual care, up to $50,000 for home custodial care in addition to costs pertaining to certain physician services, durable medical equipment and prescription medications resulting from dementia, Alzheimer's disease, and amyotrophic lateral sclerosis (ALS).

Neurological Care Program
Provides neurological specialists to evaluate and treat possible neurological conditions among retired players. Eligible players who cannot afford treatment may apply to the NFL Player Care Foundation for grants to cover some or all of the costs of treatment.

Joint Replacement Plan
Assists former players in need of knee, hip, or shoulder replacements. If a player is not covered by insurance and does not have the means to pay for this surgery, he may qualify for financial assistance from the NFL Player Care Foundation. In that case, he will not bear any of the costs associated with the surgery. In addition, most normal complications arising from surgery are covered in full, up to a maximum of $250,000.

Life Insurance
NFL rookies receive coverage of $150,000 at no cost while the annual coverage increases by $30,000 per year for veterans up to a maximum coverage of $300,000, while playing.

Tuition Reimbursement

This program provides assistance to current and former players who wish to continue their education. An eligible active player will be reimbursed up to $15,000 per year for qualified education expenses (e.g., tuition, books, and fees). An eligible retired player will be reimbursed up to $45,000 for qualified education expenses that are incurred within three years of his last NFL game.

Life Improvement Plan

This program is designed to assist vested former NFL players with various health and quality-of-life concerns. NFL and NFLPA web sites reveal a plethora of programs and opportunities for players and alumni, including education and training workshops, internships, and information concerning virtually all things relating to life after football.[3]

Glaring Omissions

For all intents and purposes, NFL retirement benefits extend only to players with longer than average careers. This leaves a vast number of ex-players without benefits of any sort, and those who played before the free agent era and more recent CBAs have been especially short-changed. Prior to 1977, vested ex-players received about $100 per month per season played.[4] Players from the 1940s and 1950s got even less. Sometimes half-heartedly over the years, the NFL and NFLPA have addressed the situation, with the most recent and generous move to establish a $620 million "Legacy Fund" as part of the 2011 CBA. The fund is primarily designed to better the financial circumstances of older retired players, and includes the following major adjustments to the pension plan:[5]

- *Every* vested player will receive a pension increase. Payments to alumni and their beneficiaries will immediately increase to no less than $600 per month. In addition, this $600 per month minimum will apply for players who are not yet receiving pensions.

- If a player is over 55 and already receiving a pension, he will get an additional $124 monthly per season for seasons before 1975, and $108 per season for seasons beginning with 1975 and continuing through 1992. If a player is over 55 and not yet receiving his pension, the additional Legacy Fund payments will be slightly higher when he starts his pension. If a player is under 55 and takes his pension early, his Legacy Fund supplement will be lower. Players whose pensions vested before 1975—those who played for the lowest salaries—will receive the largest increases.
- Legacy Fund benefits will continue not only for the lifetime of the retired player, but also for the lifetime of his eligible beneficiary.

Under the terms of the Legacy Fund, for example, a ten-year veteran player who retired in the 1960s, and who had been receiving a $200 monthly pension, will receive $1,840 a month. A ten-year veteran who retired in the 1970s will see his monthly check increase from $165 to $1,810.[6] Despite these substantial increases, old-time players with a limited number of credited years will hardly be on easy street financially.

NOTES

INTRODUCTION

1. George Koonce occupies a complex and unusual role in this book. He is both research subject and analyst for the project. We discuss his role and the challenges it posed in Appendix 1, "Methodology." Throughout the book, we've placed extended quotations from Koonce-as-interview-subject in italics to distinguish these narratives from his author/analyst voice in the project. Tunisia Koonce is also a major figure in the book. Tragically, Tunisia died from breast cancer in October 2009 at age 38. All quotations from research interviews with Koonce and other informants appear in original form and have been edited minimally for grammar, clarity, etc.

2. "NFL Hopeful FAQs." N.d. *NFL Players Association.* https://www.nflplayers.com/About-us/FAQs/NFL-Hopeful-FAQs; "What Is Average NFL Player's Career Length? Longer than You Might Think, Commissioner Goodell Says." April 18, 2011. *NFL Communications.* http://nflcommunications.com/2011/04/18/what-is-average-nfl-player%E2%80%99s-career-length-longer-than-you-might-think-commissioner-goodell-says/; both retrieved 11/12/13.

3. There's been considerable controversy surrounding Junior Seau's death and his history of football-related brain trauma. While his case has contributed to a push for extensive and systematic brain trauma research, it has also been enveloped in the struggle over control of that research and its interpretation regarding the relation between football and brain disease. See Chapter 9 and "Mind Control," *Outside the Lines.* April 28, 2013. ESPN-TV.

4. Freeman, Mike. May 4, 2013. "Anniversary of Junior Seau's Death Still Focuses NFL on CTE." *CBSsports.com.* http://www.cbssports.com/nfl/blog/mike-freeman/22183367/anniversary-of-junior-seau-death-still-focuses-nfl-on-cte; George, Rachel. January 14, 2013. "Jovan Belcher's Blood Alcohol Content Was Twice Legal Limit." *USAtoday.com.* http://www.usatoday.com/story/sports/nfl/2013/01/14/jovan-belcher-autopsy-kasandra-perkins-kansas-city-chiefs/1833251/; Hicks, Tommy. April 10, 2012. "Coroner: Former Auburn Star Kurt Crain Died of Apparent Self-inflicted Gunshot Wound." *AL.com.* http://blog.al.com/sports_impact/print.html?entry=/2012/04/coroner_former_auburn_star_kur.html; Schwarz, Alan. May 22, 2011. "Duerson's Brain Trauma Diagnosed." *NYTimes.com.* http://www.nytimes.com/2011/05/03/sports/football/03duerson.html; Tierney, Mike. July 26, 2012. "Football Player Who Killed Himself Had Brain Disease." *NYTimes.com.* http://www.nytimes.com/2012/07/27/sports/football/ray-easterling-autopsy-found-signs-of-brain-disease-cte.html?_r=0); all retrieved 5/20/13.

5. See Oriard, Michael. 1982. *The End of Autumn*. Garden City, NY: Doubleday.

6. Segura, Melissa. September 10, 2012. "The Other Half of the Story." *Sports Illustrated*, pp. 60–66.

7. Fainaru, Steve, and Mark Fainaru-Wada. November 16, 2012. "Mixed Messages on Brain Injuries." *ESPN.com*. http://espn.go.com/espn/otl/story/_/page/OTL-Mixed-Messages/nfl-disability-board-concluded-playing-football-caused-brain-injuries-even-officials-issued-denials-years; Cooke, S. Alexander. April 6, 2012. "Five NFL Players with Mental Illness Who Went Public." *Sports.Yahoo.Com*. http://sports.yahoo.com/nfl/news?slug=ycn-11202898; "Former Jet Quarterback Ray Lucas Reflects on Drug Addiction, Suicidal Thoughts." May 3, 2012. *Newyork.cbslocal.com*. http://newyork.cbslocal.com/2012/05/03/former-jets-quarterback-ray-lucas-reflects-on-drug-addiction-suicidal-thoughts/; Rivard, Ray. June 17, 2012. "Lionel Aldridge Great Man, Great Career, Troubled Life. *Lombardiave.com*. http://lombardiave.com/2012/06/17/lionel-aldridge-great-man-great-career-troubled-life/; all retrieved 5/23/13.

8. Ibid. But also see McCann, Michael. January 14, 2014. "What Rejection of Settlement Means to Concussion Cases against NFL." *Sportsillustrated.cnn.com*. http://sportsillustrated.cnn.com/nfl/news/20140114/judge-rejects-proposed-nfl-concussion-settlement/, retrieved 2/13/14.

9. *30 for 30: Broke*. 2012. ESPN-TV (hereafter *Broke*; see http://espn.com/30for30/film?page=broke); Torre, Pablo S. March 23, 2009. "How (and Why) Athletes Go Broke." *SIVault.com*. http://sportsillustrated.cnn.com/vault/article/magazine/MAG1153364, retrieved 1/12/13.

10. Torre, March 23, 2009.

11. "NFL Arrest Database." N.d. *UTSandiego.com*. http://www.utsandiego.com/nfl/arrests-database/, retrieved 6/28/13; Jenkins, Sally. July 2, 2013. "Aaron Hernandez Unfairly Stigmatizes NFL Players as Violent and Criminalized." *Washingtonpost.com*. http://www.washingtonpost.com/sports/redskins/aaron-hernandez-unfairly-stigmatizes-nfl-players-as-violent-and-criminalized/2013/07/02/cc63b648-e31d-11e2-aef3-339619eab080_print.html, retrieved 4/13/14; Associated Press. November 30, 2012. "Keith Wright Sentenced to Life." *ESPN.com*. http://espn.go.com/nfl/story/_/id/8696102/former-nfl-player-keith-wright-sentenced-life-prison, retrieved 4/14/14; Anderson, Paul. August 9, 2012. "Ex-NFL Linebacker Naposki Gets Life in Killing of Lover's Wealthy Boyfriend." *Presstelegram.com*. http://www.presstelegram.com/general-news/20120810/ex-nfl-linebacker-naposki-gets-life-in-killing-of-lovers-wealthy-boyfriend, retrieved 4/14/14.

12. See Appendix 1, "Methodology," for a more detailed description of the research methodology, data collection techniques, and analytic strategies.

13. See Gubrium, Jaber F., and James A. Holstein 1997. *The New Language of Qualitative Method*. New York: Oxford University Press.

CHAPTER 1. PURSUING "THE DREAM"

1. Research interview #42.
2. Research interview #40.
3. Favre, Brett, and Chris Havel. 1997. *Favre*. New York: Doubleday, pp. 95, 98.
4. Research interview #24. All names of players interviewed specifically for this project are pseudonyms (with the exception of George Koonce). Some identifying information (e.g., team affiliation) has been altered to ensure confidentiality. The names of players mentioned by name in research interviews by respondents have also been disguised. Names of former players interviewed for S. Coakley 2006 (Coakley, Stephany C. 2006. *A Phenomenological Exploration of the Sport-Career Transition Experiences That Affect Subjective Well-Being of Former National Football League Players*. Greensboro: University of North Carolina–Greensboro) have also been withheld. Names of interview subjects in media interviews are indicated as in original sources.
5. Research interview #41.
6. Research interview #40.
7. Research Interview #04.
8. Oriard 1982. Also see Oriard, Michael. 1993. *Reading Football*. Chapel Hill: University of North Carolina Press. Oriard's 1982 football autobiography is by far the most analytic and insightful insider's view of the everyday features of football life and culture.
9. Research interview #03.
10. See Brooks, Scott N. 2009. *Black Men Can't Shoot*. Chicago: University of Chicago Press, for an insightful study of elite urban youth basketball players and their full-time commitment to their games and "getting known."
11. Research interview #40.
12. Glicksman, Ben. December 21, 2010. "Crenshaw Football Star De'Anthony Thomas Has Hollywood Flair." *SportsIllustrated.com*. http://sportsillustrated.cnn.com/2010/specials/highschool-potw/12/21/hspotw.11/index.html, retrieved 3/19/13. Jenkins, Lee. September 24, 2012. "Can't Touch DAT." Sports Illustrated, p. 47.
13. Bassinger, H.G. "Buzz." 1991. *Friday Night Lights*. New York: Harper.
14. Such practices, however, often take insidious turns. Stories of high school athletes running amok, operating outside the law, and displaying little regard for other persons or property are common. Taken to the extreme, we hear stories of sexual exploitation and assault, with accompanying accounts of lax law enforcement and community efforts to conceal the transgressions of esteemed athletes. For a recent example, see accounts of the Steubenville, Ohio, case involving two high school football players convicted of raping a 16-year-old girl. In addition, Ohio attorney general Mike DeWine is considering further charges relating to community efforts to cover up the rape. See Almasy, Steve. March 17, 2013. "Two Teens Found Guilty in Steubenville Rape Case." *CNN*.

com. http://www.cnn.com/2013/03/17/justice/ohio-steubenville-case/index.
html, retrieved 3/18/13.

15. Research interview #40.

16. O'Shaugnessy, Lynn. June 22, 2010. "7 Things You Need to Know about Sports Scholarships." *USnews.com*. http://www.usnews.com/education/blogs/the-college-solution/2010/06/22/7-things-you-need-to-know-about-sports-scholarships, retrieved 3/17/13.

17. Helman, David. July 26, 2012. "LSU Courts Middle Schooler." *ESPN.com*. http://espn.go.com/college-football/story/_/id/8199497/soon-8th-grader-dylan-moses-offered-lsu-tigers-scholarship, retrieved 2/27/13.

18. "UO Faculty Speak Out against 'Preoccupation' with Athletics." January 7, 2012. *Dailyemerald.com*. http://dailyemerald.com/2007/01/17/uo-faculty-speak-out-against-preoccupation-with-athletics/; Associated Press. January 7, 2011. "Texas Tech on Two Years Probation." *ESPN.com* http://sports.espn.go.com/ncf/news/story?id=5999907; both retrieved 4/14/13.

19. Mandel, Stewart. January 25, 2013. "NCAA Rule Change Could Spark State of Recruiting Chaos." *SportsIllustrated.cnn.com*. http://sportsillustrated.cnn.com/college-football/news/20130125/ncaa-rulebook-changes-recruiting/, retrieved 4/15/13.

20. Staples, Andy. February 7, 2013. "How Ole Miss Landed Its Historic Recruiting Class." *SportsIllustrated.cnn.com*. http://sportsillustrated.cnn.com/college-football/news/20130207/hugh-freeze-ole-miss-signing-day/, retrieved 4/14/13.

21. Stephenson, Creg. February 7, 2013. "Ole Miss' Recruitment of Laramy Tunsil Included 800 Facebook Messages." *AL.com*. http://www.al.com/sports/index.ssf/2013/02/sicom_report_ole_miss_recruitm.html, retrieved 4/14/13.

22. "Timeline of Investigation at the University of Southern California." June 26, 2010. *USAToday.com*. http://usatoday30.usatoday.com/sports/college/2010-06-10-usc-timeline-bush-mayo-violations_N.htm; Howard, Johnette. November 5, 2010. "Cam Newton Allegations Raise Questions." *ESPN.com*. http://sports.espn.go.com/espn/commentary/news/story?page=howard/101105; both retrieved 4/15/13.

23. "Ole Miss Recruit Raises Suspicions of Recruiting Violations." January 30, 2013. *Fannation.com*. http://www.fannation.com/truth_and_rumors/view/364970-ole-miss-recruit-raises-suspicions-of-recruiting-violations, retrieved 4/15/13.

24. Bacon, John U. 2011. *Three and Out*. New York: Farrar, Strauss and Giroux, p. 392.

25. Research interview #30.

26. This includes perennial powerhouses USC, Alabama, and Florida State, among others. See, for example: Gould, Mark. N.d. "Cheating Scandals: The Legacy of College Football." *@yourlibrary.com*. http://atyourlibrary.org/sports/cheating-scandals-legacy-college-football, retrieved 4/15/13.

27. Oriard, Michael. 2009. *Bowled Over*. Chapel Hill: University of North Carolina Press, p. 263.

28. Ibid., p. 205.

29. Rhoden, William C. 2006. *Forty Million Dollar Slaves*. New York: Crown, p. 176. Rhoden is writing primarily about basketball and black athletes, but his analysis applies to all potential participants in big-time American sports.

30. Oriard 2009, p. 1.

31. Research interview #302.

32. Bacon 2011. Also see Oriard 2009, p. 204.

33. See Bacon 2011 for a discussion of the difficulties of monitoring compliance with the practice hours limitations at the University of Michigan.

34. Carnival, Barking. May 9, 2010. "College Football: Are 35 Bowl Games Too Many?" *Bleacherreport.com*. http://bleacherreport.com/articles/389979-college-football-are-35-bowl-games-too-many, retrieved 5/26/13.

35. See Eitzen, Stanley. 2009. *Fair and Foul: Beyond the Myths and Paradoxes of Sport*. Lanham, MD: Rowman & Littlefield, ch. 9; Oriard 2009. In the spring of 2014, Shabazz Napier, star of the recently crowned NCAA basketball champion University of Connecticut Huskies, sparked headlines by pointing out that even full-ride scholarship athletes often go to bed hungry due to the restrictions on their scholarship meal plans. His comments have further incited a national controversy over the equity of college players' "compensation" for their athletic participation and contributions. See Ganim, Sara. April 8, 2014. "UConn Guard on Unions: I Go to Bed 'Starving.'" *CNN.com*. http://www.cnn.com/2014/04/07/us/ncaa-basketball-finals-shabazz-napier-hungry/, retrieved 4/27/14.

36. *2012–2013 NCAA Division I Manual*. 2012. Section 15.02.01, p. 200. http://www.ncaapublications.com/productdownloads/D113.pdf, retrieved 3/27/13.

37. A few currently retired NFL players went to college prior to the advent of NCAA athletic scholarships in 1956. The one-year scholarship was adopted by the NCAA in 1973. Both of these measures changed the landscape of college football, transforming players' experience and altering the backdrop from which the NFL experience might emerge. See Oriard 2009. By 2015, some universities will begin to grant four-year scholarships.

38. "Financial Aid." 2013. *USC.edu*. http://www.usc.edu/admission/fa/applying_receiving/undergraduates2/costs.html; Sullivan, Kathleen. February 12, 2013. "Stanford Report: Stanford Raises Undergraduate Tuition 3.5 Percent, Continues Financial Aid Commitment for 2013–14 School Year." *New.Stanford.edu*. http://news.stanford.edu/news/2013/february/stanford-undergrad-tuition-021213.html; "Tuition and Fee Rates." 2013. *Miami.edu*. http://www.miami.edu/gs/index.php/graduate_school/costs_and_financial_aid/tuition_and_fee_rates/; Tuchler, Margot. February 22, 2013. "Duke Board Approves Tuition Increase for 2013. *Dukechronicle.com*. http://www.dukechronicle.com/articles/2013/02/22/duke-board-approves-tuition-increase-2013-2014; "Undergraduate Tuition." 2013. *Utexas.edu*. http://www.utexas.edu/business/accounting/pubs/tf_undergrad_fall13.pdf; "Undergraduate Campus Student Tuition." 2012. *Cost.UA.edu*. http://cost.ua.edu/undergraduate-12-13.html; all retrieved 4/23/13.

39. Hill, Jemele. October 10, 2012. "Tweet Shows Truth about Academics." *ESPN.com*. http://espn.go.com/college-football/story/_/id/8484038/tweet-revealed-truth-student-athletes, retrieved 10/6/13. Apparently Ohio State coach Urban Myer didn't appreciate this attitude. He didn't allow Jones to suit up for a game and took away his Twitter account.

40. Bryant, Paul W., and John Underwood. 1974. *Bear: The Hard Life and Good Times of Alabama's Coach Bryant*. Boston: Little, Brown, p. 325.

41. See Eitzen 2009, Oriard 2009.

42. These comparisons are based on Federal Graduation Rate (FGR) statistics for student cohorts entering college in 2005. The FGR is considered a relatively crude measure of the percentage of students who graduate from their original institution of enrollment within a six-year period. The NCAA and others prefer to use a more nuanced measure known as Graduation Success Rate (GSR), which takes into account transfer students, mid-year enrollees, and other factors that affect academic progress. Using GSRs, roughly 70 percent of football players graduate within six years, and more closely approximate the general student body GSR, especially if GSRs for male students only are compared. See NCAA Research Staff. October 2012. "Trends in Graduation-Success Rates and Federal Graduation Rates at NCAA Division I Institutions." *NCAA.org*. http://www.ncaa.org/wps/wcm/connect/public/ncaa/pdfs/2012/D1GsrFgrTrendsPdf, retrieved 4/17/13. Also see Oriard 2009.

43. Research interview #06.

44. Research interview #304.

45. Research interview #03. Siegel is being modest. He made the National Honor Society in his senior year, calling this his only academic "glory."

46. Research interview #20.

47. Bacon 2011, p. 350.

48. Oriard 2009, pp. 183–85.

49. Ibid., p. 184.

50. "The Center for Student Success and Academic Counseling." 2010. *Center for Student Success and Academic Counseling*. http://cssac.unc.edu/athletic-counseling-program, retrieved 4/18/13.

51. "Clara Bell Smith Center." 2010. *Student-Athlete Support Services*. http://www.sass.msu.edu/facilities/SmithCenter.html, retrieved 4/18/13.

52. Research interview #40. At that point, the NCAA was very vague about limits on a player's "practice time," but it has since tightened restrictions on the number of hours a player may devote to football each week.

53. Ibid.

54. Hill, October 10, 2012.

55. Oriard 2009. On our own Marquette University campus (where there is no football program), well over half of men's basketball players are enrolled in the

College of Communication, where core curriculum requirements are somewhat less demanding than in, say, the College of Arts and Sciences.

56. See Adler, Patricia A., and Peter Adler. 1991. *Backboards and Blackboards*. New York: Columbia University Press; Ridpath, David. 2012. *Tainted Glory: Marshall University, the NCAA and One Man's Fight for Justice*. Bloomington, IN: iUniverse.

57. Wolff, Alexander. October 14, 1991. "Upstairs, Downstairs." *SIVault.com*. http://sportsillustrated.cnn.com/vault/article/magazine/MAG1140491/1/index.htm, retrieved 4/15/14.

58. Sisney, Steve. May 6, 2012. "Housing Facility Seen as Boon for OU Athletics." *TulsaWorld.com*. http://www.tulsaworld.com/article.aspx/Housing_facility_seen_as_boon_for_OU_athletics/20120506_92_b1_ulnsok83242, retrieved 4/19/13.

59. Oriard 2009.

60. Wolff, October 14, 1991. Also see Oriard 2009, pp. 214–15. There are a notable number of parallel cases of athletic dorm culture contributing to campus troubles, including incidents at Oklahoma, Colorado, USC, and Missouri.

61. See Adler and Adler 1991.

62. Research interview #40.

63. Rosenberg, Michael. January 7, 2011. "Nike's Phil Knight Has Branded Oregon into National Power." *SI.com*. http://sportsillustrated.cnn.com/2011/writers/michael_rosenberg/01/06/oregon.knight/index.html; Zimmerman, Ann, and Leslie Scism. July 6, 2012. "Boone Calls the Plays as Largess Complicates Life at Alma Mater." *WSJ.com*. http://online.wsj.com/article/SB10001424052702304782404577488859279 3245510.html; both retrieved 8/16/13.

64. National Collegiate Athletic Association. N.d. "Student-Athlete Benefits." *NCAAStudent.org*. http://www.ncaa.org/wps/wcm/connect/public/NCAA/Finances/Finances+Student+Athlete+Benefits, retrieved 4/23/13.

65. Roberts, Selena. April 3, 2013. "Auburn's Tainted Title." *Roopstigo.com*. http://www.roopstigo.com/reader/auburns_vainted_title_victims_violations_and_vendettas_for_glory/, retrieved 4/23/13. Many of the allegations have been disputed. See "Report: Auburn Bribed Players." April 4, 2013. *ESPN.com*. http://espn.go.com/college-football/story/_/id/9131624/auburn-tigers-coaches-bribed-players-altered-grades-broke-recruiting-rules-gene-chizik-according-report, retrieved 4/23/13.

66. Thamel, Pete. August 16, 2011. "Hurricane Players and Recruits Accused of NCAA Violation." *NYTimes.com*. http://www.nytimes.com/2011/08/17/sports/ncaafootball/miami-hurricanes-accused-of-ncaa-violations.html?_r=0; "How the NCAA's Mishandling of the Miami Case Exposed an Enforcement Department Seemingly Powerless to Do Its Job." June 12, 2013. *InsideSpotsIllustrated.com*. http://insidesportsillustrated.com/2013/06/12/si-special-report-ncaa-miami/; both retrieved 4/15/14.

67. Dolan, Jack, Ruben Vives, and Gary Klein. September 1, 2012. "Figure in Assessor's Scandal Says He Gave Gifts to 2 USC Athletes." *LATimes.com*. http://articles.latimes.com/2012/sep/01/local/la-me-assessor-usc-20120902, retrieved 4/25/13.

68. Cash, Rana. December 23, 2010. "Pryor, Four Other OSU Players Suspended First Five Games in 2011 for Accepting Improper Benefits." *SportingNews.com*. http://aol.sportingnews.com/ncaa-football/feed/2010-12/osu-suspensions/story/reports-osu-investigating-tattoo-allegations, retrieved 4/25/13.

69. Oriard 2009, p. 211.

70. Ibid.

71. Thompson, Wright. N.d. "Outside the Lines: The Redemption of Billy Cannon." *ESPN.com*. http://espn.go.com/espn/print?id=4603346&type=story, retrieved 3/4/13. Some would argue that these instances of turning illicit profits are better characterized as efforts to capitalize financially on well-earned personal notoriety rather than simply letting colleges reap the financial rewards of the work and reputations of their players.

72. Research interview #41. Critics of the NCAA argue that such petty violations would decrease if players were provided with modest stipends to cover incidental expenses.

73. *SportsCenter*. April 25, 2013. ESPN-TV.

74. Of course, the special attention sometimes becomes a burden. Johnny Manziel, the 2012 Heisman Trophy winner, became such a campus sensation after his sterling freshman season at Texas A&M that he was mobbed everywhere he went on campus. This led him to enroll in only online courses in the spring semester of 2013. See Swerneman, Brent. February 19, 2013. "Johnny Football Taking Online Classes This Semester." *MYSA.com*. http://www.mysanantonio.com/news/local_news/article/Heisman-winner-too-cool-for-school-4288712.php, retrieved 6/17/13.

75. See Brooks 2009, for example.

76. See Cooley, Charles H. 1902. *Human Nature and Social Order*. New York: Scribners; Mead, G.H. 1934. *Mind, Self, and Society*. Chicago: University of Chicago Press.

77. See Woods, Ronald B. 2011. *Social Issues in Sport*. Champaign, IL: Human Kinetics.

78. Ibid.

79. See, for example, Fisher, Bonnie S., Leah E. Daigel, and Francis T. Cullen. 2010. *Unsafe in the Ivory Tower*. Thousand Oaks, CA: Sage; Bernstein, Nina. November 11, 2011. "On Campus, a Law Enforcement System to Itself." *NYTimes.com*. http://www.nytimes.com/2011/11/12/us/on-college-campuses-athletes-often-get-off-easy.html?pagewanted=all&_r=0, retrieved 4/23/13.

80. "Family Educational Rights and Privacy Act (FERPA)." N.d. *ED.gov*. https://www.ed.gov/policy/gen/guid/fpco/ferpa/index.html, retrieved 4/23/13. FERPA is generally interpreted to cover records relating to grades and other academic information, but also extends to disciplinary records.

81. See Benedict, Jeffrey, and Alan M. Klein. 1997. "Arrest and Conviction Rates for Athletes Convicted of Sexual Assault." *Sociology of Sport Journal* 14: 86–93. In recent cases at Marquette University, for example, Gerald Boyle, defense attorney

for mass murderer Jeffrey Dahmer, represented high-profile student athletes at criminal proceedings and university administrative hearings. See Haggerty, Ryan, Todd Lightly, and Stacy St. Clair. October 28, 2011. "One Woman's Stand against College Athletes." *ChicagoTribune.com*. http://articles.chicagotribune.com/2011-10-28/sports/ct-met-marquette-sex-cases-20111028_1_athletes-campus-security-sexual-assault-policies/3, retrieved 4/23/13.

82. A rash of incidents involving high-profile players and programs in the past few years has apparently prompted the NCAA, universities, and coaches to more aggressively deal with lawless behavior, but typically, even serious violations are handled within teams' disciplinary framework, with players less frequently answering to the criminal justice system. See, for example, Axson, Scooby. July 31, 2013. "Ohio State Suspends RB Carlos Hyde for at Least Three Games." *SIWire. com*. http://tracking.si.com/2013/07/30/ohio-state-carlos-hyde-suspended-three-games/, retrieved 7/31/13.

83. Again, Rhoden is writing most pointedly about young, black athletes, but his argument pertains across racial lines as well.

84. Rhoden 2006, pp. 176–77.

85. Ibid., pp. 176, 180, 194.

86. See Adler and Adler 1991.

87. Oriard 2009, p. 271.

88. Adler and Adler 1991.

89. Ibid.

90. Chadiha, Jeffri. May 31, 2012. "Life after NFL a Challenge for Many." *ESPN.com*. http://espn.go.com/nfl/story/_/id/7983790/life-nfl-struggle-many-former-players, retrieved 1/12/13.

91. See Oriard 1982.

92. Ibid., p. 76.

93. Underwood, John. January 10, 1983. "Casting a Special Light." *SIVault.com*. http://sportsillustrated.cnn.com/vault/article/magazine/MAG1120418/1/index.htm, retrieved 2/12/13.

94. Bateman, Oliver Lee. May 3, 2012. "Michael Oriard: Ordinary NFL Player, Extraordinary Man." *GoodMenProject.com*. http://goodmenproject.com/featured-content/michael-oriard-ordinary-nfl-player-extraordinary-man/, retrieved 1/21/13.

95. Oriard 1982, p. 155.

CHAPTER 2. INSIDE "THE BUBBLE"

1. Research interview #40. Others also refer to "the bubble" in various contexts, implying isolation, special treatment, and heightened scrutiny. See, for example, Dawidoff, Nicholas. 2013. *Collision Low Crossers; A Year inside the Turbulent World of NFL Football*. New York: Little, Brown.

2. Research interview #03.

3. Telander, Rick. 1986. "Football and Violence," pp. 173–82, in Eitzen, Stanley (ed.). 1996. *Sport in Contemporary Society*, 5th ed. New York: St. Martin's.
4. Oriard, Michael. 2007. *Brand NFL: Making and Selling America's Favorite Sport.* Chapel Hill: University of North Carolina Press, p. 199.
5. Billick, Brian. 2009. *More than a Game.* New York: Scribners, pp. 122–23.
6. Let's not exaggerate. Football isn't rocket science. Prospective NFL players score roughly the same as any other group of job applicants, averaging about 21 out of 50, the equivalent of an IQ slightly over 100. Rocket scientists (electrical engineers, to be precise) average about 30—around the range of NFL quarterbacks. See Merron, Jeff. N.d. "Taking Your Wonderlics." *ESPN.com.* http://espn.go.com/page2/s/closer/020228.html, retrieved 6/28/13.
7. Richardson, Peter. 2010. *Badasses.* New York: Harper, p. 350.
8. Ozanian, Mike. August 14, 2013. "The Most Valuable NFL Teams." *Forbes.com.* http://www.forbes.com/sites/mikeozanian/2013/08/14/the-most-valuable-nfl-teams/, retrieved 8/21/13.
9. Cunha, Darlena. N.d. "How Much Money Does an NFL Player Make?" *Chron.com.* http://work.chron.com/much-money-nfl-player-make-year-2377.html, retrieved 5/29/13. The league salary cap was $123 million per team, up a little over one percent from 2011. That means that owners paid players only about ten percent of an average franchise's worth. See Wesseling, Chris. February 28, 2013. "NFL Sets 2013 Salary Cap at $123M, Up from $120.6 Million." *NFL.com.* http://www.nfl.com/news/story/0ap1000000146046/article/nfl-sets-2013-salary-cap-at-123m-up-from-1206m, retrieved 6/25/13.
10. Silverstein, Tom. April 26, 2013. "Packers Sign Aaron Rodgers to a Record-Setting, Five-Year, $100 Million Extension." *JSOnline.com.* http://www.jsonline.com/sports/packers/rodgers27-pc9no4i-204948841.html, retrieved 5/29/13.
11. Roberts, Daniel. N.d. "Fortunate 50." *SI.com.* http://sportsillustrated.cnn.com/specials/fortunate50-2013/; Smith, Michael David. July 18, 2012. "In Salary and Endorsements, Peyton Remains the NFL's Richest." *NBCSports.com.* http://profootballtalk.nbcsports.com/2012/07/18/in-salary-and-endorsements-peyton-remains-the-nfls-richest/; "Highest Paid NFL Players on Forbes List." June 19, 2012. *NFL.com.* http://www.nfl.com/photoessays/09000d5d829f6793#photo=4; all retrieved 6/2/13.
12. Bryan, Dave. July 23, 2011. "2011–2014 NFL Minimum Base Salaries." *SteelersDepot.com.* http://www.steelersdepot.com/2011/07/2011-2014-nfl-minimum-base-salaries/, retrieved 5/29/13. In addition, the CBA established a framework for rookie salaries that limits both the amount and length of rookie contracts. The effect has been to drastically reduce the contracts of high draft picks, thus freeing up money to devote to veteran players. The long-range effect is to suppress wages for newer players, keeping their salaries in check until they earn the right to enter the free agent market. This salary scale is not carved in stone; there are several ways that

salaries may be adjusted, based on time on the roster, performance bonuses, and similar factors.

13. Dorish, Joe. November 12, 2011. "Average Salaries in the NBA, NFL, MLB and NHL." *Yahoo.com*. http://sports.yahoo.com/nba/news?slug=ycn-10423863, retrieved 5/29/14. There are three principle reasons for the NFL's third-place status. First, each NFL team has a 53-player roster, but they also pay several additional players each season as partial season replacements for injured and/or suspended players. There are 32 NFL teams, for a total of 1,696 players (not counting replacements). That's about four times the number of players in the NBA and over twice as many players as in MLB. The players' share of revenue is thus diluted over a larger membership. Second, NFL teams play only 16 games in the regular season, just a small fraction of the number of games played in each of the other major sports leagues. Fewer games mean less opportunity to generate income. Third, NFL CBAs have not been as favorable to NFL players as are CBAs in the other leagues, especially with respect to guaranteed contracts. So, even though the NFL generates more income than do the other leagues, the individual players' earnings are considerably less.

14. "NFL Average Salaries by Position." N.d. *SI.com*. http://sportsillustrated.cnn.com/nfl/photos/1301/nfl-average-salaries-by-position/, retrieved 5/29/13.

15. It's also difficult to determine exactly how much a player is making each year, given the structuring of contracts, bonuses, guaranteed, and non-guaranteed money. Nevertheless, the $2.3 million average is in the ballpark with what 2011 salary figures project.

16. Cunha, n.d. Calculation of the median also suffers from the same vagaries that plague the calculation of the mean—the actual number of players to bring into the calculation.

17. Calculating the average length of a career is also problematic. See "What Is the Average NFL Player's Career Length?" April 18, 2011. *NFLcommunications.com*. http://nflcommunications.com/2011/04/18/what-is-average-nfl-player%E2%80%99s-career-length-longer-than-you-might-think-commissioner-goodell-says/; Bennett, Dashiell. April 18, 2011. "The NFL's Official Spin on Average Career Length Is a Joke." *Businessinsider.com*. http://www.businessinsider.com/nfls-spin-average-career-length-2011-4; both retrieved 6/25/13.

18. See Oriard 2007.

19. Others have done similar speculative calculations based on slightly different assumptions that place the earnings figure at about $2.75 million for an "average" career. See Koebler, Hank. July 21, 2011. "Debunking the 'Greedy Players' Myth." *Huffingtonpost.com*. http://www.huffingtonpost.com/hank-koebler/debunking-the-greedy-play_b_906400.html?view=print&comm_ref=false, retrieved 6/23/13.

20. O'Toole, Shannon. 2006. *Wedded to the Game*. Lincoln: University of Nebraska Press, p. 135.

21. The USFL worked under a salary cap to restrict spending, but also signed many high-profile players including three consecutive Heisman Trophy winners (Herschel Walker, Doug Flutie, and Mike Rosier) and a number of future Hall of Famers, including Reggie White, Jim Kelly, and Steve Young.

22. Oriard 2007.

23. Ibid.

24. Taylor, Jim. 2010. *The Fire Within*. Chicago: Triumph, pp. 70–72.

25. Davis, Willie. 2012. *Closing the Gap*. Chicago: Triumph.

26. Research interview #03.

27. This was generally reported to be a three-year deal. "Joe Namath Fast Facts." May 29, 2013. *CNN.com*. http://www.cnn.com/2013/05/29/us/joe-namath-fast-facts, retrieved 6/4/13.

28. Oriard 2007; Anderson's deal was for three years and was guaranteed. See "Donny Anderson Signs Pro Football's Richest Pact." 2008. *Lubbockcentennial*. http://www.lubbockcentennial.com/Section/1959_1983/donnyanderson.shtml, retrieved 6/4/13.

29. Oriard 1982.

30. Oriard 2007, *Broke*.

31. Research interview #23.

32. Oriard 2007, O'Toole 2006.

33. Contrary to popular wisdom, nothing in the NFL CBA forbids guaranteed contracts. It is simply standard practice, enforced in unison by NFL owners and endured by the NFLPA. See Oriard 2007.

34. Porter, Austin. February 21, 2012. "How Far Does an NFL Contract Really Go?" *Bleacherreport.com*. http://bleacherreport.com/articles/1074216-how-far-does-an-nfl-contract-really-go, retrieved 5/29/13; O'Toole 2006; Sando, Mike. March 7, 2013. "How Do Contracts Often Work?" *ESPN.com*. http://espn.go.com/blog/nflnation/post/_/id/73449/how-do-contracts-work-glad-you-asked, retrieved 5/30/13; Oriard 2007. Contracts are described in terms of being "front-loaded" or "back-loaded." Front-loaded contracts call for large signing bonuses that are guaranteed, and may also include large salaries in the early years. Front-loaded contacts generally assure a player a substantial share of the total amount a long-term contract calls for. Teams generally resist such contracts, but for salary cap reasons, it's sometimes advantageous for teams to offer large signing bonuses because the amount counting against the salary cap will be spread out over the entire length of the contract, even if it is paid up front. Back-loaded contracts call for escalating salaries, with the later years on a contract promising extremely high rates of pay. The problem for a player comes in those later years, when he can be asked to restructure his contract or simply be released. This is especially likely if the player's on-field contributions decline due to injury or age. One technique used to serve both the interest of the player and the team is to negotiate a long-term contract with a large signing bonus or first-year salary (money that

the player is virtually certain to get), then reduced salaries over the subsequent seasons. The final years of the contract may then be "back-loaded" with high salaries. This provides the player with a huge contract total, but, after the initial outlay, allows teams to delay paying high salaries and gives the team the option of cutting players who may not be worth what the team deems prudent in the later years of a contract. The middle years of the contract end up being more modestly priced. See Vinton, Nathaniel. February 1, 2011. "Shannon O'Toole, Wife of NFL Coach, Pens Tome to Debunk Perception of 'Gold-digging' NFL Wives." *NYdailynews.com*. http://www.nydailynews.com/sports/football/shannon-o-toole-wife-nfl-coach-pens-tome-debunk-perception-gold-digging-nfl-wives-article-1.137752, retrieved 3/4/13; Oriard 2007.

35. "Nnamdi Asomugha Signs with Eagles." July 30, 2011. *ESPN.com*. http://espn.go.com/nfl/story/_/id/6816873/nnamdi-asomugha-agrees-five-year-60-million-deal-philadelphia-eagles, retrieved 4/15/14.

36. McGinn, Bob. March 18, 2013. "Less for A.J. Hawk's Nest Egg." *JSOnline*. http://www.jsonline.com/sports/packers/less-for-hawks-nest-egg-9k979sl-198900081.html, retrieved 5/30/13. One might wonder if Hawk and his agent made a terrible mistake in signing his original contract, which was heavily back-loaded. Such contracts, however, are not *necessarily* detrimental to the player. In this case, Hawk was betting that, as the fifth overall pick in the 2006 draft, he would become an indispensable impact player for the Packers. Thus, when his large paydays were due in the later years of his contract, he figured to be in his playing prime, and the Packers would be reluctant to release him. Hawk became a solid starter, but not an impact player, so his market value was more limited than he originally foresaw. With a non-guaranteed contract, he lost bargaining leverage.

37. Research interview #42.

38. "Wizard of Oz Quotes." N.d. *IMDB.com*. http://www.imdb.com/title/tt0032138/quotes, retrieved 4/14/13.

39. Research interview #42.

40. See any NFL player biography or autobiography for at least one chapter on training camp, and another on the daily grind. See Feinstein, John. 2005. *Next Man Up*. New York: Little, Brown.

41. See Favre and Havel 1997, Oriard 1982.

42. Quarterbacks and other players required to direct the offense and defense, and call signals, are especially prone to long hours of film study—often taking game film home with them at the end of the day. See Feinstein, 2005.

43. Brandt, Andrew. May 9, 2012. "Why Life after Football Can Be Bumpy." *ESPN.com*. http://espn.go.com/nfl/story/_/id/7908563/nfl-why-life-football-bumpy, retrieved 5/12/12.

44. See Feinstein 2005; Freeman, Mike. 2003. *Bloody Sundays*. New York: William Morrow; Oriard 1982. Dawidoff 2013 describes how the NFL has come to be known as the "No Fun League."

45. Brandt, May 9, 2012.

46. Murphy, Joel. October 18, 2012. "Phillip Daniels Discusses His New Role, Hopes to Coach." *Homermcfanboy*.com. http://www.homermcfanboy.com/2012/10/18/phillip-daniels-discusses-his-new-role-hopes-to-coach/, retrieved 10/18/12; Green Bay Packers. 2006. *Green Bay Packers Player Development Manual 2006–2007* (hereafter *Packers Player Development Manual*).

47. Nickel, Lori. June 4, 2013. "Johnny Jolly Gets a Second Chance." *JSOnline.com*. http://www.jsonline.com/sports/packers/johnny-jolly-gets-a-second-chance-b99263012l-210193011.html, retrieved 4/15/14.

48. See Eitzen 2009 for a discussion of sports, conservative ideology, and social control.

49. Freeman 2003. Also see Feinstein 2005, Dawidoff 2013.

50. Borden, Sam. October 4, 2012. "Standing Out after the Game." *NYTimes.com*. http://www.nytimes.com/2012/10/05/sports/football/after-the-game-nfl-players-set-their-own-rules-on-style.html?pagewanted=all&_r=0, retrieved 6/9/13.

51. See *Official Playing Rules and Casebook of the NFL 2012*, Section 4. 2012. *NFL.com*. http://static.nfl.com/static/content/public/image/rulebook/pdfs/2012%20-%20Rule%20Book.pdf, retrieved 6/9/13.

52. See Feinstein 2005. In an ironic test of allegiance, some teams employ their player development directors or other former payers as their uniform inspectors. See Murphy, October 18, 2012.

53. Social theorist Michel Foucault puts it slightly differently: "There is no power relation without the correlative constitution of a field of knowledge, nor any knowledge that does not presuppose and constitute at the same time power relations. . . . [Subjects'] visibility assures the hold of the power that is exercised over them. It is this fact of being constantly seen, of being able always to be seen, that maintains the disciplined individual in his subjection." Foucault, Michel. 1979. *Discipline and Punish*. New York: Vintage, pp. 27, 187.

54. Taylor 2010, pp. 70–72.

55. Oriard 2007, p. 68.

56. O'Toole 2006.

57. Favre and Havel 1997, p. 193. Instances like this are standard fare for some players.

58. See Pearlman, Jeff. 2008. *Boys Will Be Boys*. New York: Harper, p. 166.

59. O'Toole 2006.

60. White, Reggie. 2004. *Reggie White in the Trenches*. New York: Thomas Nelson, p. 121. For some women, the pursuit of NFL players is an art form, but for others it's serious business. There's even a web site—"Baller Alert"—devoted to tracking male celebrities, prominently including NFL players.

61. Associated Press. May 24, 2013. "Brett Favre Sexting Suit Settled in NYC." *Newsday.com*. http://www.newsday.com/sports/football/brett-favre-sexting-suit-settled-in-nyc-1.5334742, retrieved 4/23/13.

62. Also see Taylor 2010 for discussion of punishments for transgressions.

63. For more on domestic violence in the NFL, see Freeman 2003, O'Toole 2006, or recent accounts of the way the NFL has dealt with the case of Ray Rice.

64. Freeman 2003, pp. 165–66.

65. O'Toole 2006, p. 165.

66. From the beginning of his earliest troubles, the Packers have closely monitored Jolly's behavior, and he's received considerable attention from the player development staff. After his release from prison in 2012, the Packers kept tabs on him through periodic telephone calls from teammates and coaches, plus calls to his mother, trying to make sure he was staying on the path to recovery and return to football. (See Nickel, June 4, 2013.) The team's interest was at least partially altruistic—looking out for Jolly's best interest as well as keeping track of a valuable team asset. But any form of surveillance—as benign as it may seem—is nevertheless a means of exercising power and discipline, of expanding control over all aspects of players' lives. As Michel Foucault (1979) argues, constant and ubiquitous supervision and forced discipline are used to capture the will of those under surveillance, to produce "docile bodies"—that is, subjects more easily managed and controlled by authorities—all the while giving the impression that this is in the best interest of those under surveillance. Here we see the two sides of the player development coin in practice.

67. Nickel, June 4, 2013.

68. See Feinstein 2005, Freeman 2003, Oriard 1982.

69. Research interview #305.

70. O'Toole 2006.

71. See Oriard 1982.

72. Ibid., p. 225.

73. O'Toole 2006.

74. Oriard 1982, p. 225–27. Also see O'Toole 2006.

75. O'Toole 2006, p. 33.

76. S. Coakley 2006, p. 67 (research interview).

77. Brandt, May 9, 2012.

78. Rhoden 2006, p. 177.

79. Freeman 2003, p. 269.

80. O'Toole 2006, p. 18.

81. Ibid., p. 31.

82. See O'Toole 2006; Vinton, February 1, 2011.

83. Research interview #41.

84. See *Broke*.

85. This is a reflexive relationship. The bubble and the ethos are mutually constitutive. Neither is primordial or foundational. One can't fully exist apart from the other. For more on reflexivity, see Garfinkel, Harold. 1967. *Studies in Ethnomethodology*. Englewood Cliffs, NJ: Prentice-Hall.

86. "Green Bay Packers 2007 Vision Statement." *Packers Player Development Manual*.

87. See Eitzen, Stanley, and George H. Sage. 2009. *Sociology of North American Sport.* Boulder, CO: Paradigm.

88. The term's use is especially common in British discussions of sport and society, but it also appears in American contexts. See Rosen, Joel. 2007. *The Erosion of the American Sporting Ethos: Shifting Attitudes toward Competition.* Jefferson, NC: McFarland.

89. See Coakley, Jay. 2008. *Sports in Society,* 10th ed. New York: McGraw Hill.

90. See Bernstein, Ross. 2009. *The Code.* Chicago: Triumph.

91. See Clemmer, Donald. 1940. *The Prison Community.* Boston: Christopher Publishing; Anderson, Elijah. 1999. *Code of the Street.* New York: Norton.

92. See Gubrium and Holstein 1997; Holstein, James A., and Richard S. Jones. 1992. "Short Time, Hard Time: Accounts of Short-Term Imprisonment." *Perspectives on Social Problems* 3: 289–309.

93. Eisen, Rich. 2007. *Total Access.* New York: Thomas Dunn, p. 7.

94. *Broke.*

95. Freeman, Mike. April 24, 2013. "NFL Draft Prospects Continue to Throw Money Around." *CBSSports.com.* http://www.cbssports.com/nfl/blog/mike-freeman/22116358/nfl-draft-prospects-continue-to-throw-money-around, retrieved 4/25/13; *Broke.*

96. *Outside the Lines:* "Athletes and Guns." March 22, 2013. *ESPN.com.* http://espn.go.com/video/clip?id=9086459, retrieved 4/15/14.

97. Oriard 2007, pp. 208–9.

98. Ibid, p. 209.

99. Ibid, p. 200.

100. Tuaolo, Esera. 2006. *Alone in the Trenches.* Naperville, IL: Sourcebooks, p. 22.

101. Toughness and courage are predominant themes in just about all accounts of the NFL experience, regardless of historical era. See, for example, Davis 2012, Feinstein 2005, Freeman 2003, Oriard 1982, Richmond 2010, Taylor 2010.

102. LeGere, Bob. N.d. "An Inspiration: Bears Past, Present Acknowledge Payton's Legacy. *Dailyherald.com.* https://prev.dailyherald.com/special/payton/payton31.htm, retrieved 5/2/13. Also see Freeman 2003.

103. See Eitzen 2009; Eitzen and Sage 2009; Messner, Michael. 1992. *Power at Play: Sports and the Problem of Masculinity.* Boston: Beacon; Messner, Michael. 2002. *Taking the Field: Women, Men, and Sports.* St. Paul: University of Minnesota Press; Messner, Michael. 2007. *Out of Play: Critical Essays on Gender and Sport.* Albany: State University of New York Press; Oriard 1993.

104. S. Coakley 2006, pp. 107–8 (research interview).

105. The notion of compulsory masculinity refers to the assumption that everyone is heterosexual. Assuming this as the norm, masculine identity is imposed by default. Sexuality and masculinity are thus conflated. See Rich, Adrienne. 1980. "Compulsory Heterosexuality and Lesbian Experience." *Signs* 5(4): 631–60. Recently, challenges to these assumptions have surfaced around the NFL. Commentary from insiders and gay former players is skeptical, even as many remain hopeful. See Freeman 2003; Freeman,

Mike. November 6, 2013. "Ten Point Stance." *Bleacherreport.com*. http://bleacher-report.com/articles/1838030-ten-point-stance-mike-freemans-nfl-notebook-head-ing-into-week-10, retrieved 11/10/13; Tuaolo 2006; "Gay NFL Players." N.d. *Huffing-tonpost.com*. http://www.huffingtonpost.com/tag/gay-nfl-players, retrieved 4/15/14.

106. Feinstein 2005, p. 252.

107. Freeman 2003, p. xix.

108. Anderson 1999.

109. Research interview #302.

110. See Eisen 2007, Oriard 2007, O'Toole 2006.

111. *Broke.*

112. Of course, livin' large has historical and generational parameters. In the begin-ning, NFL players had neither the opportunity nor the resources to pursue the kind of decadence seen today. By the 1970s, the Oakland Raiders had raised livin' large to high art, but within the financial means of the time. Carousing and iconoclastic behavior were their "badass" calling cards (see Richmond 2010). By the 1990s, NFL salaries allowed for the kind of "stunting" and monetary madness that came to embody the contemporary version of livin' large.

113. *Mike and Mike.* February 5, 2013. ESPN2-TV.

114. Research interview #20.

115. For example, Packer Max McGee's shenanigans and humorous defiance of Vince Lombardi's locker room authority made him a folk hero around the NFL. See Taylor 2010. Taking locker room culture into the outside world in the "off hours" is a mark of livin' large.

116. See Oriard 1982.

117. O'Toole 2006, p. 128.

118. Research interview #22.

119. Lapchick, Richard. October 22, 2013. "The Racial and Gender Report Card: National Football League." *Tidesport.org*. http://www.tidesport.org/RGRC/2013/2013_NFL_RGRC.pdf, retrieved 4/15/14 (hereafter Racial Report Card). Quite remarkably, in light of the changing demographics of the U.S. and of other major professional sports, less than two percent of NFL players are Latino or Asian American, and just over one percent are "international."

120. See Oriard 2007.

121. Ibid.

122. *Mike and Mike.* November 5, 2013. ESPN2-TV.

123. Research interview #05.

124. The Racial Report Card indicates that the practice of "stacking" African Ameri-cans at particular positions by virtue of race is no longer an issue of concern. The physical demands of the various positions seem to dictate racial distributions more than discriminatory practices.

125. Dunne, Tyler. November 29, 2011. "Lang Has Turned from Life of Party to All Business." *JSOnline.com*. http://www.jsonline.com/sports/packers/

wakeup-call-a838c6k-134726453.html; Dunne, Tyler. January 3, 2013. "Packers' Dietrich-Smith Has Life in Order." *JSOnline.com*. http://www.jsonline.com/sports/packers/packers-dietrichsmith-has-life-in-order-pv8870a-185622911.html; both retrieved 11/3/13.

126. Research interview #305. Also see Feinstein 2005; Freeman, Mike. February 2, 1999. "Robinson's Arrest Looms Large after the Falcons Defeat." *NYTimes.com*. http://www.nytimes.com/1999/02/02/sports/super-bowl-xxxiii-robinson-s-arrest-looms-larger-after-the-falcons-defeat.html, retrieved 1/13/13.

127. See Eitzen 2009.

128. Oriard 1982, p. 25.

129. Coser, Lewis. 1974. *Greedy Institutions*. New York: Free Press.

130. See Adler and Adler 1991 for a discussion of other ways that organizations extract intense commitment and loyalty from their members.

CHAPTER 3. THE END

1. Research interview #42.

2. *The Late Show*. January 7, 2013. *CBS.com*. http://www.cbs.com/shows/late_show/video/13E4461C-8715-459E-857B-18C29863F193/the-late-show-1-7-2013, retrieved 3/17/13.

3. Material and quotations from this section on Koonce's retirement come from research interviews #40, 42, and 50.

4. Jerry Glanville, former coach of the Houston Oilers, is credited with coining the phrase during a 1988 discussion with a game official: "This is the N-F-L, which stands for 'not for long' when you make them fuckin' calls. I'll be selling groceries." The use of the phrase has morphed into commentary on the fleeting nature of an NFL career for players and coaches alike. See *Pick Six*: "Glanville: NFL Means 'Not for Long.'" August 5, 2011. *NFL.com*. http://www.nfl.com/videos/nfl-videos/09000d5d8213b6cb/Pick-Six-Glanville-NFL-means-Not-For-Long, retrieved 6/19/13.

5. Research interview #30.

6. As decisive as Chapman's retirement seems, however, note that it came well after he had been released and was technically out of the game—but not necessarily of his own accord.

7. Ellerson, Gary. May 16, 2012. "Life after Football." *SportsRadio1250.com*. http://www.sportsradio1250.com/Gary-Ellerson/11779164, retrieved 8/16/13.

8. Weir, David R., James S. Jackson, and Amanda Sonnega. 2009. "Study of Retired NFL Players." Ann Arbor: University of Michigan Institute for Social Research (hereafter Player Care study; see http://www.ns.umich.edu/Releases/2009/Sep09/FinalReport.pdf, retrieved 7/7/13).

9. O'Toole, 2006, p. 92.

10. See Feinstein 2005.

11. Ibid., p. 218.

12. Lane, Austen. N.d. "What's It Like to Get Whacked?" *SI.com*. http://mmqb. si.com/2013/07/25/what-its-like-to-get-whacked/?sct=hp_t11_ao&eref=sihp, retrieved 7/25/13.

13. See S. Coakley 2006, who similarly observes that uncertainty, fueled by hope and optimism, produces a cognitive unwillingness or unpreparedness to move on.

14. See Coakley, Jay J. 1983. "Leaving Competitive Sport: Retirement or Rebirth?" *Quest* 35: 1–11.

15. *Mike and Mike*. September 26, 2013. ESPN2-TV.

16. Research interview #17.

17. Research interview #60.

18. Player Care study.

19. See Berns, Nancy. 2011. *Closure: The Rush to End Grief and What It Costs Us*. Philadelphia: Temple University Press, for a discussion of how "closure talk" is used to manage the meaning of loss. Also see O'Toole 2006. O'Toole's discussion underscores the degree to which retirement is seldom voluntary and, from wives' vantage point, not really retirement at all.

20. See Sacks, Harvey. 1992. *Lectures on Conversation, Volumes 1 and 2*. Cambridge, MA: Blackwell, on membership categorization and the formulation of meaning.

21. See Adler and Adler 1991; Ebaugh, H.R.F. 1988. *Becoming an Ex: The Process of Role Exit*. Chicago: University of Chicago Press.

22. See Ebaugh 1988.

23. Ibid., p. 138.

24. Ibid., p. 142.

25. Research interview #50.

26. See J. Coakley 1983; Greendorfer, Susan L., and Elaine M. Blinde. 1985. "Retirement from Intercollegiate Sport: Theoretical and Empirical Considerations." *Sociology of Sport Journal* 2: 101–10.

27. McPherson, B.D. 1980. "Retirement from Professional Sport: The Process and Problems of Occupational and Psychological Adjustment." *Sociological Symposium* 30: 126–33; Sinclair, D.A., and Orlick, T. 1993. "Positive Transitions from High-Performance Sport." *Sport Psychologist* 7: 138–50; Swain, D.A. 1991. "Withdrawal from Sport and Schlossberg's Model of Transitions." *Sociology of Sport Journal* 8: 152–60; Taylor, J., and B.C. Ogilvie. 1998. "Career Transitions among Elite Athletes: Is There Life after Sports," pp. 647–62, in Williams, J.M. (ed.). 2000. *Applied Sport Psychology: Personal Growth to Peak Performance*, 4th ed. Mountain View, CA: Mayfield; Torregrosa, M., M. Boixados, L. Valiente, and J. Cruz. 2004. "Elite Athletes Image of Retirement: The Way to Relocation in Sport." *Psychology of Sport and Exercise* 5: 35–43.

28. Gallmeier, Charles. 1987. "Dinosaurs and Prospects: Toward a Sociology of the Compressed Career," pp. 98–106, in Mamoudi, K.M., B. Parlin, and M. Zussman (eds.). *Sociological Inquiry: A Humanistic Perspective*, 4th ed. Dubuque, IA: Kendall/Hunt; Taylor, J., and B.C. Ogilvie. 1994. "A Conceptual Model of Adaptation to

Retirement among Athletes." *Journal of Applied Sport Psychology* 6:1–20; Sinclair and Orlick 1993.

29. Lavallee, D., and P. Wylleman. 2000. *Career Transitions in Sport: International Perspectives.* Morgantown, WV: Fitness Information Technology.

30. Taylor and Ogilvie 1998.

31. Lavallee and Wylleman 2000; Torregrosa et al. 2004; Webb, W.M., S.A. Nasco, S. Riley, and B. Headrick. 1995. "Athlete Identity and Reactions to Retirement from Sports." *Journal of Sport Behavior* 21: 338–62.

32. McPherson 1980, Taylor and Ogilvie 1994, Webb et al. 1995.

33. Adler and Adler 1991, McPherson 1980, Sinclair and Orlick 1993, Webb et al. 1995. For contrast, see also Greendorfer and Blinde 1985.

34. See J. Coakley 1983.

35. See, for example, Herman Edwards on *Mike and Mike.* January 25, 2013. ESPN2-TV.

36. "NFL's Sign-and-Retire Club." N.d. *SI.com.* http://sportsillustrated.cnn.com/multimedia/photo_gallery/1007/nfl.sign.and.retire.one-day.contracts/content.1.html, retrieved 7/5/13.

37. Katzowitz, Josh. May 30, 2012. "Kordell Stewart Gets His Closure, Officially Retires from Football."*CBSSports.com.* http://www.cbssports.com/nfl/blog/eye-on-football/19205582/kordell-stewart-gets-his-closure-officially-retires-from-football, retrieved 7/5/13.

38. "NFL's Sign-and-Retire Club," n.d.

39. Research interview #40.

40. Research interview #03.

41. Research interview #17.

42. Chadiha, May 31, 2012

43. Roberts, Jeff. May 2, 2013. "NFL Retirement101: Former Giant Learns to Move On." *NorthJersey.com.* http://www.northjersey.com/sports/205723211_NFL_Retirement_101.html?page=all, retrieved 7/1/13.

44. Youngblood, Kent. August 24, 2012. "Tackling the Post-Football Void." *Star-Tribune.com.* http://www.startribune.com/printarticle/?id=167393215, retrieved 12/31/12.

45. See Messner 1992.

46. Research interview #42.

47. Chadiha, May 31, 2012.

48. S. Coakley 2006, p. 91 (research interview).

49. Ibid., p. 92.

50. Ibid.

51. Research interview #24.

52. Ibid.

53. Research interview #60.

54. J. Coakley 1983.

55. Ibid. Also see Taylor and Ogilvie 1994; Taylor and Ogilvie 1998; Taylor, J., and B.C. Ogilvie. 2001. "Career Termination among Athletes," pp. 187–99, in Singer, R.N., H.A. Hausenblas, and C.M. Janelle (eds.). *Handbook of Sport Psychology*. New York: John Wiley.

56. S. Coakley 2006, p. 94 (research interview).

57. Ibid., p. 91.

58. Research interview #28.

59. Eisen 2007, p. 241. Also see Bernstein 2009 for Ahmad Rashad's account of his "perfect exit."

60. Dunne, Tyler. June 16, 2013. "Donald Driver Showered by Love form Loyal Supporters at Softball Game" *JSOnline*. http://www.jsonline.com/sports/pack-ers/donald-driver-showered-by-love-from-loyal-supporters-at-softball-game-b9934975z1-211767161.html, retrieved 6/17/13.

CHAPTER 4. A LIFETIME OF HURT

1. Jenkins, Sally, Rick Maese, and Scott Clement. May 16, 2013. "Do No Harm: Retired NFL Players Endure a Lifetime of Hurt." *Washingtonpost.com*. http://www.washingtonpost.com/sf/feature/wp/2013/05/16/do-no-harm-retired-nfl-players-endure-a-lifetime-of-hurt/, retrieved 5/21/13.

2. Doyel, Gregg. December 23, 2010. "NFL Is Killing Its Players and League Doesn't Care." *CBSsports.com*. http://www.cbssports.com/nfl/story/14477196/nfl-is-kill-ing-its-players-and-league-doesnt-care, retrieved 7/26/17.

3. Steele, David. September 1, 2002. "Adding Insult to Injury: Most Pro Foot-ball Players Face a Future of Disability and Pain." *SFGate.com*. http://www.sfgate.com/health/article/Adding-Insult-to-Injury-Most-pro-football-2775786.php#ixzz2Okh1xKt1, retrieved 3/27/13.

4. Crossman, Mark. July 7, 2011. "John Mackey and Other Retired NFL Players Experience Living Hell." *Sportingnews.com*. http://aol.sportingnews.com/nfl/story/2011-07-07/john-mackey-and-other-retired-nfl-players-experience-living-hell, retrieved 3/27/13.

5. Epstein, David. May 21, 2012. "Dead Wrong: Two Studies Refute Reports in the Media about Former Players' Life Expectancy." *SIVault.com*. http://sportsillus-trated.cnn.com/vault/article/magazine/MAG1198483/, retrieved 4/6/13. Also see Player Care study.

6. Jenkins, Maese, and Clement, May 16, 2013.

7. King, Peter. December 12, 2011. "One Team, 25 Years On." *SIVault*. http://sportsil-lustrated.cnn.com/vault/article/magazine/MAG1192868/, retrieved 4/6/13.

8. Rosenthal, Gregg. March 20, 2013. "NFL Rule Changes Cause Controversy, Draw Ire." *NFL.com*. http://www.nfl.com/news/story/0ap1000000152262/article/nfl-rule-changes-cause-controversy-draw-ire, retrieved 9/29/13.

9. Smith, Michael. March 29, 2013. "Polamalu Says Players Should Have a Vote in Rule Changes." *NBCSports.com*. http://profootballtalk.nbcsports.

com/2013/03/29/polamalu-says-players-should-have-a-vote-in-rule-changes/, retrieved 9/29/13.

10. Jenkins, Maese, and Clement, May 16, 2013.

11. "NFL Retirees Happy with Football Career Despite Lasting Pain." N.d. *Washingtonpost.com.* http://www.washingtonpost.com/page/2010-2019/Washington-Post/2013/05/17/National-Politics/Polling/release_236.xml, retrieved 9/27/13.

12. Player Care study.

13. Jenkins, Maese, and Clement, May 16, 2013; Player Care study; Dryden, Jim. January 28, 2011. "Retired NFL Players Misuse Painkillers More than General Population." *News.WUSTL.com.* http://news.wustl.edu/news/Pages/21789.aspx, retrieved 3/27/13.

14. "In Re: National Football League Players' Concussion Injury Litigation." August 29, 2013. *ESPN.com.* http://a.espncdn.com/pdf/2013/0829/nfl_concussion_litigation_settlement.pdf, retrieved 11/3/13; Alternate Dispute Resolution Center. N.d. "NFL, Retired Players Resolve Concussion Litigation; Court-Appointed Mediator Hails 'Historic' Agreement." *ESPN.com.* http://a.espncdn.com/pdf/2013/0829/nfl_concussion_press_release.pdf, retrieved 11/3/13; Fainaru, Steve, and Mark Fainaru-Wada. September 20, 2013. "Some Players May Be out of NFL Deal." *ESPN.com.* http://espn.go.com/espn/otl/story/_/id/9690036/older-players-cut-nfl-settlement-concerns-growing-whether-enough-money-exists, retrieved 10/2/13.

15. Smith, Stephanie. August 20, 2013. "NFL and Ex-Players Reach Deal in Concussion Lawsuit." *CNN.com.* http://www.cnn.com/2013/08/29/health/nfl-concussion-settlement/index.html?hpt=hp_t2, retrieved 8/29/13.

16. Fainaru-Wada, Mark, and Steve Fainaru. 2013. *League of Denial.* New York: Crown Archetype (hereafter *League of Denial*).

17. "NFL Retirees Happy with Football Career Despite Lasting Pain," n.d.; Jenkins, Maese, and Clement, May 16, 2013.

18. Player Care study. This tremendous difference is partially a feature of comparing probabilities of an extremely rare occurrence among younger men. In the general population only 0.1 percent report such diagnoses—that is, one out of 1,000. Only 1.2 percent of former players of this age have such diagnoses—12 out of 1,000. Therefore, it takes merely 11 additional cases per 1,000 to make the set of diagnoses 19 times more likely. Looked at it this way, there is only a one *percentage point* difference. However, the same figures also show that while such symptoms virtually never appear in younger men, nearly two out of a hundred—that's about one per NFL roster—are going to experience one of these conditions as relatively young men.

19. Lehman, E., M. Hein, S. Baron, and C. Gersic. 2012. "Neurodegenerative Causes of Death among Retired National Football League Players." *Neurology* 79, published online September 5, 2012, as 10.1212/WNl.0b013e31826da150, retrieved 10/15/12.

20. Daneshvar et al. 2011. "Long-Term Consequences: Effects on Normal Development Profile after Concussion." *Physical Medicine and Rehabilitation Clinics of North America* 22: 683–700. Also see *League of Denial*.

21. "The Frontline Interviews: Leigh Steinberg." N.d. *PBS.org.* http://www.pbs.org/
    wgbh/pages/frontline/sports/league-of-denial/the-frontline-interview-leigh-
    steinberg/#seg4, retrieved 10/12/13.

22. "The Frontline Interviews: Life After Football: Steve Young." N.d. *PBS.org* http://
    www.pbs.org/wgbh/pages/frontline/oral-history/league-of-denial/life-after-foot-
    ball, retrieved 10/12/13.

23. "The Frontline Interviews: Life After Football: Jim Otto." N.d. *PBS.org* http://www.
    pbs.org/wgbh/pages/frontline/sports/league-of-denial/the-frontline-interview-
    jim-otto/, retrieved 10/14/13.

24. *League of Denial*, ch. 5.

25. *League of Denial*.

26. Gavette, Brandon, Robert A. Stern, and Ann C. McKee. 2011. "Chronic Traumatic
    Encephalopathy: A Potential Late Effect of Sport-Related Concussive and Subcon-
    cussive Head Trauma." *Clinics in Sports Medicine* 30: 179–88. Also see *League of
    Denial*.

27. "What is CTE?" N.d. *BU.edu.* http://www.bu.edu/cste/about/what-is-cte/,
    retrieved 10/15/13.

28. Stern, Robert, D. Riley, D. Daneshvar, C. Nowinski, R. Cantu, and A. McKee.
    2011. "Long-Term Consequences of Repetitive Brain Trauma: Chronic Traumatic
    Encephalopathy." *Physical Medicine and Rehabilitation* 3: S460–67; McKee, A., et
    al. 2012. "The Spectrum of Disease in Chronic Traumatic Encephalopathy." *Brain*
    2012: 1–22.

29. *League of Denial*.

30. "The Frontline Interviews: Ann McKee." N.d. *PBS.org* http://www.pbs.org/wgbh/
    pages/frontline/sports/league-of-denial/the-frontline-interview-ann-mckee/,
    retrieved 11/1/13.

31. *League of Denial*.

32. "The Frontline Interviews: Ann McKee," n.d. Recently, researchers have made
    progress toward identifying CTE in the living. At UCLA, neuroscientists using a
    brain-imaging tool have identified the abnormal tau proteins associated with CTE
    in five living former NFL players. Hall of Famer Tony Dorsett has recently been
    diagnosed with CTE and is showing the classic symptoms: his memory is fading,
    he gets lost frequently, he's depressed, and his family fears being around him
    because of his erratic behavior. See Champeau, Rachel. January 22, 2013. "UCLA
    Study First to Image Concussion-related Abnormal Brain Proteins in Retired
    NFL Players." *Newsroom.UCLA.edu.* http://newsroom.ucla.edu/portal/ucla/ucla-
    researchers-first-to-image-242445.aspx, retrieved 11/2/13.

33. For teammate Michael Oriard's speculation about Tyrer's case, see Bateman, May
    3, 2012.

34. *League of Denial*, p. 284.

35. *League of Denial*.

36. Ibid.

37. Stern et al. 2011.
38. "The Frontline Interviews: Life After Football: Jim Otto," n.d.
39. Willner, Barry. August 30, 2013. "NFL Concussion Settlement Draws Mixed Reaction from Former Players." *Huffingtonpost.com*. http://www.huffingtonpost.com/2013/08/30/nfl-concussion-settlement-former-players_n_3845954.html, retrieved 9/1/13.
40. Burke, Monte. August 17, 2013. "How the National Football League Can Reach $25 Billion in Annual Revenues." *Forbes.com*. http://www.forbes.com/sites/monteburke/2013/08/17/how-the-national-football-league-can-reach-25-billion-in-annual-revenues/, retrieved 11/2/13.
41. Gershman, Jacob. January 28, 2014. "Concern Raised Over Opt-out Terms of NFL Concussion Settlement." *WSJ.com*. http://blogs.wsj.com/law/2014/01/28/concern-raised-over-opt-out-terms-of-nfl-concussion-settlement/; McCann, Michael. January 14, 2014. "What Rejection of Settlement Means to Concussion Case Against the NFL." *SI.com*. http://sportsillustrated.cnn.com/nfl/news/20140114/judge-rejects-proposed-nfl-concussion-settlement/; both retrieved 2/4/14; Associated Press. July 7, 2014. "Federal Judge Approves NFL Concussion Settlement." NFL.com. http://www.nfl.com/news/story/0ap2000000363672/article/federal-judge-approves-nfl-concussion-settlement; retrieved 7/8/14.
42. Willner, August 30, 2013; Banks, Donald. August 29, 2013. "Former Players: Devil Is in the Details with the NFL Concussion Settlement." *SI.com*. http://sportsillustrated.cnn.com/nfl/news/20130829/nfl-concussion-lawsuit-settlement-player-reaction-kevin-mawae/, retrieved 4/22/14.
43. Wolfley, Bob. September 18, 2013. "Dorsey Levins Rips Settlement of Concussion Lawsuit against NFL." *JSOnline.com*. http://www.jsonline.com/sports/dorsey-levens-rips-settlement-of-concussion-lawsuit-against-nfl-b99101255z1-224335851.html#ixzz2jWFbq1Xq, retrieved 11/1/13.
44. *League of Denial*, p. 337.
45. Finley, Jermichael. N.d. "Jermichael Finley: Fear, Relief, Resolve." *SI.com*. http://mmqb.si.com/2013/10/29/jermichael-finley-packers-injury-first-person/, retrieved 10/30/13.
46. Jenkins, Maese, and Clement, May 16, 2013.
47. Research interview #27.
48. Player Care study.
49. Knapp, Gwen. November 2, 2008. "Otto Paid Big Price for Football Glory." *SFGate.com*. http://www.sfgate.com/sports/article/Otto-paid-big-price-for-football-glory-3262920.php#ixzz2OlAsOOV6, retrieved 3/27/13; Otto, Jim. 1999. *Jim Otto: The Pain of Glory*. Champaign, IL: Sports Publishing; *League of Denial*.
50. Research interview #42.
51. Ibid.
52. Whitmer, Michael. October 17, 2013. "Agent: No Way to Know When Rob Gronkowski Returns." *Bostonglobe.com*. http://www.bostonglobe.com/

sports/2013/10/17/agent-way-know-when-rob-gronkowski-returns/BxK1pcwx-
Vyz0acS9ZXSnxL/story.html, retrieved 10/18/13. Gronkowski's bad luck persisted
when he finally returned at midseason. On December 8, a low hit from a defensive back blew out his ACL and he was sidelined for at least the rest of the 2013
season.

53. Nack, William. May 7, 2001. "The Wrecking Yard." *SIVault.com*. http://sportsillus-
trated.cnn.com/vault/article/magazine/MAG1022464/, retrieved 6/5/13.

54. Steele, David. September 1, 2002. "Adding Insult to Injury: Most Pro Football
Players Face a Future of Disability and Pain." *SFgate.com*. http://www.sfgate.
com/health/article/Adding-Insult-to-Injury-Most-pro-football-2775786.
php#ixzz2Okh1xKt1, retrieved 3/27/13.

55. Research interview #30.

56. Jenkins, Maese, and Clement, May 16, 2013.

57. Nack, May 7, 2001.

58. Research interview #20.

59. Research interview #24.

60. Jenkins, Maese, and Clement, May 16, 2013.

61. Player Care study.

62. Ibid. Fifteen percent of older alums also report being unable to work due to disability, but this percentage is the same as for similarly aged men in the general
population.

63. Ibid.

64. Research interview #20.

65. Besinger, Ken. September 5, 2013. "Deion Sanders, Critic of NFL Concussion Settlement, Seeks Workers' Comp." *LATimes.com*. http://www.latimes.
com/business/la-fi-deion-sanders-brain-20130906; Schwarz, Alan. April 7,
2010. "Two Ex-players Leverage Connections in NFL Workers' Comp Cases."
NYTimes.com. http://www.nytimes.com/2010/04/08/sports/football/08lawyers.
html?pagewanted=all&_r=0; both retrieved 10/18/13.

66. "Total Knee Replacement Cost." N.d. *Kneereplacementcost.com*. http://www.
kneereplacementcost.com/; Kliff, Sarah. February 12, 2013. "How Much Does
Hip Surgery Cost?" *Washingtonpost.com*. http://www.washingtonpost.com/
blogs/wonkblog/wp/2013/02/12/how-much-does-hip-surgery-cost-somewhere-
between-10000-and-125000/; both retrieved 10/19/13.

67. Brownhill, Stacy. February 2, 2011. "Aches and Games." *Wweek.com*. http://www.
wweek.com/portland/article-16892-aches_and_games.html, retrieved 10/19/13.

68. Player Care study.

69. Ibid. A significant portion of former players' insurance plans don't cover prescription medications, and even fewer have dental insurance. See Appendix 2, "Retirement Benefits."

70. Ibid.

71. Segura, September 10, 2012.

72. For accounts of illicit self-medication, see *Broke*, Favre and Havel 1997.
73. *Broke*.
74. Jenkins, Sally, and Rick Maese. April 13, 2013. "Pain and Pain Management in NFL Spawn a Culture of Prescription Drug Use and Abuse." *Washingtonpost.com*. http://www.washingtonpost.com/sports/redskins/pain-and-pain-management-in-nfl-spawn-a-culture-of-prescription-drug-use-and-abuse/2013/04/13/3b36f4de-a1e9-11e2-bd52-614156372695_story.html, retrieved 5/21/13.
75. Ibid.
76. Ibid.
77. Dryden, January 28, 2011.
78. Player Care study.
79. Ibid.
80. Ibid.
81. Guskiewicz, Kevin M., et al. 2007. "Recurrent Concussions and the Risk of Depression in Retired Professional Football Players." *Medicine and Science in Sports and Exercise* 39(6): 903–9. Also see *League of Denial*.
82. The observed conversation took place *before* discussion of the 2013 concussion lawsuit and settlement reached a fever pitch, so the voiced concerns weren't simply a matter of timing.
83. *Mike and Mike*. October 21, 2013. ESPN Radio and ESPN2-TV. The segment was rebroadcast repeatedly in the following days.
84. *League of Denial*, pp. 79–80.
85. *SportsCenter*. November 19, 2013. ESPN-TV.
86. See Eitzen 2009, Messner 1992.
87. J. Coakley 2008.
88. Smith, Michael David. October 24, 2013. "Richard Sherman: I Played through a Concussion and It Paid Off," *NBCSports.com*. http://profootballtalk.nbcsports.com/2013/10/24/richard-sherman-i-played-through-a-concussion-and-it-paid-off/, retrieved 10/24/13.
89. *Mike and Mike*. October 11, 2013. ESPN2-TV.
90. Finley, n.d.
91. Schlereth, Mark. January 5, 2004. "Schlereth: It Was All Worth It." *ESPN.com*. http://espn.go.com/espn/print?id=1718301&type=story, retrieved 3/27/13.

CHAPTER 5. "ALL THAT DOUGH: WHERE DID IT GO?"
1. Feinstein 2005, p. 204.
2. "Former Pro Bowl CB Chris McAlister: I'm Broke." September 15, 2011. *Sportingnews.com*. http://www.sportingnews.com/nfl/story/2011-09-15/former-pro-bowl-cb-chris-mcalister-im-broke, retrieved 4/17/14.
3. Jessop, Alicia. October 13, 2012. "Not Broke: How NFL Players Stay Financially Stable after the Game Ends." Forbes.com. http://www.forbes.com/sites/

aliciajessop/2012/10/31/not-broke-how-nfl-players-stay-financially-stable-after-the-game-ends/; Dickey, Jack. April 6, 2012. "Warren Sapp Is Broke." *Deadspin.com*. http://deadspin.com/5899896/warren-sapp-is-broke; both retrieved 8/6/13.

4. See Appendix 2, "Retirement Benefits," and Player Care study. The Player Care study makes no mention of cumulative assets, and no systematic data on former NFL players' current net worth is apparently unavailable.

5. Research interview #02. Blackburn lived off his side income, signing bonuses, and postseason game checks.

6. Indeed, many players vastly overestimate the extent of their own assets. See *Broke*; Torre, March 23, 2009; Chadiha, May 31, 2012.

7. See O'Toole, p. 136; *Broke*; Koebler, July 21, 2011. Of course these estimates vary according to how players shelter their incomes from taxes and deductions, how they invest, how much they accrue in sales tax, and the various state and municipal income taxes they may have to pay.

8. Research interview #40.

9. Katzowitz, Josh. May 15, 2013. "James Harrison: I Spend $400K–$600K on My Body per Year." *CBSSports.com*. http://www.cbssports.com/nfl/blog/eye-on-football/22247097/james-harrison-i-spend-400k-600k-on-my-body-per-year, retrieved 7/27/13.

10. Rosenthal, Gregg. July 2, 2012. "Adam Jones Recounts Spending $1 Million in Weekend." *NFL.com*. http://www.nfl.com/news/story/09000d5d82a463aa/article/adam-jones-recounts-spending-1-million-in-weekend, retrieved 7/25/13. That's quite a reaction from Owens, who is known for outlandish spending. See Evans, Sean. April 12, 2012. "Money to Blow: A Recent History of NFL Players Going Broke." *Complex.com*. http://www.complex.com/sports/2012/04/money-to-blow-a-recent-history-of-nfl-players-going-broke/owens#gallery, retrieved 8/2/13.

11. Tober, Will. July 24, 2011. "Seven Most Ridiculous Purchases by Athletes in NFL History." *Bleacherreport.com*. http://bleacherreport.com/articles/775852-7-most-ridiculous-purchases-in-nfl-history; Whitley, David. November 2, 2012. "Warren Sapp's Sad Bankruptcy Auction Not the First—or Last—Tale of Jocks Gone Broke. *Sportingnews.com*. http://aol.sportingnews.com/nfl/story/2012-11-02/warren-sapp-broke-fired-nfl-network-bankrupt-athletes-list; both retrieved 7/25/13.

12. Torre, March 23, 2009. Emphasis added.

13. Best, Joel. 2014. *Stat-Spotting: A Field Guide to Identifying Dubious Data*, 2nd ed. Berkeley: University of California Press.

14. Mr. Torre has not responded to multiple e-mail inquiries about the story and the statistics he cites.

15. While detailing former players' current income, the Player Care study fails to report data on former players' current assets. Double the poverty level amounted to $20,800 for a single person or $42,400 for a family of four in the contiguous 48 states and Washington, D.C., when the survey was administered in 2008. U.S. Department of Health and Human Services. January 29, 2010. "The 2008 HHS

Poverty Guidelines." *ASPE.hhs.gov.* http://aspe.hhs.gov/poverty/08poverty.shtml, retrieved 7/25/13.

16. Whitley, November 2, 2012; Brooks, Matt. April 9, 2012. "Warren Sapp: The Latest Millionaire Athlete to File for Bankruptcy." *Washingotnpost.com.* http://www.washingtonpost.com/blogs/early-lead/post/warren-sapp-the-latest-multi-millionaire-athlete-to-file-for-bankruptcy/2012/04/09/gIQAErXz5S_blog.html; Stone, Jeff. October 4, 2012. "Warren Sapp, Michael Vick Just the Latest NFL Players to Go Broke and Bankrupt; But Why?" *IBTimes.com.* http://www.ibtimes.com/warren-sapp-michael-vick-just-latest-nfl-players-go-broke-and-bankrupt-why-817369; both retrieved 1/12/13.

17. *Broke.*

18. Eisen 2007.

19. *Broke.*

20. Lambert, Pam. March 15, 2004. "The High Cost of Winning." *People.com.* http://www.people.com/people/archive/article/0,,20149566,00.html, retrieved 7/29/13.

21. Landau, Elizabeth. January 7, 2011. "Winning the Lottery: Does It Guarantee Happiness?" *CNN.com.* http://www.cnn.com/2011/HEALTH/01/07/lottery.winning.psychology/index.html, retrieved 7/29/13.

22. Dahl, Melissa. N.d. "$550 Million Will Buy You a Lot of . . . Misery." *NBCnews.com.* http://www.nbcnews.com/health/550-million-will-buy-you-lot-misery-1C7291165, retrieved 7/29/13.

23. Roberts, Daniel, and Pablo Torre. April 11, 2012. "Jerry Maguire Aspires to Be You." *SI.com.* http://sportsillustrated.cnn.com/2012/magazine/04/10/steinberg/index.html, retrieved 4/18/14; Torre, March 23, 2009.

24. See Fedotin, Jeff. August 13, 2006. "George Koonce Goes from Leading Players on the Field to off the Field." *Packers.com.* http://www.packers.com/news-and-events/article-1/George-Koonce-Goes-From-Leading-Players-On-The-Field-To-Off-The-Field/94cc5822-5aa4-11df-a3b6-528cc843f916; Murf, B. October 8, 2012. "Phillip Daniels Discusses His New Role, Hopes to Coach." *Homermcfanboy.com.* http://www.homermcfanboy.com/2012/10/18/phillip-daniels-discusses-his-new-role-hopes-to-coach/; "NFL Introduces Four New Bootcamps for Current and Former Players." December 8, 2012. *Wordpress.com.* http://nfllabor.files.wordpress.com/2012/12/fournewbootcamps.pdf; "Specialized Resources for the NFL Family." N.d. *NFLlifeline.org.* http://nfllifeline.org/resources/programs-and-benefits/; all retrieved 8/15/13. See also *Packers Player Development Manual.*

25. Hack, Damon. June 16, 2011. "Playing for Profit: Ex-NFL Corner Succeeds in Business after Football." *SI.com.* http://sportsillustrated.cnn.com/2011/writers/damon_hack/06/16/eugene.profit/index.html?xid=cnnbin&hpt=hp_bn10, retrieved 4/4/13.

26. *Broke.*

27. Torre, March 23, 2009.

28. Research interview #3.

29. Chadiha, May 31, 2012.

30. Research interview #20.

31. Anderson, Elijah. 1999. *Code of the Street.* New York: Norton.

32. Oliver, Melvin L., and Thomas M. Shapiro. 1997. *Black Wealth/White Wealth.* New York: Routledge.

33. Research interview #40.

34. Research interview #20.

35. Research interview #24.

36. Research interview #23.

37. *Broke.*

38. Torre, March 23, 2009.

39. *Broke.*

40. *Broke,* Eisen 2007, Feinstein 2005.

41. *Broke.*

42. Chadiha, May 31, 2012.

43. Festinger, Leon. 1954. "A Theory of Social Comparison Processes." *Human Relations,* 7(2): 117–40.

44. Research interview #23.

45. Research interview #02.

46. Torre, March 23, 2009.

47. Research interview #30.

48. Player Care study.

49. These tend to be the investments of choice of individuals from economically disadvantaged backgrounds, especially African Americans. See Oliver and Shapiro 1997.

50. Jessop, October 13, 2012.

51. *Broke.*

52. NFL Players Association. N.d. "Agent Regulations." *NFLplayers.com.* https://www.nflplayers.com/About-us/Rules—Regulations/Agent-Regulations/; NFL Players Association. N.d. "NFLPA Financial Advisor Registration Program Regulations." *NFLplayers.com.* https://www.nflplayers.com/About-us/Rules—Regulations/Financial-Advisor-Regulations/, retrieved 8/2/13.

53. NFL Players Association, n.d., "NFLPA Financial Advisor Registration Program Regulations."

54. *Broke;* Freeman 2003; Torre, March 23, 2009.

55. Torre, March 23, 2009.

56. *Broke.*

57. Ibid.

58. Ibid.

59. Ibid.

60. Research interview #41.

61. Billick, 2007, p. 77. Rogers was the second player selected in the draft.

62. *Broke.*

63. Research interview #41.

64. *Broke.*

65. Le Batard, Dan. July 13, 2009. "As Bernie Kosar's Life around Him Crumbles, the Former QB's Game Plan Is Familiar: Emerge Unscathed." *Post-gazette.com.* http://www.post-gazette.com/stories/sports/steelers/as-bernie-kosars-life-around-him-crumbles-the-former-qbs-game-plan-is-familiar-emerge-unscathed-349253/, retrieved 7/26/13; Schoenberger, Robert. June 19, 2009. "Former Cleveland Browns Quarterback Bernie Kosar Files for Bankruptcy." *Cleveland.com.* http://blog.cleveland.com/browns_impact/print.html?entry=/2009/06/former_cleveland_browns_quarte_1.html, retrieved 7/25/13. Ironically, or tragically, depending on one's perspective, bankruptcy filings show that Kosar now owes millions to his father, brother, and ex-wife.

66. O'Toole, 2006, p. 146.

67. Research interview #41.

68. O'Toole 2006.

69. Ibid., p. 145–46.

70. *Broke.*

71. Ibid.

72. Eisen 2007, p. 185. Emphasis in original.

73. Player Care study.

74. Torre, March 23, 2009.

75. Research interview #41.

76. Research interview #304.

77. Eisen 2007. At the same time, NFL wives warn prospective pro football spouses of the vagaries of NFL marriages and the dangers of getting "dumped" after putting up with the hardships of the early years at the periphery of the league. See Feinstein 2005, O'Toole 2006.

78. Le Batard, July 13, 2009.

79. "Troy Aikman Antes Up $1.75 Million in Divorce Settlement." June 11, 2012. *TMZ.com.* http://www.tmz.com/2012/06/01/troy-aikman-wife-divorce-settlement/, retrieved 4/18/14.

80. Wahl, Grant, and L. Jon Wertheim. May 4, 1998. "Paternity Ward." *SIVault.com.* http://sportsillustrated.cnn.com/vault/article/magazine/MAG1012762/; Breitman. David. March 3, 2010. "The Top 10 Athletes with the Most Children." *Spike.com.* http://www.spike.com/articles/q1nh0o/the-top-10-athletes-with-the-most-illegitimate-children; "Jets' Cromartie, Wife Expecting Twins." April 17, 2012. *Foxsports.com.* http://msn.foxsports.com/nfl/story/new-york-jets-antonio-cromartie-wife-expecting-twins-total-of-12-kids-8-different-women-041712; all retrieved 8/5/13.

81. Wahl and Wertheim, May 4, 1998; "Monthly Child Support Payments Average $430 per Month in 2010, Census Bureau Reports." June 19, 2012. *Census.gov.* http://www.census.gov/newsroom/releases/archives/children/cb12-109.html, retrieved 8/5/13.

82. Brooks, April 9, 2012.
83. Soshnick, Scott. May 9, 2011. "NBA, NFL Players' Ex-Wives Likely to Feel Pinch." *SFGate.com.* http://www.sfgate.com/sports/article/NBA-NFL-players-ex-wives-likely-to-feel-pinch-2372426.php; Tinouye, Kunbi. April 20, 2012. "Does 'Baby Mama Drama' Make Pro Athletes Go Broke?" *Thegrio.com.* http://thegrio.com/2012/04/20/does-baby-mama-drama-make-pro-athletes-go-broke; both retrieved 8/5/13.
84. Tinouye, April 20, 2012.
85. Koebler, July 21, 2011.
86. Research interview #30.
87. Koebler, July 21, 2011.
88. Ibid.
89. Ibid.
90. Ibid.

CHAPTER 6. WHAT'S NEXT?

1. *SportsCenter.* September 6, 2013. ESPN-TV.
2. Player Care study.
3. Korn, Melissa. March 14, 2013. "The NFL Tackles Job Training for Retired Players." *WSJ.com.* http://blogs.wsj.com/atwork/2013/03/14/the-nfl-tackles-job-training-for-retired-players/, retrieved 8/15/13. This statistic was drawn from the Player Care study.
4. "From Professional Sports to Franchising." August 3, 2013. *Chicagolawbulletin.com.* http://www.chicagolawbulletin.com/Articles/2013/08/13/sporting-column-8-13-13.aspx, retrieved 8/13/13.
5. Research interview #24.
6. Research interview #20.
7. Ibid.
8. Research interview #30.
9. This amount was in the ballpark of the salary of a new tenure-track faculty member in, say, the English Department at ECU.
10. Research interview #42.
11. "Summary of NFL Player Benefits." N.d. *Delducasports.com.* http://www.delducasports.com/assets/files/Summary-of-NFL-Player-Benefits.pdf, retrieved 7/7/13.
12. Research interview #42.
13. Research interview #26.
14. "College Graduates Unemployment." N.d. *Huffingtonpost.com.* http://www.huffingtonpost.com/news/college-graduates-unemployment, retrieved 11/16/13.
15. Research interview #28.
16. Research interview #30.
17. See the web site of the Gridiron Greats Assistance Fund for a list of well over 100 instances where old-timers met hard times. "Player Stories." N.d. *Gridirongreats.*

org. http://www.gridirongreats.org/stories, retrieved 8/15/13. See Oriard 1982 for additional examples. In general, pensions have been modest, if not inadequate, for players retiring before the free agency era.

18. Hack, Damon. June 16, 2011. "Playing for Profit: Ex-NFL Corner Succeeds in Business after Football." *SI.com.* http://sportsillustrated.cnn.com/2011/writers/damon_ hack/06/16/eugene.profit/index.html?xid=cnnbin&hpt=hp_bn10, retrieved 4/4/13.

19. Materials relating to Dampeer's story come from research interview #22.

20. Research interview #17.

21. See Billick 2009, Dawidoff 2013, Feinstein 2005, Freeman 2003.

22. Research interview #42.

23. Of course this mythology leads to its own sort of debunking. Brian Billick, himself a Super Bowl–winning coach, once responded to a query about what time he arrived at his office in the morning. "About a half hour before whatever time Gruden lies about coming in," replied Billick (Freeman 2003, p. 6).

24. Average salaries among NFL assistant coaches are around $400,000; college coaches make considerably less, but still more than $200,000 on average. Assistants in major conferences average close to $300,000 per year. See Berkowitz, Steve, and Jodi Upton. June 24, 2013. "College Football Assistants Seeing Salaries Surge." *USAToday.com.* http://www.usatoday.com/story/sports/ncaaf/2012/12/18/ assistant-coaches-salaries-bowl-subdivision/1777719/; Saraceno, Jon. March 17, 2011. "Coaches Salaries Slashed in NFL Lockout Cost-cutting." *USAToday. com.* http://usatoday30.usatoday.com/sports/football/nfl/2011-03-16-coaches-salaries_N.htm; both retrieved 8/20/13.

25. "What's the Average Salary of a High School Football Coach?" N.d. *Degreedirectory.org.* http://degreedirectory.org/articles/Whats_the_Average_Salary_of_a_ High_School_Football_Coach.html; Zuvanich, Adam. January 11, 2013. "Football: Feldt Hired as Permian Coach." *Oaoa.com.* http://www.oaoa.com/oavarsity/ boys/article_e035c388-5c35-11e2-8aee-0019bb30f31a.html; Nelson, Akilah, and Kelly Davis. October 26, 2012. "Five of Highest-Paid High School Coaches in Midlands." *Thestate.com.* http://www.thestate.com/2012/10/26/2495498/5-of-highest-paid-high-school.html; Shirley, Brent. August 18, 2011. "As High School Football Popularity Soars, So Do Coaches' Salaries." *Star-telegram.com.* http:// www.star-telegram.com/2011/08/18/3300034/as-high-school-football-popularity. html; "How Much Do High School Coaches in Southeast Texas Make?" September 27, 2011. *Beaumontenterprise.com.* http://www.beaumontenterprise.com/ sports/hs/article/How-much-do-high-school-football-coaches-in-2191111.php; "Search Arkansas High School Football Coaches Salaries." N.d. *ArkansasOnline. com.* http://www.arkansasonline.com/extra/databases/coachsalaries/; Porter, Matt. May 1, 2013. "County High School Coaches Say the Pay They Receive for the Long Hours of Work Is Forcing Them to Consider Leaving the Area—or the Profession." *PalmBeachPost.com.* http://www.palmbeachpost.com/news/sports/high-school/county-high-school-football-coaches-say-the-pay-th/nXdYC/; "'What's

the Story?' with Coaches Salaries." April 27, 2013. *Fdlreporter.com*. http://www.
fdlreporter.com/article/20130428/FON0101/304280121/-What-s-story-coaches-
salaries; all retrieved 8/20/13.

26. Thelen, Paul. June 20, 2013. "Active NFL Players Destined to Become Coaches
after Retirement." *Bleacherreport.com*. http://bleacherreport.com/articles/1679155-
active-nfl-players-destined-to-become-coaches-after-retirement, retrieved 8/15/13.

27. Joyner, K.C. 2008. *Blindsided*. Hoboken, NJ: John Wiley & Sons.

28. "Bill Walsh NFL Minority Fellowships." N.d. *NFLplayerengagement.com*. https://
www.nflplayerengagement.com/next/bill-walsh-nfl-minority-coaching-fellow-
ship/; "Internship Opportunities." April 10, 2014. *NFLplayers.com*. https://www.
nflplayers.com/About-us/Join-Our-Workforce/Internship-Opportunities/; both
retrieved 4/18/14.

29. *ESPN News*. July 5, 2013. ESPN2-TV.

30. Chadiha, May 31, 2012.

31. Dozier, Leonard. N.d. "The Average Salary of Sports Radio Hosts." *Ehow.com*.
http://www.ehow.com/info_12028765_average-salary-sports-radio-hosts.html;
"Jobs in Sports: Insight Sports Radio Professional." N.d. *Jobsinsprots.com*. http://
www.jobsinsports.com/blog/post.cfm/jobs-in-sports-insight-sports-radio-profes-
sional; both retrieved 8/21/13.

32. "Discover How to Become a Sports Broadcaster." N.d. *Sportscastingcareeers.com*.
http://www.sportscastingcareers.com/becoming-a-sportscaster.php?gclid=CN_24
fv9670CFbF34godWQgA4g, retrieved 11/17/13.

33. Player Engagement, December 8, 2012.

34. *Dennis Krause Show*. September 13, 2012. Time Warner Sports–Milwaukee.

35. Eisen 2007.

36. Freedman, Jonah. N.d. "The 50 Highest-Earning American Athletes." *SI.com*.
http://sportsillustrated.cnn.com/specials/fortunate50-2011/index.html, retrieved
8/22/13.

37. See "Booking Athletes for Autograph Signing Appearances." N.d. *Athletepromo-
tions.com*. http://www.athletepromotions.com/athlete-autograph-signing-appear-
ance.php, retrieved 8/22/13.

38. Research interview #30.

39. Ibid.

40. Research interview #05.

41. "LeRoy Butler on His Pay for Charity Events." N.d. *Greenbaypressgazette.com*.
http://www.greenbaypressgazette.com/videonetwork/2838532505001, retrieved
11/23/13.

42. For example, see "Brees Dream Foundation." N.d. *Drewbrees.com*. http://www.
drewbrees.com/, retrieved 8/22/13.

43. Borchers, Callum. February 24, 2013. "In Nonprofit Game, Athletes Post Losing
Records." *Bostonglobe.com*. http://www.bostonglobe.com/business/2013/02/24/
nonprofit-game-many-athletes-post-losing records/aoeqoz6ruyorfhtotojoeo/

story.html; Lavigne, Paula. March 31, 2013. "Athlete Charities Often Lack Standards." *ESPN.com*. http://espn.go.com/espn/otl/story/_/id/9109024/top-athletes-charities-often-measure-charity-experts-say-efficient-effective-use-money; Vincent, Isabel. "NYC Star Athletes Like Sabathia, Ferguson Run Lousy Charities." *NYPost.com*. http://www.nypost.com/p/news/local/it_jock_crock_rb6wV1sD4x-hjejETfpRP3I; all retrieved 4/1/13.

44. Research interview #27.
45. Research interview #41.
46. "Specialized Resources for the NFL Family." N.d. *NFLlifeline.com*. http://nfllife-line.org/resources/programs-and-benefits/, retrieved 8/15/13.
47. Youngblood, August 24, 2012.
48. Marvez, Alex. June 1, 2013. "NFL Prepping Players for Second Life." *Foxsports.com*. http://msn.foxsports.com/nfl/story/league-assists-retired-players-transition-to-life-after-football-053113, retrieved 8/15/13.
49. Eichelberger, Curtis. May 14, 2013. "Wall Street Internships Offer NFL Players Option When Game Ends." *Bloomberg.com*. http://www.bloomberg.com/news/2013-05-15/wall-street-internships-offer-nfl-players-option-when-game-ends.html, retrieved 8/23/13. Vincent's remarks need to be understood in context. He is currently a vice president for the NFL, and responsible for providing programming for players and alumni. He had previously served as president of the NFLPA, and was reportedly a finalist for the position of executive director of the union, but did not get the job.
50. "Internships and Entry Level Programs at the League." N.d. *NFL.com*. http://www.nfl.com/careers/internships; Eichelberger, May 14, 2013; Fastenberg, Dan. May 23, 2013. "NFL Players Get Internships in Attempt to Build Second Careers." *AOL.com*. http//jobs.aol.com/articles/2013/05/23/nfl-players-internships-second-careers/; "Internship Opportunities." April 10, 2014. *NFLplayers.com*. https://www.nflplayers.com/About-us/Join-Our-Workforce/Internship-Opportunities/; all retrieved 4/18/14.
51. Eichelberger, May 14, 2013.
52. King, Peter. February 7, 2011. "The Man of the Hour." *SIVault.com*. http://sportsil-lustrated.cnn.com/vault/article/magazine/MAG1181467/5/index.htm, retrieved 8/23/13. It also didn't hurt that Goodell is the son of a U.S. senator and has a college degree in economics.
53. Research interview #24.
54. Research interview #23.
55. Research interview #50.
56. Research interview #57.
57. "Executive Profile: Willie Davis." N.d. *Businessweek.com*. http://investing.busi-nessweek.com/research/stocks/people/person.asp?personId=540364&ticker=FNF&previousCapId=320570&previousTitle=MANPOWERGROUP%20INC; "Willie Davis." N.d. *Forbes.com*. http://www.forbes.com/profile/willie-davis/; both retrieved 8/24/13.

58. The details of the story are drawn mainly from Davis's recent autobiography. See Davis 2012.
59. This is a variation on a quotation variously attributed to Branch Rickey ("Luck is the residue of design") and John Milton.
60. Research interview #30.

CHAPTER 7. PLAYING WITHOUT A PLAYBOOK
1. Research Interview #26.
2. Chadiha, May 31, 2012.
3. Youngblood, August 24, 2012.
4. S. Coakley 2006, p. 87 (research interview).
5. Chadiha, May 31, 2012.
6. S. Coakley 2006, p. 86 (research interview).
7. Chadiha, May 31, 2012.
8. Research interview #26.
9. Research interview #79.
10. Ibid.
11. Research interview #26.
12. Research interview #42. Also see Greendorfer and Blinde 1985, for a discussion of the limitations of the "social death" perspective for understanding professional sports retirements.
13. Research interview #42.
14. Research interview #26.
15. Research interview #42.
16. Ibid.
17. Player Care study, pp. 14–15.
18. See Lasch, Christopher. 1977. *Haven in a Heartless World.* New York: Basic Books.
19. See Skolnick, Arlene. 1997. *The Intimate Environment,* 6th ed. New York: Pearson.
20. O'Toole 2006.
21. See Goyette, Caroline. October 29, 2007. "True Grit." *Milwaukeemag.com.* http://www.milwaukeemag.com/article/242011-TrueGrit1, retrieved 11/9/2013; O'Toole 2006.
22. See Davis 2012, Goyette 2007, Oriard 1992, O'Toole 2006.
23. O'Toole 2006, p. 81.
24. Ibid., p. 76.
25. Ibid.
26. Ibid., p. 115. Emphasis in original.
27. Ibid., p. 177.
28. Ibid.
29. Research interview #49.
30. Research interview #03.

31. S. Coakley 2006, p. 102 (research interview).

32. Silver, Michael. February 4, 2013. "Raven's Super Bowl Success Is Ultimately a Ray Lewis Love Story." *Yahoo.com.* http://sports.yahoo.com/news/nfl—morning-rush—ravens—super-bowl-success-is-ultimately-a-love-story-134058071.html, retrieved 4/18/14.

33. Research interview #07.

34. Campbell, LaMar. September 8, 2011. "For Retired NFL Players, Most Challenging 'Season' Just Beginning." *CNN.com.* http://www.cnn.com/2011/OPINION/09/08/nfl.life.after.the.game/index.html, retrieved 9/17/13.

35. Research interview #20.

36. Research interview #17.

37. Research interview #04.

38. Research interview #25.

39. See, for example, Davis 2010, Feinstein 2005, Oriard 1982, Richmond 2010.

40. Research interview #21.

41. *Mike and Mike.* January 28, 2013. ESPN2-TV. Also see Feinstein 2005, Freeman 2003, Oriard 1982.

42. Research interview #42.

43. Player Care study. Also see Feinstein 2005; Krattenmaker, Tom. 2010. *Onward Christian Athletes.* Lanham, MD: Rowman & Littlefield.

44. See Feinstein 2005, p. 267.

CHAPTER 8. TRIALS OF TRANSITION

1. Research interview #42.

2. See J. Coakley 1983, Greendorfer and Blinde 1985.

3. Research interview #47.

4. Research interview #60.

5. Oberg, Kalvervo. 1960. "Culture Shock: Adjustment to New Cultural Environments." *Practical Anthropology* 7: 177–82; Pedersen, Paul. 1995. *The Five Stages of Culture Shock.* Westport, CT: Greenwood; Schmid, Thomas, and Richard S. Jones. 1999. "Personal Adaptations to Cultural Change." *Perspectives on Social Problems* 11: 317–42.

6. See Berger, Peter. 1963. *Invitation to Sociology.* Garden City, NY: Anchor.

7. "Slurs in Incognito's Messages." November 5, 2013. *ESPN.com.* http://espn.go.com/nfl/story/_/id/9926139/richie-incognito-miami-dolphins-used-slurs-messages-jonathan-martin, retrieved 11/7/13. Wells, Theodore V., Brad S. Karp, Bruce Birenboim, and David W. Brown. February 14, 2014. "Report to the National Football League Concerning Issues of Workplace Conduct at the Miami Dolphins." *Turner.com.* http://ht.cdn.turner.com/si/images/2014/02/14/PaulWeissReport.pdf, retrieved 4/19/14 (hereafter Wells Report). Wherever possible, we intentionally reproduce vulgar, vile, degrading language in unexpurgated form in order to capture the actual texture of the culture from which it emerges. Indeed, we might

argue that this language itself constitutes the culture. To "sanitize" the language would compromise the cultural depiction.

8. We're not taking sides in this controversy, nor do we intend gratuitously to disparage Incognito, Martin, or any of the other participants in the conversation. Our interest is in the cultural milieu that both prompts and emerges from this dialogue.

9. "Exclusive: Incognito's Team Reveals Texts with Jonathan Martin." January 30, 2014. *Miami.CBSlocal.com.* http://miami.cbslocal.com/2014/01/30/incognitos-team-reveals-texts-with-jonathan-martin/, retrieved 4/19/14; Wells Report.

10. "Slurs in Incognito's Messages." November 5, 2013. *ESPN.com.* http://espn.go.com/nfl/story/_/id/9926139/richie-incognito-miami-dolphins-used-slurs-messages-jonathan-martin; Schrotenboer, Brent. November 5, 2013. "Richie Incognito's Bully Reputation Goes Back to 2002." *USAToday.com.* http://www.usatoday.com/story/sports/nfl/2013/11/05/incognito-bully-accusations-nebraska-fresh-man/3439819/; "Ndamukong Suh Voted Dirtiest Player." November 9, 2012. *ESPN.com.* http://espn.go.com/nfl/story/_/id/8608300/ndamukong-suh-detroit-lions-voted-nfl-dirtiest-player-sporting-news-poll; all retrieved 11/7/13.

11. See, for example, Chris Carter and Mike Golic on *Mike and Mike*. November 5, 2013. ESPN2-TV.

12. Murtha, Lydon. N.d. "Incognito and Martin: An Insider's Story." MMQB.si.com. http://mmqb.si.com/2013/11/07/richie-incognito-jonathan-martin-dolphins-lydon-murtha/, retrieved 11/7/13.

13. Beasley, Adam. November 7, 2013. "Miami Dolphins Players Mostly Voice Support for Richie Incognito." *Miamiherald.com.* http://www.miamiherald.com/2013/11/07/3735089/miami-dolphins-center-mike-pouncey.html, retrieved 4/19/4.

14. *Mike and Mike.* November 15, 2013. ESPN2-TV.

15. Murtha, n.d.

16. Almond, Elliott. November 12, 2013. "NFL Bullying: Why Ex-Stanford Star Jonathan Martin Became a Target." *Mercurynews.com.* http://www.mercurynews.com/sports/ci_24462878/nfl-bullying-why-ex-stanford-star-jonathan-martin, retrieved 11/21/13.

17. *Mike and Mike.* November 8, 2013. ESPN2-TV.

18. Murtha, n.d.

19. Beasley, November 7, 2013.

20. *Mike and Mike.* November 7, 2013. ESPN2-TV.

21. *Mike and Mike.* November 8, 2013. ESPN2-TV.

22. Ibid.

23. Clemmer, Donald. 1940. *The Prison Community.* New York: Holt, Rinehart and Winston; Sykes, Gresham M. 1958. *The Society of Captives.* Princeton, NJ: Princeton University Press; Wieder, D. Lawrence. 1988. *Language and Social Reality: The Case of Telling the Convict Code.* Washington, D.C.: University Press of America.

24. Murtha, n.d.

25. Ibid.

26. Durkheim, Emile. 1938. *The Rules of Sociological Method*. New York: Free Press; Erikson, Kai. 1964. "Notes on the Sociology of Deviance," pp. 9–15, in Becker, Howard (ed.). *The Other Side*. New York: Free Press.

27. "Richie Incognito Drops N-Bomb on Video." November 4, 2013. *YouTube.com*. http://www.youtube.com/watch?v=SW9C4qi5Y80, retrieved 11/11/13.

28. "Richie Incognito Accused of Molesting Woman with Golf Club in 2012." November 8, 2013. *Huffingtonpost.com*. http://www.huffingtonpost.com/2013/11/08/richie-incognito-molesting-woman-golf_n_4240725.html, retrieved 11/11/13.

29. Babb, Kent. February 14, 2014. "NFL-Commissioned Report Finds Culture of Intolerance in Miami Dolphins Locker Room." *Washingtonpost.com*. http://www.washingtonpost.com/sports/redskins/nfl-commissioned-report-finds-culture-of-intolerance-in-miami-dolphins-locker-room/2014/02/14/5d10bf3c-95a8-11e3-afce-3e7c922ef31e_story.html, retrieved 4/19/14; Farrar, Doug. February 14, 2014. "Report on Incognito–Jonathan Martin Saga: History of 'Persistent Bullying, Harassment and Ridicule' with Dolphins." *SI.com*. http://NFL.SI.com/2014/02/14/richie-incognito-jonathan-martin-report/, retrieved 2/19/14; Wells Report.

30. Burke, Chris. March 24, 2014. "NFL Competition Committee Passes on N-word Rule, Considers Extra Point Changes." *NFL.SI.com*. http://nfl.si.com/2014/03/19/nfl-competition-committee-passes-on-n-word-rule-considers-extra-point-changes/, retrieved 4/29/14.

31. Wells Report.

32. Ibid.

33. Ibid. Emphasis added.

34. See Freeman 2003, Tuaolo 2006.

35. Wells Report.

36. Lariviere, David. February 11, 2014. "Coming Out Will Hurt Michael Sam's NFL Draft Status." *Forbes.com*. http://www.forbes.com/sites/davidlariviere/2014/02/11/michael-sams-gay-admission-will-hurt-his-nfl-draft-status/, retrieved 4/19/14.

37. Jenkins, Sally. February 10, 2014. "Michael Sam's Courageous Decision to Come Out Resonates from the NFL to Sochi." *Washingtonpost.com*. http://www.washingtonpost.com/sports/olympics/michael-sams-courageous-decision-to-come-out-resonates-from-the-nfl-to-sochi/2014/02/10/e6cc1c1e-927c-11e3-b46a-5a3d0d2130da_story.html, retrieved 4/19/14; McGinn, Bob. May 5, 2014. "Scouts Down on Sam's Talent." Milwaukee Journal Sentinel, p. 2c; Yan, Holly, and David Alsup. May 12, 2014. "Reactions Heat Up after Michael Sam Kisses Boyfriend on TV." CNN.com. http://www.cnn.com/2014/05/12/us/michael-sam-nfl-kiss-reaction/, retrieved 5/12/14; Outside the Lines. May 11, 2014. ESPN-TV.

38. Brinson, Will. November 7, 2012. "Jonathan Martin's Lawyer Alleges More Verbal Abuse." *CBSsports.com*. http://www.cbssports.com/nfl/

eye-on-football/24199408/david-cornwell-alleges-more-verbal-abuse-of-jona-than-martin, retrieved 11/8/13. Redacted text is from cited source. An unexpur-gated version was unavailable.

39. *Mike and Mike*. November 8, 2013. ESPN2-TV.
40. Kimmel, Michael. 2008. *Guyland: The Perilous World Where Boys Become Men*. New York: HarperCollins.
41. Ibid., p. 13.
42. See Racial Report Card.
43. See Stack, Carol. 1974. *All Our Kin*. New York: Harper & Row.
44. *Broke*. African American interview subjects in O'Toole's study also hint at racial differences in family demands, but the suggestions are subtle.
45. Many vulgarities routinely make their way into print, but "nigger" is virtually forbidden. It's also culturally telling that "fag" and "faggot"—terms similarly offensive with reference to sexuality—are relatively commonplace in vernacular speech as well as the public media.
46. Beasley, November 7, 2013.
47. Salguero, Sal. N.d. "Incognito Considered Black in Dolphins Locker Room." *Miamiherald.com*. http://miamiherald.typepad.com/dolphins_in_depth/2013/11/richie-incognito-considered-black-in-dolphins-locker-room.html, retrieved 11/7/13.
48. See, for example, Chris Carter on *Mike and Mike*. January 7, 2013. ESPN2-TV.
49. Durkheim, Emile. 1933 [1893]. *The Division of Labor in Society*. Glencoe, IL: Free Press; Durkheim, Emile. 1951 [1897]. *Suicide*. New York: Free Press.
50. Merton, Robert K. 1957. *Social Theory and Social Structure*. Glencoe, IL: Free Press.
51. See Hilbert, Richard A. 1992. *The Classical Roots of Ethnomethodology*. Chapel Hill: University of North Carolina Press.
52. See MacIver, R.M. 1950. *The Ramparts We Guard*. New York: Macmillan; Ries-man, David. 1950. *The Lonely Crowd*. New Haven, CT: Yale University Press; Srole, Leo. 1956. "Social Integration and Certain Corollaries." *American Sociological Review* 21: 709–16.
53. Merton 1957.
54. Ibid.
55. Holstein, James A., and Jaber F. Gubrium. 2000. *The Self We Live By*. New York: Oxford University Press.
56. Research interview #27.
57. Feinstein 2005, p. 190.
58. See Adler and Adler 1991.
59. See Holstein and Gubrium 2000.
60. S. Coakley 2006 (research interview).
61. Ibid.

62. See Adler, Patricia A., and Peter Adler. 1989. "The Gloried Self: The Aggrandizement and the Construction of Self." *Social Psychology Quarterly* 52: 299–310; Adler and Adler 1991.

63. See Mead 1934, Cooley 1902.

64. See Becker, Howard S. "Notes on the Concept of Commitment." *American Journal of Sociology* 66: 32–40.

65. At the time of their study, very few players were likely to extend their careers in the pros. Today, however, with the proliferation of international basketball leagues, more and more journeyman players are continuing their careers and sustaining more than mere vestiges of their gloried selves.

66. Goffman, Erving. 1961. *Asylums*. Garden City, NY: Anchor.

67. Ibid., pp. 12, 5.

68. Ibid., pp. 6–10.

69. Ibid., p. 13.

70. Ibid., pp. 14–35; See Gubrium, Jaber F., and James. A. Holstein (eds.). 2001. *Institutional Selves*. New York: Oxford University Press. NFL hazing rituals also contribute to this function.

71. Goffman 1961, p. 43.

72. Ibid., p. 73.

73. See Clemmer 1940; Cordilia, A. 1983. *The Making of an Inmate: Prison as a Way of Life*. Cambridge, MA: Schenkman; Holt, N., and D. Miller. 1972. *Explorations in Inmate-Family Relationships*. Sacramento: California Department of Corrections, Report 46; Lenihan, K. 1975. "The Financial Condition of Released Prisoners." *Crime and Delinquency* 4: 226–81; Richards, S.C. 1995. *The Structure of Prison Release*. New York: McGraw-Hill; Richards, S.C., and R.S. Jones. 1997. "Perpetual Incarceration Machine: Structural Impediments to Post-Prison Success." *Journal of Contemporary Criminal Justice* 13(1): 4–22; Richards, S.C., and R.S. Jones. 2004. "Beating the Perpetual Incarceration Machine," pp. 201–32, in Maruna, S., and R. Immarigeon (eds.). *After Crime and Punishment: Pathways to Offender Reintegration*. London: Willan; Ross, J.I., and S.C. Richards. 2002. *Behind Bars: Surviving Prison*. Indianapolis: Pearson; Ross, J.I., and S.C. Richards (eds.). 2003. *Convict Criminology*. Belmont, CA: Wadsworth; Wormith, S. 1984. "The Controversy over the Effects of Long-term Incarceration." *Canadian Journal of Criminology* 26: 423–35; Zamble, E., and F. Porporino. 1988. *Coping, Behavior and Adaptation in Prison Inmates*. New York: Springer-Verlag.

74. See Jones, Richard S., and Thomas Schmid. 2000. *Doing Time*. Greenwich, CT: JAI; Petersilia, Joan. 2003. *When Prisoners Come Home*. New York: Oxford University Press; Richards, S.C., J. Austin, and R.S. Jones. 2004. "Kentucky's Perpetual Prisoner Machine: It's about Money." *Policy Studies Journal* 21: 93–106.

75. Obviously there are many significant differences between prisons and the NFL. NFL players choose to enter the league, while prisoners are incarcerated against their will. NFL players cherish their experience in the league, whereas

few prisoners have anything good to say about their prison experience. Perhaps most importantly, NFL players typically resist their "release," while most prisoners eagerly anticipate theirs. These differences cast players' experience inside the bubble in an entirely different light, making it a sought-after destination rather than a fate to be avoided.

76. See Doyle, Michael E., and Kris A. Peterson. 2005. "Re-entry and Reintegration: Returning Home after Combat." *Psychiatric Quarterly* 76: 361–70; Tanielian, Terri L., and Lisa H. Jaycocks (eds). 2008. *Invisible Wounds of War: Psychological and Cognitive Injuries, Their Consequences, and Services to Assist Recovery*. Santa Monica, CA: Rand Corp.

77. See "PDHRA Battlemind Training." N.d. *OSD.mil.* http://fhp.osd.mil/pdhrainfo/media/battlemind_brochure.pdf, retrieved 4/21/14.

78. Research interview #353.

79. See Whyte, William H. *The Organization Man*. Garden City, NY: Doubleday.

80. Oriard 1982, p. 323.

81. Bateman, May 3, 2012.

82. Sager, Mike. April 23, 2010. "Todd Marinovich: The Man Who Never Was." *Esquire.com.* http://www.esquire.com/features/the-game/todd-marinovich-0509, retrieved 12/12/13.

83. Murray, Mark. N.d. "Poll: Forty Percent Would Steer Kids away from Football." *NBCnews.com.* http://www.nbcnews.com/storyline/super-bowl/poll-forty-percent-would-steer-kids-away-football-n19646, retrieved 4/19/14. The poll also found that lower-income parents were more likely to overlook the dangers of football than those with more substantial incomes, suggesting that the game itself may begin to reproduce economic and class distinctions.

APPENDIX 1. METHODOLOGY

1. See Adler, Patricia A., and Peter Adler. 1994. "Observational Techniques," pp. 377–92, in Denzin, N., and Y. Lincoln (eds.). *Handbook of Qualitative Research*. Thousand Oaks, CA: Sage; Gubrium and Holstein 1997.

2. See Adler and Adler 1994; Davis, Christine S., and Carolyn Ellis. 2008. "Emergent Methods in Autoethnographic Research," pp. 283–302, in Hess-Biber, Sharlene, and Patricia Leavy (eds.). *Handbook of Emergent Methods*. New York: Guilford; Ellis, Carolyn. 2004. *The Ethnographic I: A Methodological Novel about Autoethnography*. Walnut Creek, CA: AltaMira Press.

3. Lofland, John. 1976. *Doing Social Life*. New York: John Wiley; Prus, Robert. 1996. *Symbolic Interaction and Ethnographic Research: Intersubjectivity and the Study of Human Lived Experience*. Albany: State University of New York Press.

4. Adler, Patricia A., and Peter Adler. 1987. *Membership Roles in Field Research*. Newbury Park, CA: Sage.

5. See Ellis, Carolyn. 1991. "Sociological Introspection and Emotional Experience." *Symbolic Interaction* 14: 23–50.

6. Jones and Schmid 2000.
7. Player Care study.
8. Glaser, Barney G., and Anselm L. Strauss. 1967. *The Discovery of Grounded Theory: Strategies for Qualitative Research*. New York: Aldine.
9. See Charmaz, Kathy. 2006. *Constructing Grounded Theory: A Practical Guide through Qualitative Analysis*. Thousand Oaks, CA: Sage; Glaser and Strauss 1967.

APPENDIX 2. RETIREMENT BENEFITS

1. Player Care study.
2. "Summary of NFL Player Benefits," n.d.; "Player Benefits." February 2, 2010. *NFLcommunications.com*. http://nflcommunications.com/2010/02/02/player-benefits/; "Bert Bell/Pete Rozelle NFL Player Retirement Plan." April 1, 2007. *Wordpress.com*. http://nflalumniasssociation.files.wordpress.com/2011/03/nfl-player-retirement-plan.pdf; both retrieved 4/19/14.
3. Also see "Archive for 'Player Benefits.'" February 12, 2014. *NFLcommunications.com*. http://nflcommunications.com/category/player-benefits/; "Player Care Foundation." N.d. NFLplayercare.com. https://www.nflplayercare.com/; National Football League Alumni. N.d. "Moving Forward Together." *NFLalumni.org*. https://www.nflalumni.org/; all retrieved 4/19/14.
4. Freeman, Mike. May 19, 2002. "Pension Raised for Pre-1977 Players." *NYTimes.com*. http://www.nytimes.com/2002/05/19/sports/pro-football-inside-the-nfl-pension-pay-raised-for-pre-1977-players.html?pagewanted=print&src=pm, retrieved 7/10/13.
5. "NFL Announces Distribution of $620 Million Legacy Fund Benefit for Pre-'93 Retired Players." November 10, 2011. *NFLcommunications.com*. http://nflcommunications.com/2011/11/10/nfl-announces-distribution-of-620-million-legacy-fund-benefit-for-pre-%E2%80%9993-retired-players/, retrieved 7/12/13.
6. "NFL Announces Pension Plan for Retired Players." November 11, 2011. *Profootballweekly.com*. http://www.profootballweekly.com/2011/11/14/nfl-announces-pension-plan-for-retired-players, retrieved 7/12/13.

INDEX

Academics, support and college experience in, 25–26
Adler, Patricia, 39, 238–39, 300n65
Adler, Peter, 39, 238–39, 300n65
Adulation, 16, 27–28, 173; bubble's adoration and, 64–65; Driver and, 64; Green Bay Packers and, 64; Koonce and, 64; Starr and, 64; women and, 64, 274n60
Advertising, 186–88
AFL. *See* American Football League
African Americans, 24, 68, 266n42; business success, 179; "the Dream" and, 14; locker room culture majority as, 78; new social territory for, 232; NFL and representation of, 230; opportunities cultivated for, 247–48; as predominant in NFL, 148; unprepared for wealth and, 147–48
Agents, 54–55; bad, 154–57; life-management tasks of, 70–71; NFPLA's requirements for, 155–56; as overcharging clients, 156; shady advisors as, 155–57; as taking over all aspects, 156–57; white collar crime and, 157; wives as, 70–71, 205
Aggression, 221, 224
Aiello, Greg, 114
Aikman, Troy, 5, 109, 162
Alcohol, 131–32
Aldridge, Lionel, 3
ALS. *See* Amyotrophic lateral sclerosis
Alzheimer's disease, 107–8, 258, 282n18
American Dream, 136
American Football League (AFL), 52–54, 272n28

Amnesia, 109
Amyotrophic lateral sclerosis (ALS), 107–8, 258
Anderson, Donny, 54
Anderson, Elijah, 147–48
Annuity program, 257
Anomia, 234
Anomie, 233–35
Anti-Defamation League, 231
Arrington, Michael, 210
Asomugha, Nnamdi, 56
Athletes. *See* Student athletes
Athletes in Action, 80
Atlanta Falcons, 80
Atlanta Journal-Constitution study, 19
Autograph signings, 12, 21, 36, 49, 64–65, 140, 252; employment after football and, 174, 187–89, 213, 252
Autopsies, 110–13
Ayanbadejo, Brendon, 209

Baltimore Ravens, 134
Band of brothers, 229
Bankruptcy, 3–4, 7–8, 142–45, 169, 287n14
Barber, Tiki, 97–99
Bart Starr Award, 80
Beale, Jillian, 201–2
Beals, Alan, 31
Behaviors, acceptable, 223–24, 232
Belcher, Jovan, 2–3
Belotti, Mike, 17
Benchmarking: bubble and, 152–53; employment after football and, 174–76; jobs as falling short with NFL salary, 174; problematic, 152–53

ABOUT THE AUTHORS

James A. Holstein is Professor of Sociology in the Department of Social and Cultural Sciences at Marquette University. He is the author, with Jaber F. Gubrium, of *The Self We Live By: Narrative Identity in a Postmodern World* and has authored or edited over 40 scholarly books.

Richard S. Jones is Professor of Sociology and Faculty Athletics Representative at Marquette University. He is the author of *Doing Time: Prison Experience and Identity* with Thomas J. Schmid.

George E. Koonce, Jr., played professional football for a decade, the majority of those years with the Green Bay Packers, with whom he won Super Bowl XXXI. After his playing days, he held positions as Special Assistant to the Athletic Director at East Carolina University, Director of Player Development for the Green Bay Packers, Senior Associate Athletic Director and Director of Development at Marquette University, and Athletic Director at the University of Wisconsin–Milwaukee. Dr. Koonce is currently Vice President of Advancement at Marian University.